"This is a scary book. It threatens to expose the tricks we pastors use to influence some and to motivate others; it threatens to uncover our egoism and reveal how often we protect our fiefdoms. *The Relational Pastor* is a call to live authentically. It's an invitation to be honest about who we are and what keeps us awake at night; and finally it's a call to the only life worth living—a real one. "

Rev. Laura S. Truax, senior pastor, LaSalle Street Church

"In an age where connecting with people via technology and social media has quickly become the norm, Andy Root has spent much energy reminding youth pastors what it means to connect and *be* in relationship with others in the context of their ministries. *The Relational Pastor* is a convicting call to pastors at all levels to remember what it is to be Christlike and incarnational in regards to our relationships. This is a must-read for any pastor who believes that relationships with people are at the core of not just ministry but of our understanding of Jesus Christ and our intimacy with him."

Kris Fernhout, pastor of student ministries, Christ Community Church

"I have always been fascinated by the African Ubuntu saying: 'I am because we are.' The suggestion that without you I cannot be myself is radical and transformative. Such a way of understanding human persons opens up a very different relational space, one which stands in stark contrast to our individualistic assumptions and the whole idea that we are 'our own people.' Andrew Root understands this dynamic; more than that, he shows us how we might live it. With grace and imaginative commitment he carves out a quite beautiful model of relational discipleship and relational church. If you are interested in what love looks like, this book is for you."

John Swinton, chair in divinity and religious studies, University of Aberdeen

ANDREW ROOT

THE

RELATIONAL

PASTOR

SHARING IN CHRIST
BY SHARING OURSELVES

IVP Books

An imprint of InterVarsity Press
Downers Grove, Illinois

InterVarsity Press
P.O. Box 1400, Downers Grove, IL 60515-1426
World Wide Web: www.ivpress.com
E-mail: email@ivpress.com

InterVarsity Press® is the book-publishing division of InterVarsity Christian Fellowship/USA®, a movement of students and faculty active on campus at hundreds of universities, colleges and schools of nursing in the United States of America, and a member movement of the International Fellowship of Evangelical Students. For information about local and regional activities, write Public Relations Dept., InterVarsity Christian Fellowship/ USA, 6400 Schroeder Rd., P.O. Box 7895, Madison, WI 53707-7895, or visit the IVCF website at <www.intervarsity .org>.

Scripture quotations, unless otherwise noted, are from the New Revised Standard Version of the Bible, *copyright 1989 by the Division of Christian Education of the National Council of the Churches of Christ in the USA. Used by permission. All rights reserved.*

While all stories in this book are true, some names and identifying information have been changed to protect the privacy of the individuals involved. Stories are shared with permission.

Design: Cindy Kiple
Images: silhouette of crowd: © Kirsty Pargeter/iStockphoto
        green texture: © hudiemm/iStockphoto
        silhouette of urban crowd: © edge69/iStockphoto
Interior design: Beth Hagenberg

ISBN 978-0-8308-4102-8

Printed in the United States of America ∞

A catalog record for this book is available from the Library of Congress.

P 24 23 22 21 20 19 18 17 16 15 14 13 12 11 10 9 8 7 6 5 4 3 2 1

Y 34 33 32 31 30 29 28 27 26 25 24 23 22 21 20 19 18 17 16 15 14 13

To Kara
My friend, my wife, my pastor, my heart

Contents

Preface

My friend and teacher Kenda Creasy Dean calls me "a well socialized introvert," and it's true, I am a severe introvert. Apart from the juxtaposition of loving to stand up in front of large rooms and talk, I prefer to be alone, to be in my head reading, writing *or most wonderfully* watching TV. As an introvert I'm far more energized by time by myself than with others. I feel particularly stretched and exhausted by things like elementary school carnivals, small talk in elevators and dinner parties with (even good) acquaintances. (Though I can imagine I'm not alone with the carnival thing!)

This very confession makes it quite odd for someone like me to write this book on relationships. This book makes the claim that at our core we human beings *are* our relationships, that God encounters us in relationships and that pastoral ministry at its base is about facilitating relational encounters. It seems a contradiction that a loner introvert would conceive of such a perspective.

But I see it differently. I've come to recognize that the very fact that I possess this personal disposition gives me a perspective on the depth and mystery of relationships themselves. Because relationships are not a reflex for me, I've been forced to think deeply about them. And when reflecting on my own experience I've been overcome by the spiritual significance relationship has played in my life (even in the life of a TV-loving introvert). When I'm broken, afraid and needing to celebrate, like an impulse I (again, the severe introvert) seek out others; I need others to share with me, to share in me. There is something about relationship that is deeper than the introvert-extrovert personal traits; there is something about the human spirit that yearns (needs at the deepest level) for others to share in our lives.

This book you hold is for pastors; that is its primary audience. But it is a book, I hope, with ramifications beyond the vocation of pastor, connecting to the whole of the Christian life. Nevertheless, in these pages the pastor is the focus. It is a book for pastors which seeks to ignite the imagination on how relationships draw us into the very presence of Christ. It is a book that critiques the way we pastors have *used* relationships in the past, thinking that our ministries need to be relational because the relationship can win us the loyalty we need to get people to come and stay at our church.

My goal with this book is to make a case that "relationship" is the very goal (not a tool) of ministry. That *in* sharing in each other's lives we share *in* God's own life through Jesus Christ. I look to place the theological, the spiritual, within the concrete practice of ministry.

As an introvert focused to reflect on my relationships, it has been clear to me that in those moments where God moved—those moments where what is dead in me gave way to life—that others, that relationships, were present. Our relationships are the very field, the very place, where God is encountered.

Pastoral ministry can be nothing more and nothing less than making space for people to encounter the very presence of God. Here, in this book, I claim that space is created in the sharing of relationships of persons.

This is a book born out of my own work of training and educating pastors for the last eight years, listening to their stories and hearing their challenges. It is a book born out of not only teaching pastors but living with one. My wife, Kara, who shows up in these pages, is a pastor, is my pastor. I've watched her lead a small church with skill, sensitivity and theological depth. I've watched her do this from the inside; I've listened to her as she articulates the frustrations, fears and many failures that come with this calling. This is a book, I dearly hope, that is sensitive to the pastor's experience. While I desire for it to push and prod, I yearn for it to do so in appreciation for the pastor her- or himself.

This is a book about the relationships of persons, and there are many such persons who have blessed me in the journey of writing this book. Dave Zimmerman, my editor, has worked hard to make this book tight and readable. As an editor Dave is all an author could ask for, someone with wisdom, intellectual depth and appreciation for the process of writing. This is actually my second project that seeks to explore the issue of relationships in ministry, and Dave Zimmerman was behind the first as well.

The first project, *Revisiting Relational Youth Ministry*, explored relationships in the context of youth ministry. I received word from many (mainly youth workers) who read that first book that they wished I would broaden the audience so their pastor too would wrestle with the ideas. I did end up writing a more popular version of the youth ministry book for Zondervan, but resisted a broader text, not because I didn't think it would translate but because I wasn't interested in writing a derivative book that somehow simply replaced "youth pastor" with "pastor." But as time went on I saw some exciting new ways of making the argument (particularly with neuroscience and the hypostatic union). So with the blessing and wisdom of Dave, I have, in no small terms, pulled down the structure in which I built the thesis of *Revisiting* and rebuilt it here with all new theoretical frameworks and theological dialogue partners. (I've also sought to address *some* of the questions raised after the first book, for instance, questions about education, evangelism, why influence is so bad, etc.) I've done this *not* because *Revisiting* is in any way deficient but rather as a way of driving my perspectives and points deeper, of making another case for imaging ministry as place sharing.

This project was written while I was on a sabbatical generously given by the board, President Bliese and Dean Martinson of Luther Seminary. I'm thankful for the space it provided me.

Two of my dearest colleagues at Luther Seminary read and commented on the whole of the manuscript. I've known both Jessicah Krey Duckworth and Theresa Latini for more than ten years now, and our history of dialoguing with each other's work goes all the way back to the seminar rooms of Princeton Theological Seminary. I'm thankful for the blessing of now working with both of them and for their insight into this project. Theresa, particularly, saved me from some potential pitfalls.

Two other friends took the time to read the manuscript, two friends with pastors' hearts and scholars' minds, Blair Bertrand and Jeff Keuss. Their insight was invaluable. Thanks to Victoria Smith for working on the index and for being a partner in pedagogy for so many of us at Luther.

You'll find at the end of this book an appendix with practices and examples that seek to ground the perspectives of this book further in pastoral practice. I was blessed by a group of pastors doing ministry in different contexts, whose monthly gatherings are funded by a grant from Austin Theological Seminary. They made space to read and interact with this text, and to provide these needed snapshots of practice in the appendix. Big thanks to Jodi Houge, Marc Oslie-Olson, Jamie Schultz, Travis Gerjets, Phil GebbenGreen and Kara Root.

And it is to Kara Root whom I owe the greatest debt of gratitude. We are partners in all things.

1

Reshifting Pastoral Ministry

An Introduction

Every church has a Dave. In the church my friend Shane pastors, Dave was in his early sixties, was a member of the church for decades and thought he knew everything about everything. Dave was overly involved in any church business. Hearing the need for more consistent stewardship, Dave took it upon himself to corner new members, providing a little muscle to begin or increase their giving. Confidently sure he could fix the broken entryway door, he only made it worse, locking everyone out of church on a Sunday morning. The problem wasn't that Dave *thought* he was always right and always needed. The problem was that Dave *told* everyone so, explaining to parents of small children why they were parenting their kids wrong, or announcing all the reasons why the car you bought was stupid, or asserting why worship needed to happen in a certain way. Dave was exhausting. As my friend Shane explained, when you saw Dave, you walked in the other direction.

On the other end of the continuum was Jodi; every church has or wishes for a Jodi. Jodi was in her early thirties, a petite redhead, bubbly and constantly upbeat. She had come to the church right out of college by happenstance. She had just taken a new ("first real," as she said) job. The church was in her neighborhood, and feeling lonely one Sunday, and being a real people-person, she showed up. Since then Jodi had been a fixture. In no overstatement, the church simply couldn't function without her; her energy was infectious, giving new life to this aging congregation. In generosity she made sure things happened, making all the arrangements for the annual outdoor service at the beach and single-handedly hosting a jazz cocktail party to fund the confirmation retreat.

If Dave was the great know-it-all annoyance of the church, Jodi was its young saint, quietly and competently leading. Jodi literally kept the church going as they went through the fourteen-month transition from the previous pastor to my friend Shane. Everyone loved Jodi for her kind, upbeat and selfless leadership.

It was then no surprise to anyone that both Dave and Jodi were elected to the church council. Though in two radically different ways, they were both leaders. Even though most people couldn't stand Dave, truth be told, it didn't matter. The church needs people willing to do things, and Dave was more than willing to do so.

As the council met for its annual retreat, there was business to be done, but this business would be intense, and Shane knew it. So he decided to start with an exercise, something he heard from somewhere now forgotten, an exercise that was radical in its simplicity. He knew that in his church, issues so easily became more important than people, so he began by setting chairs facing each other no more than three feet apart. He then passed out notepads and pencils. As the room got heavy with confusion Shane invited the council members to sit facing another person, with just notepad and sharp pencil in hand. They were instructed to say nothing. One half of the pair was to look at the other person, just to see, for a whole minute, and then for two more minutes to sketch the other person's face. The discomfort was palpable; to cope, giggling and funny faces began the process, and a handful of council members kept protesting that they had no artistic skills. But Shane kept reassuring them that it had nothing to do with artistic skill but with seeing, and asked them to please honor the silence. After a few minutes, they switched roles, the sketched becoming the sketcher. Then Shane had them switch seats and repeat the process a couple more times, spending a few silent minutes staring and drawing each other until they had each drawn, and been drawn, three or four times.

As the exercise came to completion, the once uneasy atmosphere in the room became calm, almost relaxed. Then they debriefed their experience, and Shane asked how it felt. People expressed what they sensed in the room as a whole, that after pushing through a level of unease, these short few minutes of silent attention to this other person drew them to the other, looking into their face in order to draw it forced them to really see each other. It was a galvanizing experience for everyone— well, everyone but Dave.

As people took their turns stating what it was like to share these few silent minutes with the person across from them, Dave spoke up. He stated, "I felt very comfortable with everyone as I drew them, I mean I really did." People nodded, affirming that this was their own experience as well, but Dave wasn't finished, "I mean, I felt really comfortable with everyone, everyone . . . except Jodi."

It was as if the air had been sucked from the room. Dave continued, "Yeah, looking at Jodi just made me feel really uncomfortable, I mean, I felt judged just looking at her." The tranquil atmosphere turned toxic. People sat shocked. *Did he really just say that?* Shane thought. *Did he really say that Jodi, little, smiley, kind Jodi, made him feel uncomfortable?* No one knew what to say; after all, the absurdity of Jodi making *anyone*, let alone *Dave*, uncomfortable seemed crazy. But Dave continued to insist, stating again, "I mean truly I felt comfortable and safe looking at everyone, but Jodi, I really have no idea why, she just made me feel uncomfortable, just uncomfortable. She just did."

As Dave continued to spew his reactions, the rest of the council, as inconspicuously as possible, looked over at Jodi. Her face was bright red, almost matching her curly hair. And her eyes opened wide, she sat frozen, as if knowing any move would bring a flood of tears. Shane now knew something needed to be said; he regretted ever doing this exercise in the first place, cursing his memory for ever recalling it.

He took a breath, hoping to repress the response his flabbergasted anger desired, like, "Hey, Dave, why are you being such a jerk?" Shane imagined such a response receiving a standing ovation from the rest of the group. But he resisted. Instead, to his own shock, he turned to Dave and asked, "OK, we definitely hear that she made you feel uncomfortable, but that is only a reaction to a feeling. Why do you think you are reacting with discomfort?"

Dave responded without as much as a beat between Shane's question and his answer, "I don't know, she just does. Jodi just makes me uncomfortable." Shane tried again, "I know, Dave, you've told us your reaction and reactions are important, but tell us more about what you're feeling."

Jodi still sat frozen and Shane's pushing of Dave only seemed to amp up the tension in the room. It was clear that people couldn't take much more. Dave folded his arms across his chest and stared at the floor. Shane watched him, not sure if he was reflective or shut down, searching for an answer or ready to explode.

Finally, Dave broke the silence. He stated, "Well . . ." and then stopped. His voice cracked and the muscles in his cheeks twitched. He sat silent another long few seconds before mustering the strength to continue, "Well," he started again, "you all know my daughter Donna. She grew up in this church, and I told many of you that she just moved back in with us. When she was thirteen she kind of stopped coming often to church, and now that she's back with us, she has only made it to church once every month or two. I've said it is because she works late on Saturday. Well, she does work Saturdays, but she's done by four. And she is done with that job now anyhow; she was just fired for not going. I'm sure a few of you know this, but Donna suffers from severe depression and she can't come to church because she can't get out of bed, and now she can't get out of bed to go to work. She lost her job, her apartment and even her car, because of the depression."

Now, everyone's attention shifted from Jodi and rested squarely on Dave. The tension in the room evaporated and in its place was only attention, attention to Dave. Where tension tends to thrust us into ourselves to be concerned with how we are feeling, attention to another person and their story pushes us through ourselves into the other's experience.

The council sat hanging on Dave's every word. Dave breathed another deep breath, his eyes filling with tears, and then he continued. "And I guess, that's it. Yeah, no, that is it, that's why Jodi makes me feel so uncomfortable."

"What is?" Shane added quickly.

"Well, I guess I feel so defensive and uncomfortable looking at Jodi because when I see her, I see who Donna could be if she didn't suffer from depression. I see my little girl in Jodi. It just reminds me of my sweet Donna, and all that she could have been."

Something had just changed, something holy. Something transformational had just occurred. Dave was seen, and seen in the fragility of his humanity. As my friend explained to me later, "It was from that moment that everything changed; Dave was no longer an annoying know-it-all hindrance, but a person. He became someone we shared not just leadership, but life with."

PERSONS AND RELATIONSHIPS

And this is what this book you hold is about. This book is about seeing ministry as the encounter of human person to human person, sharing deeply in relationship as the way to encounter the presence of Jesus Christ. But who would deny this? Who would think that ministry isn't about relationship? I can imagine that there are few.

While we in the church frequently discuss the importance of relationships for our ministry, we have often failed to recognize that relationships, or something called *relational ministry*, is dependent on *persons*. It is dependent on personhood, on seeing those in our churches and communities as persons, not as consumers of programs, not as "giving units" or volunteers, nor as rational calculators that decided that they and their families can get the most out of their involvement at this church over another. And we have done this too often. We have deeply wanted our ministry to be relational, but not for the sake of persons, for the sake of the *ministry*, for the sake of bringing success to our initiatives. In other words, we've wanted people to feel relationally connected so that they might come to what we are offering or believe what we are preaching or teaching.

So when we speak of "relational," we usually mean it as another strategy, another buzzword, to get people to do what we want them to do. Relationship becomes a kind of glue that keeps individuals involved or coming. The point of our ministry isn't the relationships between persons, but how the relationship wins us influence. In other words, the relationship in ministry becomes something we use for influencing individuals, for the purpose of winning some leverage to get individuals to commit. And this makes sense if we view human beings as individual, rational calculating wills. Then relationships are simply the repetitive choices that people *willfully* and *rationally* make, which influence them to give their resources like time, money and energy. Individuals decide to be in relationship with Skippy Peanut Butter, buying it every week, in relationship with Central Methodist Church, attending three times a month, and in relationship with Joe from work, joining his fantasy football league.

In this way of thinking, *relationship* becomes a generic term used to signal what people are loyal to. People can be in relationship with things as much as people, with ideologies as much as fellow human beings. So the church's relational ministry becomes about *using* relationships to win such loyalty from individuals. It becomes about using a relationship to get them to become loyal to the *idea* of Jesus, as opposed to encountering the *person* of Jesus Christ. Again, as I said earlier, the relationship is never the point but is the tool used to get individuals to decide to give their resources (time, money and energy) to the church. Relationship becomes more about loyalty to a brand.

I realize that this sounds harsh, and truth be told, I'm confident that no one is seeking to use relationship *intentionally* as the candy coating that wins loyalty—I don't think! But, I do think we have tended to *use* relationships this very way. I think we've done this because this is the very water we contextually swim in; our American context is constructed to mistakenly see people as individuals and not as persons, pitting the church in a battle for people's resources and making Jesus into an idea (ideology) that I'm individually loyal to. The church has adopted this cultural reality at the expense of the central Christian commitment to personhood.

These words (*individual* and *person*) may seem to be synonymous, but they are fundamentally different (a difference we will explore later on). But for now it is enough to say that personhood, as opposed to individualism, sees relationship with others as the very ontological structure of humanity. Or to say it in a less jargon-y way, personhood claims that we *are* our relationships. Relationships are not what we decide to be loyal to, not devices that bring loyalty to ideologies, but what give us our very selves. We are our relationships; they are the very core of our existence, the source of life. As Jewish thinker Martin Buber said, "In the beginning was the relationship."[1]

In the journey of this book we will seek to shake pastoral ministry free of individualism, to place it again on the Christian confession of personhood.[2] We will explore relationships as the mysterious core of what it means to be alive and human, as the very confession that God becomes *person* in Jesus Christ and therefore personhood becomes the form in which human beings encounter the God who becomes human.[3] I'll claim that relationships of persons encountering persons are the very way that we encounter Jesus Christ. Drawing on what the church fathers called "the hypostatic union" (the relationship between the divine and human natures in the person of Jesus), I'll claim that relationships in ministry are an end. Relationships are the very point of ministry; in and through relationships people encounter the person of Jesus Christ and are therefore given their own personhood—a true personhood free from sin and death.

But all this is easier said than done. Making a distinction between individualism and personhood works through theological musings on paper, but what concretely signals that we are doing ministry in the logic of the *personal* and not bound to *individualism*? What gives witness that our relationships are ends and not means? I'll contend that there are two concrete realities that signal this, two realities we saw in the story of Dave and Jodi; these realities are empathy and sharing as transformation.

When Dave confessed why Jodi made him uncomfortable, when he revealed Donna's depression and his own broken heart, the group reacted with empathy. They felt Dave's pain and opened their own person to his. Through his expressed suffering, like a reflex, the rest of the group opened their person to Dave's, because through his expressed suffering they saw not an individual, but a person. It is no coincidence that his suffering was the yearning and pain of stressed relationship. We are our relationships, and for Dave to express the burden of this relationship was to open his very being to the being of others.

Empathy is a personal reality. We find it hard to be empathic for someone whose car is broken, this is the loss of individual resources. But we find empathy spilling from our pores when we hear that someone's car is broken, and therefore they'll be unable to get their daughter to physical therapy. As persons we empathize with the personhood of the daughter who yearns and suffers, and with the parent who struggles. The car is at issue because of what it means to persons. It is only stuff, but material becomes important (even sacred) when it becomes the material of personal, relational existence. It becomes the material of personal *place*.

Individualism has no room for empathy, no room to feel the other's *place* as your own. The popular phrase "It sucks to be you!" is the mantra of individualism and the enemy of empathy. It is the crass retort expressing that your life is yours and only yours, your suffering has nothing to do with me, and we aren't connected as persons but as free-floating individuals. It, then, just sucks for *you*, because now your own individual freedom and self-fulfillment is threatened. The *I* or *me* is so distinct in individualism that there is no *you*, just other individual competing *I*s. So "It sucks to be *you*," but your sucky situation is actually good for *me*, because it means that I'm winning, that my *I*, my *me* is more successful.

We are only in the land of the personal, where relationships are an end, when we are pulled into empathy. (We'll explore this further in chapter six.) As Jeremy Rifkin says, "Turning relationships into efficient means to advance productive ends destroys the empathic spirit."[4]

But there is more. The personal, empathic encounter possesses the power to bring forth transformation, to bring change to the person. Personal encounter is transformation (even conversion); encountering the person of Jesus, people are called to follow him, to sell everything and follow him (Mt 19:21).

But even the theological concept of conversion has been overtaken by individualism. In our churches we desire ministries that change people, that transform and convert people from death to life, from the old to the new. But too often, caged by individualism, we contend that transformation or conversion is solely an epistemological reality. Even when we dress it up with personal language, like saying we want people to "have a personal relationship with Jesus," what we actually mean is not something *personal* but something *individual*; we want them to individually, in their own minds, assimilate knowledge about Jesus and become loyal to the idea of Jesus.[5] We use our relationships as leverage to get people to *know* things about their own individual ideas or behaviors, to change to new ideas and behaviors. We use the relationship to convince them that *our* Christian subculture is better than another. And so often in ministry we become burned out or discouraged, or burned out *because* we're discouraged, because transformation never seems to stick. People can individually be converted to an idea, only later to be individually captivated by another competing perspective. Bound within individualism, transformation is like fashion, it is important for the now, but eventually we'll move on.

But, to encounter another person, to have your own person empathetically embraced, is not to (solely) go through a conversation of knowledge or ideas but to find new possibility, new life, in the life of others. Dave is never seen the same way again after his confession. It ultimately doesn't matter if he changes his own knowledge of himself. In this community he now is different, in this community he is embraced. And this new way of seeing him becomes, as I'll argue, more real than what Dave ultimately thinks about himself. (We'll see that it stretches so deep it even has neurological changes.) In the end, because we are persons, we will see ourselves and we will know ourselves through others. To have our person embraced is to find our person bound to others and therefore transformed in and through the relationship.

Jesus calls himself a vine and us the branches. We are invited to remain in him as he remains in us—participating in his personhood (Jn 15:5). Now, in the community of others, in relationships of persons, Jesus is present ("Where two or three are gathered in my name, I am there among them" [Mt 18:20]) transforming death into life, so that our person might live forever with his own.

This book will explore how relationships are bound in personhood, and how this personal reality is fundamentally theological, making relationships in ministry ends and not means. We'll see how relationship with persons in ministry becomes about sharing deeply in the lives of others, for no other reason than to be with and for them as Jesus Christ is with and for us as the one who is incarnate, taking on two natures in one person.

This project will end by turning to practice; how do you, as pastor, actually take action in ways that participate in the personal? How do we do ministry that avoids seeing relationships as a means when it feels like we have so much pressure to build a church or lead people? We will explore how what I'll call "place sharing" (personal relationships of empathetic encounter) sets the direction for rethinking prayer, leadership, preaching and education in the church.[6]

But before diving in, it might be helpful to take a flight to 10,000 feet and look again at the cultural situation of the church. Believe me, I understand that this isn't new; for the last few decades thinkers have been taking pastors up to 10,000 feet, showing them the cultural typographical changes, often pointing out how some obtuse philosophical construction like *postmodernism* has changed the landscape, or how digital technology has flooded once dry sections of earth with information and choices. But I do think there is something to be seen by climbing again to this altitude, something unique that points to cultural changes which will greatly affect pastoral ministry and reveal the need for rethinking pastoral ministry along the lines of the personal relationships we have just discussed.

So let's begin.

2

New Energy,
New Communications,
New Consciousness . . .
New Ministry

I vividly remember being a third-year MDiv student on the cusp of graduation, taking one of my last required courses on the practices of pastoral ministry. In this class we learned how to do baptisms and funerals, discussed keeping a budget and explored a theology of stewardship. It was a class on the basic how-tos of pastoral ministry. Yet, outside of some of the basic topics, I really don't remember much else. That is, except for the day our instructor, a retired pastor—now professor—in his early seventies said in a tone of disappointment, "I remember back at the beginning of my career, being a pastor was important. People in town shook your hand and said, 'Hello, pastor!' And if you got pulled over, the officer rarely gave you a ticket, you were the pastor!" Then, pausing, with a hint of sadness, he added, "Not anymore. No one cares if you're the pastor now, no more free lunch for you people."

The change in the cultural conception of pastoral ministry stung, but a second experience made the change bleed. A seminary classmate of mine was having lunch with a highly esteemed professor, a famous theologian known for a long career of brilliant work. As they talked about theology and pastoral ministry, the great theologian launched into a short but potent diatribe. Turning to my classmate, lowering his voice and pointing around to the other students walking through the cafeteria, he said, "In my day, going to seminary was important, and not just everyone got in. If a family had three kids and one went to med school, one to law school and one to seminary, the seminarian wasn't less than his siblings; the seminarian was doing something just as rigorous and important, something to be proud of. Often parents were more proud of their seminarian! Now, well . . ." He sighed, "Now it just isn't that way. I mean we used to get the best and the brightest; now look at these people!"

It might be best to chalk up his comments to low blood sugar. (I actually have come across a number of very bright students.) But while these words may have been harsh and nostalgic, they do point to the truth that even the best and brightest of seminarians feel inadequate, even those that could compete with any med or law student. The simple truth is that the cultural conception of the pastor and of ministry in general has changed. Or it may be better to say that it is in the process of changing; we are in the whitewater of a wave pushed from what once was to something else.

Of course there are a number of theological commitments that give continuity to the practice of ministry. After all, ministry is nothing more and nothing less than joining in God's continued action in the world. But God's continued action happens *in the world*, therefore the pastor or minister is always seeking to discern God's action in a time and place.[1] This means that while our theological conception of God's action, as I will argue, is inextricably linked with persons and personhood, our cultural contexts have not always made it easy to see this theological perspective clearly, and particularly clearly enough for it to inform our practice of ministry.

So as the cultural ground shifts below our feet, it may be time for us to push beyond our (unaware) weddedness to the individual and make a case for the personal. There has been an overall awakening to the personal in the social sciences, an awakening for which *some* give credit to the Christian tradition.[2] Psychology, sociology, political science and other fields have begun to make pushes for the social and personal orientation of human beings. But at times this pushing feels like it's up a steep hill as cultural individualism has soaked so deeply into the very soil in which we seek footing to climb.

Things are changing, the world is shifting, whether for good or ill is still to be determined. But it has now become a truism of our time that we are resting squarely in a time of transition, a time of *post-* or *late* or *hyper*modernity, a time at the end of Christendom, a time of a new missional era. In this time business as usual will not do, but what to do seems unclear.

PLAYING WITH OUR TRANSITION

To articulate this transition, I want to *play* with Jeremy Rifkin's historical typography in his book *The Empathic Civilization*. This chapter is a sandbox and Rifkin's theory my toy. The historical structure I'm building here is made of sand, and Rifkin's typology can easily be dowsed and drowned in critique.³ But, like play, though the reality may be more complicated and many things left unsaid, it nevertheless allows for a creative performance that, though simplified, points to something true. Playing with Rifkin's theory allows us to say something true about our pastoral situation, while acknowledging that things are always more complicated outside the sandbox.⁴

The buckets and shovels I'll borrow from Rifkin are his assertions that through human history we can see a number of transitions that come when a new energy regime is created (like the industrial revolution, for example), which lead to new forms of communication to manage this new regime, which then lead to new ways of understanding ourselves, others and even God. If there is anything clear about our own time, it is that we are plotting (or fighting over) new energy and new communications. It may help to hear Rifkin in his own words,

> Energy is critical, but it doesn't stand alone. The great economic revolutions in history occur when new energy regimes converge with new communications revolutions. The convergence of energy and communications revolutions is what changes the human condition for long periods of time. New communications revolutions become the command-and-control mechanisms, the means of structuring, organizing, and maintaining the energy flow-through of civilization.⁵

He continues, "The convergence of energy and communications revolutions not only reconfigure society and social roles and relationships but also human consciousness itself. Communications revolutions change the temporal and spatial orientation of human beings and, by so doing, change the way the human brain comprehends reality."[6]

But it isn't play to simply copy the creations of others. It becomes play when we adapt and add to the structure in the sandbox. Using Max Weber, I'll playfully offer my own contribution by adding how ministry, the pastor and evangelism were seen in Rifkin's later times of transition, and therefore what our own transition might mean for ministry, pastors and evangelism. This sandbox history may help us not only understand why the two professors in the stories at the beginning of the chapter felt this transition, but beyond their complaints we'll also seek a new vision.

HISTORY

Hunter-gatherer transition. The oldest energy regime that we are aware of is hunting and gathering. In this period there was simply no managing of the resources of the earth; people in small tribes often responded to the earth itself. In many ways the earth and its creatures were personal. In some tribes killing an animal and eating its flesh meant taking in its life power. The earth was alive, giving rain or fruit, and god was creator, often bound within the earth itself.

To manage the energy of hunting and gathering, oral communication through language became essential. Cooperation in gathering and hunting was an absolute necessity. Stories of past hunts or droughts or storms socialized the young. Unique languages were created among small groups of people who were actually (in our terms) living close together. But though other tribes were within miles of each other there was little reason to communicate. Communication is for cooperation, and often the only interaction with other groups was not cooperative but violent.

Language became the best way to manage the energy of hunting and gathering. What is ironic is that though the earth was personal, those outside the communication system, those with other language, often weren't. Humans showed personal connection to only those with whom they had blood ties. This is why warring tribes, upon forging peace, would marry off their daughters to each other, intertwining their bloodlines. It made the other tribe persons.

Ministry. It's hard to discuss ministry in this primitive period, especially if we think of ministry as a fundamentally Christian or a Judeo-Christian reality (as I'll presume as this history unfolds). But to stretch the term for argument's sake, we could assert that in this period ministry or spiritual leadership existed as cosmic storytelling.[7] As any first-year seminarian has heard, the creation story in Genesis has interesting correlation with older mythological stories from the area, for instance the Babylonian story of Gilgamesh. These ancient stories, while from the view of our post-Enlightenment definition of truth as provable fact, couldn't have actually happened, nevertheless gave the hearer a conception of self, world and god. This energy regime of hunting and gathering, managed by language, led to what Rifkin calls mythical consciousness. So spiritual leadership was about telling cosmic stories of why or what the world was and who was in control of it.

The spiritual leader was then a storyteller, performing and protecting the stories of his or her people. Interpreting new phenomenon (wildfire, early winter, war) within the cosmic stories of the past. The spiritual leader was embedded within the energy regime and communication system. The spiritual leader explained why the energy regime thrived or failed, and used the communication system, language, to give cosmic significance to the practice of managing the energy. Hunting (and to a lesser degree gathering), through cosmic story, became spiritual.

The spiritual leader wasn't just a storyteller but also an endorser of war or was himself a warrior.[8] Up against others with different languages, which led to different stories, resulting in different gods, the spiritual leader would need to defend the tribe's cosmic stories, showing that this tribe's gods were powerful in making it rain, assisting in slaying the beast.[9] The spreading of mythological perspective (call it evangelism) often happened then through war, through the battle of gods. It is no wonder, as we read in the Old Testament, that when Israel was conquered, the Philistines took their ark—which they assumed to be their god (1 Sam 5). Of course the point of that text is that Yahweh is no territorial, tribal god. The Philistines soon witness that Israel's God can act outside of the orbit of the original tribe's cosmic story, that Israel's God is not in need of a cosmic storyteller to be animated.[10] But this only illustrates that gods were tribal and the only way to evangelize was to capture the people or the people's gods. As Rifkin says, "In the age of mythical consciousness, being heroic was the measure of a man."[11]

Agricultural transition. The next energy regime to come on the scene following hunting and gathering is the agricultural age. Eventually the hunter-gatherer people discovered how to store the energy of the sun in crops. Now instead of encountering the earth as a person, plants could be managed, put in rows, and animals fenced and fatted. This period of agriculture would last thousands of years.[12] As human populations grow and the entropy (i.e., waste and cost) of energy becomes exponential, the time between the regimes shortens, moving from millions of years to thousands, and then, as we will see in chapter three, from centuries to decades. Yet, new energy regimes aren't around every corner. There is only a handful of regimes for the whole of human existence, which makes our own search for a new, clean regime all the more onerous.

As the agricultural regime became more sophisticated over time, people learned not only how to manage plants in rows and animals in fences, but how to get the essential resource of water through hydro-ducts from one area to another. As water traveled, so too did people, and the once distinct languages had to evolve to some common tongue so the resources of agriculture could be managed and traded. After all, as people got better and better at growing, soon they had more than they (or their people) needed, allowing the excess to be traded for other goods.

As this common tongue became necessary across vast stretches of space, soon writing was needed. Rifkin explains that in every great agricultural society script or writing was soon developed. This writing was used to manage the new energy regime. But just as soon, the cosmological stories were transferred from oral tradition to text. Now in text, gods were no longer local, transferred only through war, but transcended one locale and could place a demand on anyone or any people that had the text itself. Talcott Parsons explains,

> Once there are sacred texts, . . . these are subject both to continual editing
> and to complex processes of interpretation and tend to become the focus
> of specialized intellectual competence and prestige in the religious field
> and on the cultural level of rationalized systems of religious doctrine.

> Groups who have a special command of the sacred writings may then
> attain a special position in the religious system as a whole—the Jewish
> rabbis of the Talmudic tradition present a particularly salient case.[13]

This pushed the personal connection from blood ties to religious ties.[14]
In other words, those who shared your religion by reading your sacred
texts were called brother or sister. This is why the parable of the good
Samaritan is so significant (Lk 10). (We'll return to this in more detail
later.) The parable throws hearers off balance by calling the followers of
Jesus to risk danger for the sake of someone who is not a Jew, for one
that does not read the law, for a stranger that lives beyond that context's
circle of personal connection.

Ministry. To think about ministry, the pastor (or spiritual leader) and
evangelism in this period is more than difficult. After all, this is the
period that stretches over the heart of the Christian tradition, starting
sometime, imperiously, around Moses and going until the period of the
Reformation (if not after). Therefore, to keep it broad, we can state that
this was the period of the rise of the priesthood,[15] whether at the beginning with Aaron and the first and second temple periods in Israel, or
at the end of this period with the rise of the priesthood in the period of
the church fathers leading into European Catholicism. And the priest's
job, according to Weber, was *not* to proclaim spiritual or social change
(this was the job of the prophet), but to manage divine things.

The spiritual leader as priest was the one who offered sacrifices or
mediated the sacraments, and did so as the sacred text stipulated. But
the pastor as priest did more. The pastor in this period was the devoted
and authorized reader of the sacred text. Whether it was rabbis reading
Torah and providing midrash or medieval priests reading the New Testament in Greek and performing mass in Latin, the pastor was the
manager of divine things by being the sole devoted reader of the sacred
book.[16] After all, at least part of the Protestant Reformation related to
loosing the priests' grip on the Bible, translating it into the common
vernacular so all people could read it.

Managing of this energy regime through writing allowed for large
empires to dominate huge spaces.[17] Caesar Augustus could keep his
hand on the Jews in Israel in the first century because of the communi-

cation system, and he could use writing to direct his governors or his generals. This allowed for the sweeping impact of civilizations (complex cultures) on others. Around the Mediterranean it is nearly impossible to find a place not affected by Roman culture in this period. People were literally evangelized to this way of being by the currents of imposing civilizations. It is no wonder that this may be when the largest evangelistic impact in Christian history occurred (for good or ill), when Constantine converted the empire overnight to Christianity. Too often the priest, the pastor, was spiritual defender of the civilization, using the sacred text to support the ruling system.[18]

We can see evangelism as imposed civilization; as with all periods of evangelism there are both positives and negatives. Yet, for the sake of example, it may be most helpful to look at one of the most shameful evangelistic operations of Christian history, the Crusades. The way to recover the Holy Land and evangelize the heathens was to bring forth the force of civilization, the power of a civilization's knights. It was justified because the Christians were civilized, and after all, the Muslims didn't share the same religious sacred text and therefore deserved personhood only if they converted. As we'll see, such a perspective obscures Jesus' teaching on love of neighbor.

It is worth adding that in the time of the Reformation, which was a transitional time when the communication system was changing, and on the horizon was a new energy regime, the Catholic Church in many ways was the proprietor of civilization. Religion and civilization were inextricably linked. To give one popular example, King Henry, the lord of the realm of England, a divinely appointed master of civilization, had to answer to the pope for his sex life. For the pope was true lord of all of European civilization. But at the same time a dirty monk of the peasants in Germany, Martin Luther, a crass, uncivilized man, was using that very sacred writing, the very text of the Bible, to point to the hypocrisy of the pope as lord of civilization, and giving the sacred text to the common person, fracturing the exclusive right to it by the lords of civilization, the kings of empire.

To be continued . . .

3

Transitioning from the Pastor as Self-Help Entertainer

What Relational Ministry Can't & Must Become

As we continue to play with Rifkin's history, it will become clear how much the conception of the pastor, ministry and evangelism has shifted in the last 100 to 150 years. It will be the pursuit of this chapter to place the pastor, ministry and evangelism as our central focus.

In chapter two we explored two periods (hunting-gathering and agriculture) that each lasted thousands to millions of years. Yet, in this chapter we'll see three significant transitions occurring in quick succession and having radical impact on our understanding of pastoral ministry. In chapter two our purview was vast. In this chapter it will be narrow, examining more directly how the conceptions of pastor, ministry and evangelism coalesced in these periods for American Protestants.

It is important to remember that there is no such thing as a clean break in history. These transitions can still be spotted in our denominations and congregations. To talk about transitions is *not* to assume that the bone breaks cleanly between one epoch of time and another. Rather, all historical change comes as frayed transitions taking at least pieces and fragments of a passing era into the new one. As I play with Rifkin and Weber, making broad points in my sandbox, it will be helpful to remember that no clear break is possible. And that remnants of the past persist into the future, leading from broad perspectives in the last chapter to narrower views of pastoral ministry in this one.

HISTORY CONTINUED

Steam and coal transition (the first Industrial Revolution). The long-reigning energy regime of agriculture would transition slowly, and with stops and starts. But when the slow change finally took hold, it was impossible to not feel its iron grip. According to Rifkin the energy regime transitioned from stored sun in seeds to the steam and coal of the Industrial Revolution. This new energy regime, coupled with a new communication system to manage it—print—allowed for an all-new conception and organization of people. Now, because coal and other resources of the Industrial Revolution were found in some places and not others, boundaries and borders became important; who owned the resources of the land was a vital question. While in the hunting-gathering period the earth was alive, it was personified, now the earth was inert, it was simply a basket, maybe a beautiful one, but just a container of resources needed to animate manmade machines.

This attention to borders due to resources meant a new focus on the nation-state (countries). Now, as Rifkin explains, personal connection (who you defined as a person) moved from blood ties to religious ties to, in this period, ideological ties. The rise of the nation-state due to the energy regime of the first Industrial Revolution brought forth ideological consciousness. This ideological consciousness would have its darkest days in the trenches of the world wars, bloody wars fought (at least in Europe) by those sharing religious commitments but nevertheless opposed ideologically. A German Christian could kill an English Christian because they lived in two ideologically opposed nations. It no longer mattered that they read the same sacred book.

But of course it wasn't simply locale; to live in Germany, England or America was to breathe the ideological air, it was to see *oneself* as a citizen of these particular people. While thinkers like Ann Swidler have reminded us that cultures are always more complicated than simply saying "Americans are like this" or the French like that, there nevertheless appears, especially postwar, to be an ideological divide between East and West.[1] It was ideology that made another a companion or enemy.

And often this air became infused with ideological significance through the press, through the distribution of pamphlets and posters made possible by the new communication system of printing. It was, after all, this very system that made it possible for the Reformation to wrestle power away from the priests of Catholic Europe at the end of the last period. But, when this new communication system was full-blown in newspapers and pamphlets, it created ideologically loyal citizens of industrial nation-states. And steam and coal connected these ideological citizens bound within fashioned boundary lines called countries.

Ideological citizenship made possible through the communication system of the press did even more. It potentially sowed the seeds of an individualism that would become full-blown in the twentieth century. After all, it was the individual who read; "I am" the reader.[2]

Ministry. It is not that religion gave way with the transition into this new period. Rather, religion remained a constant reality, but now it too became embedded within the nation-state. Western countries were considered "Christian nations," and the number of consistent worshipers at churches justified this label. It wouldn't be until the next period that religious hegemony would be overcome. In the new energy regime and communication system, ministry was broadly seen as perpetuating or protecting a way of life. Through law and government the way of life of a nation-state was upheld functionally, but it was through religion that this way of life was fortified culturally, spiritually and morally.

Perhaps the best example of this comes at the close of this period, an intensely ideological time in which President Eisenhower is reported to have said that he didn't care what faith American people participated in, just that they did. What was important for the nation-state, especially one in conflict with a secular communism, was to hold to some religion—not for the sake of religion but for the nation-state's ideology. The early Billy Graham is an example of this. In the mid-twentieth century Graham's rhetoric not only spoke of an individual relationship with Jesus but also had strong overtones of American nationalism. Some even think that Graham's escalation to America's great preacher had much to do with the support of business and political leaders' appreciation for his hot, nationalist message against the backdrop of the cold war.[3]

Or to give a counterexample, it was because of this very sensed reality that Karl Marx railed against Christianity in the nineteenth century, calling all religion the opiate of the people, drugging them to focus only on being good and seeking heaven, overlooking that the machines of the new energy regime were beating and oppressing them. And the very moral system pastors presented as "the Christian way" overlooked such a state, calling people to be dutiful to what, in the end, Marx contended, was hurting them.

Though this may be overstated, even so it appears at least in some way that ministry in this period was about pushing individual citizens to be moral and upstanding. Both abolition and temperance, while having a collective thrust about them, were often legitimated with an ethic of national and individual uprightness; drunkenness was bad for the nation and bad for an individual's soul.

And no one was more upstanding than the pastor. The *man* of the cloth was an honorable and holy man, a model of the good "citizen."[4] The way a pastor functionally lived out being both the good citizen and calling *his* flock to do the same was through moral exhortation, through imploring *his* congregation to act morally and be good citizens. This was a particularly strong phenomenon in American pulpits. For instance, Dietrich Bonhoeffer, while in New York in the first years of the 1930s, writing to friends back in Germany, discusses visiting Riverside Presbyterian Church, calling the preaching simply moral pragmatism—something he found stomach-turning. So the pastor was moral exemplar, using *his* pulpit to implore his congregation to be good citizens themselves.[5] This fit perfectly with the ideological consciousness of the time made possible by the energy regime of industrialization and the communication system of print.

Yet, it must also be mentioned, if only shortly, that there was another, very strong, pastor response in this period of ideological consciousness and a coal energy regime. Another response of the pastor was to engage with exerted force into *justice*. Pastors and ministers like Walter Rauschenbusch, Dorothy Day and Reinhold Niebuhr took action in words and deeds against the dehumanizing practices of the industrial revolution. Pastoral ministry as moral exhortation, whether through the call to upright citizenship or social engagement, rested squarely (as a salve or a bristle) in the craw of the nation-state.

Evangelism. As in the other two periods, evangelism too can be seen in line with the consciousness formed by the energy regime and communication system. Where war and the spread of civilization bore the evangelistic thrust of the other two periods, here evangelism as missionary activity may have found its golden era in the focus on overseas geographical mission. In the coal regime evangelism went global. After all, everyone in the "Christian" nation-state was (at least civically) a believer. Therefore, evangelism became about missionary activity done "out there," as people from one "Christian" nation-state were sent on steamships to convert "non-Christian" people in exotic lands. Through the technology made possible by the nation-state young men and women could board ships in industrial centers and head out for adventures in lands never touched by steam or coal. Coming from a different (perceived as advanced) energy regime, they could morally justify imposing the Western way on others as they sought to share their own consciousness, communication and conceptions of God. Just as those in nation-states went on campaigns to win office or to war to protect their borders, so missionaries went on campaigns to Africa or South America to evangelize the heathens, the heathens being those who had not yet found themselves in the new energy regime.[6] Of course, even in this period there were outliers to this perspective, such as John William Colenso. But we remember (and honor these people) because of their prophetic opposition to the dominant perspective.

Electric and managed oil transition (second Industrial Revolution). In cities all over America you can easily spot the church buildings constructed in the coal era and those in the oil era. Usually resting in city neighborhoods, church buildings of the coal era have no parking lots, because people walked to the denominational church of their neighborhood. Successful churches of the oil era, however, tended to be bigger, needing more space for programming and having huge parking lots, in order to accommodate those driving miles to participate in these programs.

It was a radical transition from stored sun in seeds to iron machines puffing dark smoke, and the juxtaposition was intense, leading to labels

for people with machines like "advanced" and "developed." Technology
has been part of the story of all the energy regime and communication
system transitions through history, but now that feeding machines
became the objective, technology, as advancement and development,
became everything. As capitalist markets expanded, so too did the drive
for the new, through technology. Soon the machines creating the new
things we desired needed a stronger cocktail than coal and steam to
animate them. A new resource, found in the earth, like coal, was uncovered and discovered to fuel combustion engines. Rifkin explains that
oil became the blood of the new energy regime, coursing through the
car motors of the American public and beyond, and it was pulled from
the ground by huge oil pumps dotting the landscape of the Southwest.

Of course, oil fueled much more than cars. The very machines that
allowed for the creation, processing or transporting of anything, even
our food, made us dependent on this liquid gold. But it was through the
car that most people directly engaged this new energy regime, even
pumping it themselves into their tanks. The car was invented toward the
end of the previous energy regime; the Model-T became the quintes-
sential product of the assembly-line factory of the first Industrial Revolution. But it was not until after World War II that the car became as
American as apple pie and the second (oil) Industrial Revolution would
be in full stride. As cities like Los Angeles moved away from public
transportation (streetcars) and toward freeways, cars gave people the
feeling of freedom to go and do what they individually wanted whenever
and wherever they individually wished. The car encased people in steel
and glass, moving them as individuals. The coal and steam industrial
revolution would slowly start us down a track of individualism in its
burgeoning urban centers and assembly-line factories. But it was in this
period, this second industrial revolution of oil and electricity, that the
individual was assumed to be his or her own universe.

In this energy regime what had been slowly evolving throughout the
previous energy regimes became actualized; we became (*or so it seemed*)
independent, and relationships with other human beings became not a
necessity but an individual choice. This is what Anthony Giddens calls
the pure (self-chosen) relationship.[7] Machines and technology freed us

from dependence on other people, making us full-blown individuals.

The communication system created to manage this energy regime, according to Rifkin, was the wave created by the electrical pulses pushed through circuits originating from power plants run by oil and coal. This electrical system ran right into the individual home, allowing us to plug into a machine and receive information through the wave itself. At first these individual devices accepted the wave and decoded the sounds of voices and music, but soon, with the right receiver, we could obtain not only sound through the wave, but moving pictures as well. Oil (and coal) allowed for electricity to be pushed to huge parts of the country, forming a new communication system around the radio and television, which had the result of defining people further (and radically so) as individuals. We not only drove our car alone, but could sit in front of our TV alone (or with our small nuclear family) watching the programs beamed through our walls by the wave. We were individually free to watch whichever program we individually chose, or if bored we could get into our car and drive wherever we individually desired.

It is no wonder, then, that the new way we understood ourselves in this period pushed forth by the oil-electric energy regime and the communication system of the radio/television was a "pseudo-therapeutic (self-help) consciousness."[8] As full-blown individuals we became *obsessively* concerned with ourselves as independent feeling subjects. Now that technology was meeting so many of our basic needs, like giving us food in sealed packets at grocery stores, we could move our attention from survival to fulfillment. The very fact that in the second sentence of this paragraph I used the word *obsessively* shows the depth of this consciousness. *Obsession* is a psychological term; others like it (*inferiority complex, anxiety, Freudian slip, mother issues, transference*, etc.) became part of common speech.[9] This is not to disparage psychology or therapy. Rather, concepts and examples drawing from these perspectives will be clear as our project unfolds. But a form of amateur self-help analysis soaked deeply into our cultural context of unquenchable individualism at this time.

While in the last period relational connection broadened, making "persons" those who shared your national ideology, this period turned us inward with force, making everyone a feeling, self-actualizing individual with choices. The question was how would you individually make these choices, and how would these choices affect your individual (or your child's, for instance) self-esteem.

Ministry. Ministry in this period turned to programs of intervention. Surely, some ministries were more focused on *programs* and others on *intervention.* But it appeared in some ways that programs and interventions were united. In other words, at one level what ministry had to provide was programs that would get individuals to decide to come to *this* church. And by *programs* I mean extra-worship experiences, like men's group, youth group, children's group, marriage support group, over-sixty group, knitting club, slow-pitch softball teams, and the list could go on and on. If individuals had their own cars, then they could choose to go to church anywhere. And a church's program would serve as the magnet to get mobile individuals in metal cars to be pulled to one church over another.

These programs made the church attractive in a competitive religious marketplace of individual choice. The programs seemed to push individuals into membership (or at least commitment) in one place, over driving to another. People would say, "I love this church, it has something for everyone in my family," meaning it has a program for every individual. And it is no wonder that the church called these activities "programs," something that you individually chose to participate in, just as TV and radio had been running programs of their own.

The communication system of "programming" became the strategy of the church's ministry. But the church seemed to want to claim moral ground over TV and radio; after all, the church's ministry of programs weren't only for the purpose of entertainment but also provided pseudo-therapeutic intervention of self-help, such as three ways to be a good husband, how to live the life God wants you to live, or praying to overcome past issues.

As the list of programs in the previous paragraph points to, most had a pseudo-therapeutic bent to them.[10] Not in the sense that they were therapy (and grounded in psychological theory and practice), but in the sense that through participation we could work on our individual self, becoming a better, more godly parent, spouse, man, mother or business partner. These programs allowed us individually, in the tone of the pseudo-therapeutic self-help consciousness, to become the self we wanted to be. It is no wonder that megachurches offering huge rosters of programs, the Crystal Cathedral and a *Purpose-Driven Life* became so successful in this period. They were the perfect mix of program and self-help intervention created for individuals.

The pastor. The pastor changed radically in this period too, transitioning from a moral exemplar in the last period into an entrepreneurial manager in this one.[11] In the oil era it would be essential for the pastor to create and manage the church's many programs. So instead of a learned, moral *man*, the ideal pastor became a creative, energy-bursting visionary that individuals could identify with and therefore would want to come to that church, bringing more and more individuals into participation with the offered programming.

Of course, not all pastors fit this ideal type, and some chafed against it. I understand that in different denominations and traditions things may have looked differently. It may appear that I'm only speaking of evangelicalism, and while this may be true, the evangelical pastor did set the terms for all pastoral ministry in this period. Or at least, the evangelical pastor became the cultural picture of "the pastor," just as in the coal era the mainline pastor was the portrait of the minister.

The pastor as entrepreneurial manager with a congregation as large in participants as his personality won the day. After all, programs run on numbers, number of viewers or listeners, and the programs of the church were no different. And so often these visionary entrepreneurs could grow a church, but as it compounded they couldn't manage it. Therefore, this period brought on the creation of the executive or business management pastor. The pastor who would manage the day-to-day programs so the entrepreneur would be available to provide what individuals came to church for—an entertaining, pseudo-therapeutic connection with the entrepreneurial pastor.

In many ways the pastor became an entertainer with a strong self-help bent, preaching sermons that would make people drive miles to hear them, preaching sermons with (three) basic pseudo-therapeutic

points that were directly applicable to the individual life, helping us
become a more successful parent, friend and therefore follower of Jesus.
So the pastor was not just an entertainer, but a self-help therapeutic
entertainer that allowed individuals to identify with him or her and
therefore give their loyalty to the church. It was worth the drive across
town, passing a dozen other churches on the way, because Pastor Held's
sermons were engaging, inspiring and individually helpful. You were as
loyal (or more) to him for how his advice affected your life, as to the
church community itself.

And Pastor Held led no longer as a cleric or an elite moral man, but as
a wise friend, giving advice on how "you" could live a successfully godly
life. It is no wonder that the pastor's outfit changed from the tie and
jacket (or religious vestment) to casual golf attire or even a Hawaiian
shirt of an advice-giving, fun friend.[12]

Evangelism. When it came to evangelism in this period, things shifted
from geographical mission so popular in the coal era, to what could be
called the *relationalistic*. Where evangelism in the other periods con-
sisted of large movements like boarding steamships and heading to
Africa, or moving on the currents of empires to bring forth Christian
civilization, in this period evangelism went small, it went individual.
After all, if the way we understood ourselves, to follow Rifkin, went from
ideological to self-help, then evangelism would need to follow suit. In
this oil regime the individual became the center of existence; it became
our job to construct our individual self.[13] Ministry followed this focus on
the individual by centering on programs of intervention, and the pastor
became a pseudo-therapeutic self-help entertainer that individuals could
identify with (liked listening to), providing them the advice and direction
they needed to be healthy and holy individuals who followed Jesus.

The church then didn't so much *send* evangelistically as it had in the
past, but instead took the stance of inviting people to *come* to the church,
to come and find the individual self-help insight they needed to live
good and holy lives.[14] But there is the rub: how do people know to come
and receive what the church is offering? How do they know that the
preaching is entertaining and the programs helpful? How do they know
of the individual benefits the church offers?

It then became the job of church members to tell others, to make a case to their neighbors, friends and coworkers on why they should individually participate in the church. The rise of friendship and neighbor evangelism saw the individual congregation members mobilized to serve as spokespeople for the programs, offering their own successful individual lives as proof that the programs worked, that following Jesus had individual benefits, that the preaching was helpful and the preacher funny.[15]

Evangelism as endorsing the benefits of the church to individuals, made relationships essential, but it also made relationships *for* something, for a purpose, for *influencing* individuals to come or act in a certain way.[16] And of course this wasn't any different, really, from the relationalistic focus of the TV spokesperson, building a relationship with a viewer to influence them to eat Wonder Bread or drive a Chevy.

People in churches were encouraged to reach out to neighbors and coworkers, not for the sake of the other person but for the purpose of getting the other person to come to Jesus or come to church. This is why I call it *relationalistic*, because in so many ways these engagements took the shape of relationships (like the TV spokesperson), but in the end the point was not the relationship itself but how the relationship won leverage to get the individual to decide to do something.[17]

When ministry takes on an ethos of self-help, offering pseudo-therapeutic programs as its form of ministry where numbers matter (and numbers always matter in programs, as we mentioned), then *influence* becomes the heart of ministry. Influence becomes the point. Influencing people to come, to do, to be, becomes central. (It is no wonder authors like Henri Nouwen and others writing against the performance of doing became prophets to baby-boomer churchgoers.)

A new day? To follow Rifkin one more step is to claim, with many others, that we are on the verge of something new. Rifkin believes that if something new doesn't happen soon, we'll find ourselves and the natural world in peril. This is so because the oil energy regime is nearing its limit, and to escape peril a new energy regime is needed. Pushes for hydrogen, solar and wind power have been explored and may with a few advances become the new energy regime. But if they will, Rifkin explains, it will depend on distribution, on being able to turn existing homes and buildings into energy producers and not solely consumers, allowing them to distribute their excess energy to others.[18] There will be a need for sharing, the kind of sharing that the new communication system has already created.[19] The Internet, the already-arrived communication system, makes it possible, Rifkin believes, for people to share energy as they do files and information.[20]

What is yet to be determined is what impact this will have on how we understand ourselves. Rifkin believes that consciousness changes in concert with energy regimes and communication systems, and it seems unequivocal that we are at the doorstep of a new regime as we find ourselves in an Internet age. Yet, for Rifkin, there are signs that we are already moving toward this new consciousness; following neuroscience, he believes we may be entering a time of sharing made possible by empathetic consciousness and the ability to see others as persons—something actually central to the Christian tradition but often obscured in our Western context, perhaps ready to be seen anew today. The child is willing to share her snack, almost as reflex, after witnessing the sadness of another child. She shares not for return but because she has seen; she acts for the other child not to win loyalty or even to alleviate the other child's distress. No, she acts because she feels the other's pain and is moved to join her in it. She simply but profoundly seeks to join the other child's place. The perspective that human beings are solely rational-choice calculators, always doing what serves their own interest, is dissolving.

Yet Rifkin isn't naïve. The new communication system seems to highlight that we are on the cusp of either sharing/cooperation or narcissistic self-involvement. Rifkin states, "The shift into a Third Industrial Revolution and a new distributed capitalism is leading both to a greater sense of relatedness . . . as well as a more fractured sense of self, and increased narcissism."[21] He continues, "The likely reality is that a younger generation is growing up torn between both a narcissistic and empathic mind-set, with some attracted to one and some to the other."[22]

A distributive energy dependent on sharing will only work, Rifkin believes, if a new way of understanding ourselves as *persons* arises. Yet the goal of this book is not to argue for a geo-political energy policy, or the need for government subsidized solar panels, or to reshape the Internet in a safer, more inclusive way. Rather, what Rifkin's perspective addresses and my adding to it, I hope, reveals is that a new conception of ministry is needed. The business as usual forms and perspectives of ministry done in the oil regime will need to give way to new ones.

Signs and growing pains for this needed new form of ministry in a new burgeoning era have already arrived in stops and starts. House churches, alt-worship and communities of faith with emergent sensibilities have sought to reconceptualize the church, the pastor and evangelism beyond the strictures of self-help programs of large corporate megachurches. They have sought a return, yes, in some ways to ancient practices and, yes, in some ways have stereotypically used the new communication system of the Internet to connect participants. But even more so, these communities have taken strides in hopes to be relational, to be smaller communities of *sharing* (whether it be thoughts or resources).[23]

Yet, as the atrophy and confusion around the emergent church in the last handful of years shows, while these movements have made significant stabs at reconceptualizing ministry in a distributive energy age, seeking relational connection in smaller and reflective communities of *sharing*, those feeling their way into this rethinking have not yet been able to offer an alternative vision of ministry other than the deconstruction of the passing regime, other than the need to be *communal* and *relational* (which without substance quickly become buzzwords). They have little theological conception of what relationships are and how they mediate the mystery of God's very presence.

This then will be my task for the rest of this book, to offer a conception of ministry and the pastor that fits with the arriving new world, and yet rests on a richly theological vision. My objective is to provide a vision of the church and pastor congruent with Rifkin's insight but standing on a deep and central Christian commitment. The rest of this book will make a case for a consciousness of personhood, built on the second person of the Trinity. I will argue that to be a person is to be in relationship, not for the sake of influence but for the sake of place sharing, for the sake of being with and being for. I could call this reality in theological language "incarnational," or in Rifkin's language "empathetic." As we go on we'll see how these very realities of incarnation and empathy are interconnected, the latter being the outer action of the former's inner reality. This will allow us to reconceptualize ministry as participation in the life of Christ through the personhood of the other, through relationship. But this personhood can only be opened to us through the ministry of the Spirit, which stirs our hearts and opens our eyes to see the other not as a calculating will to influence but as another to empathetically encounter, as another whose place I'm called to share.[24]

Then it appears that the time is right contextually to recover and deepen this theological perspective, helping to redefine pastoral ministry beyond the priestly reader, moral exemplar or self-help entertainer. Instead, the aim is to see the pastor as *convener of empathic encounter of personhood*, as the one who invites congregation members into relationships of place sharing with those in and outside the church. What this means and what this looks like will be the pursuit of the following chapters.

4

Sipping the Sweet,
Hard Liquor of Individualism

Ministry as the facilitation of empathic encounter through personhood occurred when the church council heard Dave's confession in the story in chapter one. To almost no one at the church had Dave been a person: he was a problem, an annoyance, or positively he was a volunteer, someone who did stuff for the church, someone who cared a lot about the church. But when Dave confessed the burdens that weighed the relationship most central to his being, he became just *Dave*, just beautifully broken Dave, a person, and a mysterious one at that, someone bound to others. As Shane said, "That day everything changed, Dave became a person." Shane explained that it changed not only peoples' perception of Dave but it changed Dave as well. It allowed him to be known as a person, but more than known, encountered. Now that Dave was seen as a person, free to act and be acted toward as a person, other people opened their own personhood to him. They began to share each others' place, to do ministry with and for each other, as, a concept I'll develop more later, place sharers.

THE PROBLEM OF INFLUENCE

Pastoral ministry in our new era must surround the practice of facilitating personal encounter, of setting a space for people to be in relationships not of individualized self-help but of human person to human person. Relationships in ministry cannot be for the purpose of influencing people (a blind spot of the era of pseudo-therapeutic self-help programs in the oil era), because such a motivation of influence blinds us from personhood. The other person becomes a problem to solve, something to fix, someone to win loyalty and resources from rather than another to encounter, a person to see and be with and for.

Influence becomes central because the self-help consciousness of the oil regime turns people into individuals. It shucks personhood and defines people solely as individuals, as free choosing wills disconnected from all others but through their decision. People are believed to be the sum total of their decisions, and therefore the church must influence these decisions. But these decisions cannot be influenced by force. The pseudo-therapeutic waters of self-fulfillment will not stand for any top-down coherence that cages individual freedom.

Still, people are their choices, it is believed, so how do we help them make good choices? How do we help them choose Jesus? We do this by becoming close enough to them through relationship that we can influence their decisions.[1] As friends, through relationship, we are given the place to offer advice and direction as the individual constructs his or her self. So through our relationship we influence others toward the ends we wish for them, toward the ends we believe are best for the individual. So influence becomes the currency both of individual spiritual growth and participation in programs.

If the critique isn't obvious, let me spell it out further: the problem with relationalistic influence is that it makes a fetish of the individual. Influence actually can only work as a strategy of ministry when we have misplaced the Christian commitment to persons and followed the Baal of individualism. Relationship as a means to influence isn't problematic if people are only individuals, for individualism assumes that people are bound only to their own will, and as long as they can will (think) correctly then they can be whole. But as I'll argue later, people are more than their wills; people are their relationships. Personhood demands that the other see me, and see me not as a will that decides, not as someone to get to a program or a church, but as a human being bound to others in love and fear. Personhood demands that I see the other as mystery to encounter, and not as a will to mold through influence.

ON THE PRECIPICE

This is all a must because it is in the field of personhood, it is in and through person-to-person relationships, that people encounter the ministry of God's action in the person of Jesus Christ. In and through personhood people, according to Paul, are drawn into union with Christ's own person, where Jesus' person becomes bound to their own person ("I no longer live, but Christ lives in me" [Gal 2:20 NIV]). Ministry in this new era becomes about *sharing*, sharing our person with and for each other as God, in Jesus, shares God's own person in the incarnation. When Dave shared his person, the divine and human collided. That very moment of confession, which unveiled Dave's person, became holy, as my friend said, because it was where personhood was revealed and the personhood of God was encountered.

But as Rifkin's ideas warned us at the end of chapter three, on the precipice of this new era it appears that we are teetering between awakening to the personal and rigid ossification to individualism (and even a narcissistic one at that). We could then say we are at the point of the "crisis of the personal," not because it is an impossibility but because we stand at the point of an either-or, either we will turn our theology and practice of ministry toward personhood *or* we'll be mesmerized by market mentalities and consumer calculations and therefore worship the false Baal of individualism. Will a pastor be one who can win the loyalty of individuals or one who opens space in preaching, liturgy, study and fellowship for persons to encounter persons in the confession of God's own incarnate person?

The crisis of the personal. When my son Owen went to daycare for the first time, he was sixteen months old and was a novice at language, to say the least. He really only knew a handful of words and even less that anyone but we, his parents, could understand. He was our firstborn, so his world revolved around us; he had very little interaction with older kids, like those scary rabble-rousing two-year-olds. But after just two days something strange happened. Owen had picked up on some language, some language that he knew even in his sixteen-month-old head was soaked in meaning. It was language that communicated anger and desperation and even power. It was the word *mine*. Owen had witnessed two- and three-year-olds shouting it for two days: "Mine, mine, mine!" He had no real idea what it meant or more truly how to use this word, but he knew the ethos, the feeling, it communicated.

So after two days when he became frustrated with us he'd use his new word. In frustration and desperation he would shout it out of context. We'd say, "Owen, it is time for bed," and he'd run away from us shouting "Mine! Mine! Mine!" We'd say, "Owen, you need a diaper change," and he'd shout, "No, mine!" You could almost see him with every bursting "mine" becoming drunk with power. In a healthy way he was differentiating himself, becoming in touch with his feelings, but in a negative way, a negative way our Western world exasperates to the nth degree, he was making *himself* his own boss. His uttered "mine" was the hard but sweet liquor of individualism.

Already I have tried in the pages of this book to draw a contrast between individualism and personhood, giving some detail on what I mean. But I'm sure more is needed. So, what is the issue with individualism, and why does it threaten the personal? And even if it does, who cares? What does this have to do with pastoral ministry? How does individualism make relationships of ministry problematic?[2]

PERSONS VERSUS INDIVIDUALS

You are your interests. There are ways that juxtaposing persons and individuals seems like a showdown between Coke and Pepsi. Truth be told, there isn't much difference between the cola giants, other than what can be measured in degrees—Pepsi is a little sweeter, Coke tastes a tad fuller, but both are cola, after all. It can feel the same with *persons* and *individuals*, as if when using one word we basically mean the same as the other. For instance, the concepts of persons and individuals respect the *I*, both seem to uphold the importance of freedom and life.

Yet, when we scratch beyond the surface we can see a great difference between these perspectives. Individualism is constructed around the core commitment of seeing people as fundamentally rational animals that are loyal to what enhances or fulfills their individual self-interest. Individualism says you are your interests, where personalism says you are your relationships. In individualism I marry because of what it offers me. I work because of the esteem or resources it yields me. I have sex because of how it makes me feel. So people are their interests, and those interests are individually formed—my interests are mine, I get to pick them, and my pursuit of them shouldn't be hampered. All of our lives, like two-year-olds we're cajoled to shout, "My interests are mine, mine, mine!" and so mine that they are me.[3]

Individualism, as a theory, contends that because we are our interests (as it is individually and for the most part rationally conceived), they should never be opposed by outside forces. We see this within political persuasions in America. Liberals contend that individual interests, for instance, to be pregnant or not, or to marry whom you want, should never be opposed. Conservatives too are wed to individualism, believing that no government program or tax law should be able to thwart your own individual interest; you should be able to spend your money how you want, even on a handgun to take to a bar. The American political system is so fiercely divided because ultimately both groups are so similar, resting their feet squarely in the warm, mucky waters of individualism, where we are our interests. There is blood in the water because both are fighting over such narrow views framed by individualism.[4]

Yet, this isn't just about politics. Those of us in pastoral ministry have found ourselves wading in the same lukewarm waters of individualism, having our own purview narrowed. When we define people as their interests, when we assume that they choose one church over another because it meets their interests, then we see influencing their decision as the key to pastoral ministry. And so we use relationships in pastoral ministry to influence the interests of individuals, seeking to convert not their person, but their interests (after all, they are their interests). We want them to be interested in spiritual things rather than secular, interested in spending time at church rather than at the golf course, interested in listening to our sermons instead of watching football.

And we use relationships to influence; because changing someone's individual interests is not easy, we need to persuade them toward another subjective desire. It then becomes the relationship that seems to open the door of your individual self to allow for your interest to be converted. So the relationship becomes a key that allows you to recalibrate someone's interests. It is an inception, yes, as in the Christopher

Nolan movie. In the movie trained thieves enter people's subconscious through dreams, stealing their ideas. Yet the movie turns when the group of thieves decides not to enter someone's consciousness to steal a thought, but to do something much more difficult, to implant a thought from outside the dreamer. They call this an inception. When relationships are used to influence, they becomes a way of implanting new interests in an individual's consciousness, believing that if you can implant a new idea you have influence over him or her. The relationship (like the dream in Nolan's movie) seems to make the individual's consciousness vulnerable enough that you can implant ideas that will convert his or her interest, that will influence the individual's commitment toward some end. To say it crassly, the relationship is believed to weaken the person's consciousness, so the pastor or ministry can convert his or her interest. In pastoral ministry bound within individualism, it is not the person's humanity that matters but his or her interests.

Wants. When people are their interests, when people are individuals, then we assume that they are their wants. And when pastoral ministry mounts the treadmill of attending to individuals' wants, the dial gets turned to eleven and fatigue and burnout are next. Wants are the tentacles of our interests; the clearer we are about our interests, the more direct and intense our wants become. The more we are individually committed to our interests, the more we know what we want. For example, I come to this church because I want my daughter to be in a good youth group, because I'm interested in her being good and not getting pregnant. I like this church because I want to feel connected, because I'm interested in feeling better about myself, so I want the preaching to be good and inspiring.

Now your job as the pastor is to serve the wants of your people, and the more defined their interests, the more they smack you with their wants. If you can't accommodate their wants, they may become interested in finding another church or another pastor.

When people are individuals who are their interests through their wants, the consumer mentality of our context has entered the church. This mentality is built on individualism; it can only exist in its intensity because of it. The best consumer is someone that knows what he or she wants, and knows what's wanted because he or she is clear about particular interests—to wear the fashion of this subculture, to drive a car that projects a certain image or promises to protect his newborn child. The best consumer wants a product because it meets his or her interest, and it becomes marketing's job to influence those interests and to fortify the doctrine of individualism, asserting continually in images and jingles that we are our interests—so want away.[5] We can see this in marketing strategies through the twentieth century. Once a product was advertised for what it *did;* now it is advertised for what it *means,* for how it serves our deepest interest. Nike isn't about shoes, it is about much more; it is about our interest, it is about our individual self. To use relationships for influence is to welcome the logic of mass consumption.

When Jesus teaches his disciples to pray, he invites them to pray, "Give us this day our daily bread" (Mt 6:11; Lk 11:3). Karl Barth beautifully explains that this petition is the invitation for the disciples to pray their needs and not their wants.[6] To pray for daily bread is to extract the need from the want—something ever so difficult and delicate in our time. But when the interest of individualism becomes our master, then ministry is encouraged to ignore or bypass need. Yet the very lifeblood of love, the very motivation of the incarnation is not *want* but *need.* It is the need of humanity that leads God to become human. I'll unpack this further in the following chapters. But for now it is enough to say that when ministry bows to the wants of interest, overlooking needs, it fails to see persons. Need becomes the starting point of imagining pastoral ministry as the facilitation of encounter with personhood. Need is to see persons.

Objects. Individualism has a hard time seeing need (even if it is the idealistic want to do away with need) because when we are our interests, then the world outside of us, even other people, becomes an object. Objects are the fetishes of our wants. When we are told that we are our interests and our interests are attained through our wants, then the world is a candy store, making everything an object we can possess. When we are our interests and our wants form our actions, then everything becomes an object, and this becomes a frontal attack on the personal. When other people become objects, they are either assets or detriments to achieve my interests. Individualism teaches us that the world is made up of objects to possess or reject, and those possessed are mine, and they are mine because I want them, because they meet my interest.

So to say it again, when I am my interest, as individualism asserts, then people become objects.[7] We acknowledge that they too are individuals with interests, sure, but what makes us, us, and them, them, is the goal of attaining our distinctive interests. So even as acknowledged individuals, because they are their interest and their interests are distinct from my own, they become objects that either help or hurt the goal of meeting my individual interest; they either help me get what I want or frustrate it. If our distinctive interests can be united, if we have the same explicit or tacit goals, then we are friends; if not, we either choose to be indifferent, or if that isn't possible, then enemies.

The good Samaritan is good because he sees a person in need; he is lying beaten, his need cannot be missed. For the priest and Levite the beaten man is an object, an object that threatens their most securely held interests; they want to stay safe and stay religiously pure. The Samaritan acts for this other in need, to the threat of his own interest, he risks his safety and shares his money in response to the *need* of the other, who has become a person to him, become another he is bound to (Lk 10:25-37).

The Samaritan recognizes that he is bound to the one suffering because he has seen the beaten man through his need, and through need the beaten man cannot be made into an object. Soaked in his need, he is a person yearning for another to share in his broken person. The Samaritan is called into a relationship of persons, a relationship where the Samaritan *shares* the place of the beaten man, not because he wants to change the loyalties of the beaten man's interest but because the Samaritan sees the beaten man's person by participating in his need. Seeing the beaten man's need, the Samaritan sees a person and responds to his person by *sharing* in his suffering, by *sharing* his resources, by *sharing* his place.

What makes the Samaritan "good" is not his own religious piety but his willingness to see the *person*, to see the need and *share* in it, which pushes his own interest to the background so that he can see the personhood of the beaten man. And when we see persons, we find ourselves acting, because *to act with and for another is the heart of what it means to be a person.* Jesus' audience wouldn't have missed that the Samaritan, a half-Jew (a half-human), became an impossible-to-miss person by seeing the humanity of the beaten man and *sharing* in it. It is impossible to *share* in objects, to dwell in or with objects; we can only use objects, but it is dwelling in and with that is the very current of God's action in and through the incarnation of Jesus Christ.

Cooperation. Rifkin has made a case that *sharing* will become central in this new period we are entering, but only if we can avoid the sticky traps that individualism sets. I am arguing that *sharing* in the need of others is how we participate in personhood, even, as I'll develop later, how we participate in the life of Christ. Yet sharing as *cooperation of mutual participation* is nearly impossible when individualism has become full-blown. (Again, just pointing to the American political system is enough to make this clear; politicians can never cooperate because to do so is to be forced to see the other as a person, and the political game is to make your opponent not a person but an object of threat to your deepest interest.) Cooperation demands we see persons, that we share in their place to the point of at least indwelling their expressed need.[8]

The best option where individualism reigns is the you-scratch-my-back-I'll-scratch-yours agreement. Here people are nuanced objects, or better, they become a mutual competitor with whom we have a truce, a partnership where as individuals I help you meet your interests so that you help me meet mine. We are friends or lovers as long as our individual interests are being met, and our wants not frustrated; you only have value as a partner in honoring my wants and meeting my interests.

When the world is made up of objects, and objects are to be possessed, then life is just one big competition. *Whoever dies with the most toys wins*, as the bumper sticker of embraced individualism (with a speedball of consumerism) boasts. But we could add, though it is never as boldly shouted as the bumper sticker, that at synod meetings, presbyteries or other pastoral gatherings the hidden mantra exists, *Whoever dies with the biggest church and most programs wins.* Competition is intense for pastors. It seems that too often we judge the value of our ministry by the ability to get individuals to come; we turn our ministries into objects, things to possess. Ministry becomes programs because we imagine people need objects to possess, and programs are objectified—we tell people what the program offers them, what they will individually get out of it, and how it will help them meet their own individual interests. We even say, "You're really going to *want* to come to this!"

This isn't to say that *programmed* (even themed) spaces are bad or unimportant for pastoral ministry. After all, the church council meeting where Dave became a person was a programmed event. But in retrospect it was much more than an objectified program, it was a space where people encountered each other by sharing in each other's need; *need* and not *want* became the air they breathed through the exercise of drawing each other's faces. Spaces are important, church calendars are necessary, but the heart of ministry is not giving people objects to possess (either in programs or even doctrines) but spaces to be encountered, places to become persons one-to-another, to confess their need and to be known, to dwell in and with one another. Our relationships in ministry are for encountering persons, not to win loyalty to objects (whether church, program or religious perspective); they are the invitation to *share* in the other's place, to dwell one with another.

No relationship with objects. There is no relationship with objects, or rather there is only the relationships of individual to possessions, of loyalty to things (which is *not* the relationship of persons). Too often our context has used the word *relationship* to mean that which I'm associated, connected or affiliated with, that which I've desired or want or meets my interest. Yet this logic of possessed connection or affiliation misses the theological meaning of relationships. Theologically, relationship means to indwell. It has the sense of spiritually sharing in, such as when we say the presence of Christ shares in (indwells) the bread and wine. Or, as I will unpack in chapter ten, we say that Jesus' divine and human natures are so in relationship that they indwell each other in his single person. Human beings cannot indwell objects; we cannot be in relationship with them. Human beings can only indwell other persons, because to be a person is to be an *embodied* spirit, and spirit can only indwell spirit.

I may have a strong association with my computer (I love using it), and my kids may have significant connection to their swing set (they're on it all the time), but we cannot indwell these things, for neither my computer nor their swing set is spirit; it is not a person.[9] Neither the computer nor the swing set can die; only embodied spirit tragically confronts its end. To lose my computer or for the swing set to be overtaken by atrophy is sad; we used and enjoyed the object, it facilitated work or fun, but when it is gone, I lose nothing of myself; I simply need to replace it.[10] But spirit cannot be replaced. When a loved one dies, he or she is gone and the part of us that was bound to this person through relationship is lost. We grieve because the person is irreplaceable and is ripped from our spirit, taking part of it into darkness. Objects can be replicated, but persons are infinitely unique, because objects are material but persons are embodied spirit.

Assuming what can't be, that we can be in relationship with objects, has confused us in pastoral ministry. We haven't been able to see the difference between relationships that are about persons and those about objects, those that seek to indwell the person and those that seek to influence the individual. We've allowed individualism's obsession for the object to be the hidden danger in the Trojan horse of our flippant, indiscriminate use of *relationship*. When pastors say that they want the church to be relational, for it to be about relationship, too often they've fallen into the cultural, confused language of individualism, using the relationship to get individuals to change their interests, to be objects that they can possess and place in the ledger of members. But the minute we seek to use the relationship as a tool, people are no longer persons but have become objects (or projects) that we seek to influence to a new interest. We cannot share, to the point of indwelling, an object, for objects have no need, no mystery of yearning that shakes their spirit.

And when we as pastors encounter others as objects that we possess through the flypaper of our relationalism, we too lose our humanity; we lose our personhood and become sales reps trying to convince others, through our faux relationships, that our perspectives or programs are worth wanting to be part of, that individuals can possess them like objects. When relationships are about influence, it encourages us to see people as objects to possess.

The monstrous, impersonal pursuit of the ideal. One of the reasons individualism is so seductive is that it rests squarely on the foundation of idealism.[11] It believes that all people actually can get their interests, that all our wants can be fulfilled. If we could just find the right idea, if we could just convince people to give loyalty to the right perspective, we could all have what we want. Individualism is so sweet and savory in the mouth because it is marinated in an idealism that lacks the courage to admit darker realities of our existence. And ironically, unable to admit these darker realities, idealism always runs the danger (as history has shown) of doing the monstrous to keep the purity, integrity or power of the idea.

This is one of the great dangers of democracy as it blends with consumer individualism. In the end it becomes an idea, an ideal, an ideology (and a good one), but dangerously cut off from the communal realities that bore it (at least in America) in agrarian communities. Jeffersonian democracy contends that all people are equal and should be free to have life and liberty and to pursue happiness. But when threat comes to this very idea in, for instance, the oil regime, governments have felt justified in killing and imprisoning in order to keep the ideal safe. There is no room to push this argument further, but it is interesting that the biblical text uses monarchy (kingdom of God) as opposed to liberal democracy. If the king can be 100 percent trusted as good (which no human monarch can), then it is more personal; we are ruled by a person, not an idea. In this world where no monarch is trustworthy, I'll take democracy, but there will be no elections in heaven.

The personal, as opposed to individualism, holds not to an ideal perspective but to the concrete life of the other before us. John Macmurray states, "The essence of idealism, whether in its popular or in its philosophical form, lies in an emotional attachment to ideas rather than to [persons]."[12] It is not an individual loyalty to an ideal that we seek to know but the real, concrete human person we seek to encounter. It is through the realism of *need* that we are invited to share in the life of the other. Jesus actually breaks the law, healing on the sabbath, stating that the sabbath is made for humans and not humans for the sabbath (Mk 2:27). Jesus shatters the ideal, claiming that his disciples are called not to individually be loyal to an idea (even an important one like the law), but to be, and be with, persons. As Jesus states, the law is to clear the ground so we encounter persons; it is a servant to the personal God, to the person of my neighbor. It is not an ideal to which I'm called to assimilate but a pathway into the personal. So for Jesus the point of the law (and breaking it) becomes the way to make human life more human, rather than keeping the idea pure. The law is to open our eyes to see the need of our neighbor.

The problem with idealism is that even when it sees need, it converts it into an idea, allowing us to actually avoid the concrete life of our neighbor. Loyalty to our interest in the ideal is what we worship. To use an extreme example, a woman asks her roommate if her outfit makes her look fat. The roommate, who holds to an ideal of *always* telling the truth, says, "No, that outfit doesn't make you look fat, you just are fat." The roommate is 100 percent committed to this ideal and has success-fully (and boldly) kept it. But her use of the truth crushed the concrete humanity of another, using the truth untruthfully to hurt another. When the woman in the outfit cries because of the response, the roommate throws up her arms, stating, "I'm just saying!" It is true that she has kept the ideal; she is still individually loyal to the idea of telling the truth. But the integrity to this ideal has come at the expense of the concrete per-sonhood of the other.

So to see need is not to convert it into an idea or program but to open your person to it, to seek to walk into the place of need to encounter the embodied spirit of the other. Idealism seeks the integrity of the ideal; the realism of personal encounter seeks the God who became person found in the need of the suffering of the cross. Idealism uses the idea as the measure of sharing. You are called to share the idea with another, but only called to the other person as long as the ideal remains pure. If the person challenges or threatens the ideal you have given your interest to, then the other person must go, so the integrity of idea remains and you as an individual remain pure.

It doesn't take much imagination to see how individualism as the ideal has set terms for evangelism in our passing oil regime. Relationship in ministry became the vehicle for assimilating other individuals to an idea; relationships became the chaser that makes the new religious ideas (call them ideologies) go down more easily.

To pick up again on the inception analogy, the point of relational ministry is to influence people with new ideas. We use the relationship as a way into people's consciousness, implanting a new idea that converts their individual interests and wants in a new direction. Like in the movie, an inception is dangerous business; if the individual perceives at any time that the new idea is being implanted over and against his or her own volition, the person will revolt. If someone comes to see that you as pastor only sought to know and be in relationship with him or her for the sake of the ideological inception, to influence his or her interest, the disappointment and pain will be deep. Because in the end the truth is revealed: you never cared about her as a person, just her assimilation to *your* idea.

CONCLUSION

In this chapter I've sought to draw a thick distinction between individualism and the personal. I've made bold statements that a person is not an individual, spilling ink to show that individualism contends that people are their interests, leading us to see people more as their wants than as others in need. This has the impact of deforming the world (most profoundly other people) into objects, making it harder for us to *share* in each others' lives. We are then deceived into believing that what matters is getting people to assimilate to our ideas, which further pushes us from the personal.

But all of this was to say what a person is not. Now we must turn from the negative to the positive, turning from what a person is *not* to what a person *is*. I've already pointed in the direction that we'll be headed, asserting that persons are embodied spirits that seek to indwell others through need.

5

All the Lonely People

*Pastoral Ministry &
the Field of the Personal*

It was true; we'd watched way too much *Supernanny*. You know, the reality show where British Jo Frost, the supernanny, arrives on the doorstep of struggling parents, helping them find new ways to get control of their disobedient (sometimes deviant) children. The supernanny gives overrun parents schedules, directions and methods. Like Jesus calming the battering storms that had swept up on the Sea of Galilee (Mk 4:35-40), so Jo, with some fancy editing, calms the storms of child disobedience.

One of the supernanny's best strategies to get control and implement boundaries is the "naughty seat," a step or mat that you place your kid on when he or she needs a timeout for not listening or breaking a clear rule. When Owen turned two, the show, and particularly the "naughty seat," turned from entertaining voyeurism to practicality. Entering the terrible twos with force, we turned an old bathmat into the Alcatraz of our house, grabbing the disobedient criminal in overalls and whisking him to the mat with only the words, "Owen, you are not to color on the wall; we color only on paper; now you're on timeout." With our verdict stated clearly, the supernanny had taught us to engage no further, but to walk away, leaving him to do his hard time, on his polka-dotted Ikea bathmat.

As we'd walk away the tears would begin. They'd start with contrition, but soon contrition turned to anger, revealing that tears were more about doing the time than the crime. (Years later his little sister, Maisy, at the same age, would scream like a brokenhearted lover bearing an indiscretion that would send her lover packing, "I'm sorry, I'm sorry, I'm sooo sorry!" But she, like her brother, was more sorry for the punishment than the crime.)

After the anger would subside, the pleading would begin. These two minutes were just too much for his little being—he yearned for release, now wishing he'd never even seen a cursed crayon. Sitting alone he'd start chanting the burden on his punishment. With about forty seconds left in his timeout he'd start, sullenly chanting, in a two-year-old lisp, "I'm wonewy, I'm sooo wonewy" (lonely). It was no confession, but hearing his caged bird song of loneliness would melt our hearts. There was this odd reflex in us, even when we were so angry with his disobedience. The song of loneliness was too much for us; it took all our willpower to stick out the remaining seconds. We yearned so badly to pick him up and heal his loneliness with our own person. There was something magical, something spiritual, about his plea of suffered loneliness that caused our own person to respond with the overbearing desire to give ourselves to him.

When he was six, his now six-minute timeout came with no caged bird songs of loneliness; now with frustration chiseled on his face, he'd chant, "I'm sooo bored; this is sooo boring." Shamefully, my response possessed little compassion. Rather, triggered like a gun, I wanted to shout, "Tough! Suck it up!—Shut that trap or I'll add five more minutes!"

It was the expression of *loneliness* that became a confession that was too deep, too intertwined with our own humanity, to be ignored. At six when he chanted "I'm bored," I had no compassion, because in the moment, he was no person, he was an individual who shouted the frustration of his *own* interest and the caging of his wants. He'd even shout, when the boredom got too much, "I *want* to be *finished* with this *stupid time out!* I *want* to be *done*!" But this only added fuel to my anger; now we were two individuals set against each other, fighting to see who would get their *wants* met, whose ultimate interest would frame our lives. It was a competition now, his want versus mine; I was parenting not to his person but to win. My anger bubbling red hot.

But his "wonewy" was no confession of an individual with wants; it was the revelation of a person, a person longing for a relationship to save him, for another to come and be with him, for his broken, shameful, even discontent heart to be cleaved to another. He was lonely and yearned for a relationship. Disappointment remained, the bad act still existed, but his confession opened his little person to us; the only response, our very reflex, was to give him our own person in return.

ALL THE LONELY PEOPLE

Loneliness reveals personhood because loneliness is the confession of lost relationship; it is clutching to find your personhood. And it can be so radical that some psychologists actually say that the hardest thing to get clients to discuss is loneliness; they hypothesize that this is so because the feeling of loneliness is the closest experience that we have to death. It is to be dead to all others; it is to be alone.

There is simply no life in being alone, no such thing as a singular person. God's very command in Genesis states as much, "It is not good that the *adam* should be alone" (Gen 2:18). To be alone, we could even stretch it to say hyperindividualism, is the very judgment of God. The human being cannot be alone and must be put to sleep—like the merciful act to a fifteen-year-old Labrador—when the human is alone and lonely. We could shout, *No, wait, God! The adam is still an individual, the adam still has interest, the adam is still wanting to name the animals!* But God's judgment is profound in its directness, in its revealing of our anthropological state that Israel cannot miss, "It is not good . . ." It stands in the very opposition of the goodness of creation, the goodness that is God's word of stratification after God creates (Gen 1:4, 10, 12, 18, 21, 25, 31).[1] God has been saying "it is good" throughout this narrative. But now, the bitter words of judgment come, and they are staggering next to all the proclamations of goodness. God states, "It is *not good* that the *adam* [the earth creature] should be alone" (Gen 2:18).

Israel cannot miss that there is no humanity without relationship, that we human beings, we upright walkers on the earth are fundamentally persons, given our very personhood not through tasks, interests or wants, but through being bound one to another, through indwelling and sharing deeply with one another as bone of our bones and flesh of our flesh (Gen 2:23). This is why Jewish philosopher Martin Buber states, "In the beginning was the relationship."[2]

In the new era, when *sharing* needs to become the heart of our new consciousness, it is essential that pastoral ministry recovers the person and recognizes that we do ministry with persons, finally putting to rest the fascination and accommodation to the individualism of the oil regime. But this leads us to a very important question, *What is a person?*

A PERSON IS HIS OR HER RELATIONSHIPS

Why did Shane say that Dave became a person after his confession? After all, this statement was much more of a reaction than a rational assertion. What happened that made him and all the others see that Dave was most fundamentally a person? And why did that change them?

To turn our attention to persons is to reinitiate and then expand what I've already said, that a person is not someone's interest projected into the world by his or her wants. Individualism says that we are our interests, but a person is defined by relationships.[3]

"Brother," "friend," "mother" are the designations given to persons. An individual is a boss, consumer, professor, voter and so forth. The very label denotes a function; you are given this label by individually doing something toward some interest. The labels of individualism (boss, consumer, professor, voter, etc.) exist because they denote your function toward a goal. Bosses manage, consumers buy, professors teach and voters pick candidates; you are this thing because of the function bound in the goal of meeting or expressing your interest. But the denotations of "brother," "friend" or "mother" are not constructed to signify a function but a relationship.

You are only a brother because there is another who calls you such, there are no brothers without other siblings. You are a brother because you are a person; it is through relationship with a sister or another brother that you become a brother yourself.[4] Macmurray shows the depth of the personal when he says, "I need you to be myself. This need is for a fully positive personal relation in which, because we trust one another, we can think and feel and act together. Only in such a relation can we really be ourselves."[5]

Persons do things too, sure, but it is hard to say what. What do brothers or mothers do? Well, they brother or mother.[6] A mother does a lot of mothering, but what is mothering? Only someone in the relationship, only the one being mothered can tell you what it is. She may work forty hours, coach volleyball, cook or mow the lawn, but these functions and activities are not the heart of being a mother. Motherhood is bound in relationship. She is at her most mothering when she takes her five-year-old on her lap, holding him near her chest, and strokes his head. She is mother when she mothers him, when she opens her person to him and he opens his to her.[7] She is mother not in her functions but in giving her life to him as he opens his to her. She is his mother because she shares in his life, by inviting him to share in hers.[8]

What do brothers do? "Brothers gotta hug," to quote the great 1990s movie *Tommy Boy*. Brothers hug because a brother cannot be denoted by a function toward an interest. We could answer that what brothers do is they *brother*. The absurdity of that statement, and the overall difficulty to come up with a clear function for being a brother, shows that brotherhood is bound in the relational reality of personhood; being a brother is being in relationship with another who becomes sister or younger-older brother. It is to act brotherly because you are his or her brother.

Saying that what brothers do is brother sounds like nonsense, but it is true. What a brother does is be a brother, being bound in a kind of relationship with another that makes him a person called brother. It makes more sense in the negative, when a sister says, "It hurts because my brother really has never been a brother to me." We actually know what this means; we understand that the brother has violated her personhood by never opening up his own person to her.

By refusing to share himself in relationship he, in a real sense, negates her sisterhood, or she is only a sister in generic label, not in and through person-to-person relationship. She feels deep pain because her connection to her brother only lives in the functional, she is only bound to him by giving him Christmas gifts or receiving his stilted "happy birthday" messages on Facebook. All they have is the function, with the goal to do what's obligated, but his very person is hidden from her. And the more she searches for it, even pleading for him to be a brother, to brother her by becoming a person to her, the more he sinks deeper into the functions of his individual interests, the more his person becomes locked behind thick iron walls.

When she states her desire for more, for him to be a brother to her, he'll respond, "What? What do you want me to do? I'll do it! What do you want from me?" Yet his defensive, frustrated response is the verdict that his person is not available. She now cries because she *wants* nothing; he has no idea what she wants him to do; want is vacant from the pleading of the personal. What she needs is *him*, what aches in her bones is to be with his person, but he is unable to reveal his person to her. Her inability to say what she wants from him, that she truly wants nothing, witnesses to the fact that the personal reality of encounter is too myste-rious to quantify in a list of functions or behaviors. But because she can't give him her wants it frustrates him more. "You just have all this pressure on me, but you can't tell me what you really want," he retorts. He images her crazy because she can't state her goal. But she has no goal, just the desire to glimpse his person, just to be a person next to his person, to *sister* him. After all, he is her brother.

Dave became a person with his confession at the church council meeting because Dave was seen as his relationships. When he con-fessed what many people already knew, that his daughter Donna suf-fered from depression, a window was opened up to see Dave not as an individual but as a person, as someone who most fundamentally *was* through the relationships he had with others. To see his overbearing wants next to the suffering of the relationship that made him "him," was to see Dave exposed; it was to see his person, in its loneliness, longing and connections. And when a person is exposed, as with Owen's two-year-old loneliness, we find ourselves drawn to the other, we find ourselves opening up our own person to the personhood of the other.

Personhood as a gift. If mothers are only mothers by mothering and brothers are brothers by brothering, this cannot, as we've seen, happen in a vacuum. There are no mothers without children. Then the personal reality of being a brother or mother is given to you as a gift by the very being of another. It is a gift given without an interest; it falls outside the way I give the gift of helping my neighbor move his fridge. I help him because I hope he'll return the favor when I have the interest of moving my own. But the gift of personhood, the gift of becoming a father, comes through the profound but simple presence of the being of the other; the being that seeks the *sharing* of relationship. When she *is*, when she comes into the world as a person dependent on your own person, you are given the gift of being her father. You are changed from something to something else, not because your interest is met but simply because you find yourself in relationship with her. Everything changes because you share in her life and she shares in yours; you dwell with her and she with you. It is sheer grace.

You can see again why our relationships in pastoral ministry can't be for influence; to make them about influence is to see people only as individuals. Our most profound ways of being in the world exist in and for themselves—they are gift. Brothers and mothers have no ends; what they desire is to be brothers and mother for others who call them such. The personal stretches so deep in the discipleship of Jesus Christ that the young church calls one another brothers and sisters, for they are bound to one another through the person of Jesus Christ. And Jesus himself tells his listeners that whoever follows him by doing his command of upholding personhood finds true life by sharing in his person, and this person is his brother, sister and mother (Mk 3:34). It can't be missed; the familial language makes it shockingly clear that the faith of the Nazarene is one of personhood for all.

I have been using familial language, for good biblical reason, to make the point of the personal, but friendship too is most profoundly bound in this same reality. We are friends because we are friends, because we have encountered each other's person.

There is no means to an end in friendship because it is about persons, and personal relationships exist only for themselves. If I say, "I thought he was my friend, but really all he wanted to do was sell me car insurance," we understand this as a violation. Friendship, like motherhood or fatherhood, has no functional end. The point is not an interest; the point is to be with and for, to share in the life of the other. "Friendship evangelism," which seeks to use friendship for the sake of meeting the interest of conversions, violates the personal; it ignores personhood—a dangerous move, as we'll see, because this God who becomes incarnate fully takes on personhood.

That's why Chris Farley is right in *Tommy Boy*. What do brothers do? Brothers gotta hug. What they do is bound within the encounter of the other that has given them the gift of being a person. The most primary action of a brother is to hug, it is to embrace the personhood of the other who gives you your person; it is to love.[9] What does a brother, mother or friend do? They love, they hug, they embrace the personhood of the other as the gift that makes them *them*. They love, not by using their relationship as a means to another end but by being with and for the beloved. So-called friendship evangelism doesn't love the person; the love of person has no ends, it only acts so that the beloved can live and love. Friendship evangelism actually loves the idea, the third thing it is trying to get people to know, do or come to. In friendship evangelism I don't really love the person, but the idea of church membership, the idea of converting you. I love not you but the thing I'm using the relationship to get you to do. That, in the end, is what I want and am therefore committed to. This eliminates the personal by making an interest its very point of connection in the first place. You are not a person in relationships that have another end, you are an individual; I seek not to see your person transformed but your interest converted.

But we are not individuals, we are persons, and persons delight in the mystery of the gift of personal encounter, of sharing in the life of the other. Brothers, friends and mothers are together, that's what they do, they *are* together. And Jesus reminds us that those that hear his word and follow his command of personal love (which is his very person) are his brothers, sisters and mothers (Mk 3:34); we are called into the world to love the world as our Father loves—as persons.

Jesus' friends. Jesus in John 15 calls his disciples friends: "I do not call you servants," servants who dutifully seek the interest of their master, no, Jesus says, "I have called you friends" (Jn 15:15). In other words, because my life is in you and your life is in me, because we abide (are together) in each other, you are my friends because I have shared in your person and drawn you into my connection with God. Calling his disciples friends makes it crystal clear that it is personhood that matters to God and rests at the center of Jesus' ministry. As we saw earlier, friendship has no goal, no interest outside the friend. I am your friend not to get you to a new interest but to share in your person.

Jesus is friend, and what do friends do? Friends share in the life of friends—"I no longer live but Christ lives in me" (Gal 2:20 NIV). Friendship can have no goal of influence—it seeks only to share our place, to invite us to share in the life of the other. Jesus calls his disciples friends, telling them that in his Father's house are many rooms and he will go make a place for them (Jn 14:2), because the point is not getting them to a goal but living with them, embracing their person. They are given a room in a house where God's own person is given to share in as a gift.

Jesus invites people to come and share in his own person, to find their own personhood in sharing in his life as person. "Come and see," he invites (Jn 1:39). So we call people (do evangelism) as the invitation to come, see and share in the personhood of God through sharing in the personhood of this community.

At its most fundamental, what it means to be, what it means to be the one who encounters God, is to be a person. It is to be given our personhood through the gift of relationship. To be a person is to be our relationships.

So what is a pastor? This takes us full circle, leading us to ask, What is a pastor? Is it the label that denotes someone that meets the goal of his or her interests (or better, meeting the interests of God)? Or is "pastor" more like a brother or mother or friend? Is it hard to say exactly what they do, because what they do is bound so deeply within their own person and the persons they encounter? You can only be called pastor, as a mother can only be called mother, because there is a relationship that gives you this personal reality, this identity. In other words, is being a pastor defined by the functional or the personal?

We could try to define a pastor by *his* or *her* functions, and it has been en vogue for the last century to do so. The pastor is the one who preaches, gives the sacraments, runs the meeting, visits the sick, provides a vision for the church and so the list continues. But to define the pastor by the functional is to lock him or her into the "priest." The "priest" is the projector and distributer of divine things, the true reader of the sacred text. This is a function.

But isn't a pastor more? Surely, the pastor has to do some priestly things, but the pastor is only a pastor because of a flock of persons to whom he or she is called. A person is pastor because she or he is called by the Spirit to open her or his own spirit to the spirit of the flock. The pastor does this by preaching the Word of the God who encounters our persons, and by being present through the personal act of sharing in the sacraments, prayers and the story of her or his people. What pastors do is *pastor*, and pastoring is the brave action of leading by opening your person to the person of others so that together we might share in the life of God.

Shane recognized that he had many things to do as pastor; on this church council retreat there were functions that needed to be animated, to-do lists that needed to be finished. But instead of becoming overwhelmed by them, he provided a simple space for people to encounter each other's personhood, looking at each other for a few minutes to sketch each other's face. He was their pastor by binding himself to them and giving them a space to be person, one to another.

A FEW LINGERING QUESTIONS

Question 1. Now, I know some of you are thinking, *OK, maybe, but still as a pastor I do have functions and goals I need to meet.* And some of you are disturbed, thinking, *As a Christian, I want to see people converted; I have that goal.*

Yes, as pastors we still have things that must be taken care of; we still take on goals to get the institution to function. This isn't bad in itself. But it is bad, or at least warped, when the functional wants of our job drown out and can't support the reality of the personal. Good mothers or good fathers take on many functions: they work, clean, cook. Every week they have goals of getting things done. But a good mother or father does these busy functions for one purpose, she or he does them to facilitate the creation of an environment that allows mother or father and the rest of the family to encounter each other as persons. The functional goals are finally only for encounter of the personal.

Our busy pastoral schedule and our to-do lists should be similar. We brainstorm goals, not for the goal, not even for the results, but for the space it will open up to allow person-to-person encounter, the ways it will free us to share in each other's lives as participation in God's own life. The mother does functions to facilitate space for her to be with her children. But it is not a closed space she wishes for: because she desires to encounter her children's persons, she also does functions that help them to be encountered by other persons. She does her functions so she might share in the life of her children and so that others too might see the gift of the personhood of her child, and share in his or her life. Pastoral ministry is filled with busy functions, but they are stillborn if they ignore the personal. Like good mothers or fathers, we as pastors have to remember that all our functional doing is for the sake of facilitating encounters of persons in our churches and trusting that the God who becomes person meets us in such ways.

Question 2. But what about the second question? As Christians, don't we have the goal of converting people? Haven't I been too hard on friendship evangelism? And isn't some influence in our relationships necessary? Too often this question is asked in the logic of individualism; in other words, evangelism really is about getting the world to hold to our (so-called Christian) interests. So we even use relationships that wear the costume of the personal, but really care little for personhood, and want only the conversion of individuals' interests.

Yet, through the Gospels Jesus calls people to see the kingdom, but what is interesting is that this kingdom does not come through individual conversion to the interests of the kingdom. No, this kingdom is different than an earthly political system or social movement, because it comes solely through the personal, it comes by the faithfulness of a person. Jesus throughout the Gospels calls people to his own person, *I am* the way, and the truth, and the life (Jn 14:6); *I am* the true vine (Jn 15:1, 5); *I am* the bread of life (Jn 6:48); *I am* the good shepherd (Jn 10:14); *I am* the light of the world (Jn 8:12; 9:5); *I am* the gate (Jn 10:7). "Come to me" is his continued mantra (Mt 11:28; Lk 18:16). It is through his person that the kingdom comes. We find the kingdom only when we find ourselves *sharing* in his life; it is about being in his person.

To confess the incarnate Christ is to confess the centrality of the personal to ministry. God ministers to the world, freeing it from sin and death, by becoming person and calling all of creation to find new life in his crucified and resurrected person. The cross and resurrection aren't simply functions that give us something to possess (even salvation). The cross and resurrection are the acts of the personal that seek to confront and overcome all that keeps persons from sharing in the life of one another and God. Salvation is finding your person bound to God through the person of Jesus Christ. Salvation is not something that can be possessed, it is a personal reality of sharing fully in the life of God, where sin and death have no say. Sin and death must be overcome so we can find our life bound to God and one another, so that we can be in relationship.

It is in the gift of sharing in Jesus' own person that we are give our person; it is through sharing in his life that we are given our own. The goal of evangelism is not to convince people to take on a Christian interest in the world but to help them open their very person to the person of Jesus Christ. But they can only be helped to open their person to Jesus' own person if we too will open our person to them. The gospel lives in the logic of the personal; ministry *must* then too find its lifeblood in the personal. Kathryn Tanner says powerfully, "Human beings are made for fellowship with God by being made for fellowship with one another."[10] Relationships in ministry then are bound in the personal, which means they can have no other goal than to share in the life of the other.

It is time for us to imagine pastoral ministry in and through the logic of the personal.

6

What Is a Person?

Recovering a Christian
Definition of People

In the little-seen movie *The Big Kahuna*, Bob is a zealous young Christian who finds himself on a business trip with Larry (Kevin Spacey) and Phil (Danny DeVito), seeking to land a big contract for industrial lubricants with Mr. Fuller, whom they call the Big Kahuna. Without the contract, the company and their jobs are lost.

Trying to make contact with Mr. Fuller they throw a party in their Wichita hotel room, hoping a few free drinks and light conversation can land them the needed deal. Yet after the beer is gone and the hotel room emptied out, it appears that they have failed. No Mr. Fuller; the whole point was to meet the man they'd never seen, and it now looks like the company and their jobs are over. Until they realize that Bob actually did talk with Mr. Fuller, and that Mr. Fuller had invited Bob to further their conversation later the next night at a dinner party. What they discussed, Bob explains to the others, was religion; they talked about faith in Jesus.

In any case, this is good news. They have one more shot at closing the deal, at doing what it was they were sent to do, keep the company afloat. Bob is sent the next night to the dinner party and told to discuss the company's line of lubricants.

With Bob gone, Larry and Phil anxiously pace the empty hotel room like caged animals, the anticipation almost too great to bear. When Bob finally returns they can take it no more. They bombard him with questions, asking him what he and the Big Kahuna spoke about, seeking to know if he got the contract and saved their jobs.

Bob explains that they never actually discussed lubricants. When asked why, he explains that it never came up; instead, they discussed Jesus. Larry is flabbergasted, "And who brought up the conversation of Jesus, Bob?"—accusing him of doing evangelism on company time.

An intense argument ensues, leaving both Bob and Larry yelling at each other and finally rolling on the ground, until Phil separates them. Once apart, Larry is humiliated, apologizing to Bob, who, even with his tussled hair, stands in self-righteousness. Larry departs, leaving Bob and Phil alone.

Throughout the movie Phil has been in deep contemplation, regretting decisions that have stressed or ended some of his most significant relationships. As the chaos of the room dissolves into deafening silence, Phil speaks, telling Bob that he has something to say to him.

Sullenly flipping a cigarette in his mouth, Phil explains that Larry is his friend, and he is his friend because he is honest. And he is honest, Phil explains to Bob, because he has opened his person to Phil. Phil has seen him, and in seeing him, even though he is at times bombastically blunt, Phil has experienced him as honest.

Phil then turns to Bob and says that he understands that Bob too wants to be honest, that Bob strives for it. But Phil continues, telling Bob, "The question you have to ask yourself is, 'Has it touched the whole of your life?'"

"What does that mean?" Bob asks with confusion.

"That means," Phil continues,

> that you preaching Jesus isn't any different than Larry or someone else preaching lubricants. It doesn't matter if you're selling Jesus, or Buddha, or civil rights, or how to make money in real estate with no money down. That doesn't make you a human being [a person]; it makes you a marketing rep.
>
> If you want to talk to someone honestly as a human being [as a person], ask him about his kids, find out what his dreams are. Just to find out. For no other reason. Because as soon as you lay your hands on a conversation to steer it, it's not a conversation anymore—it's a pitch. And you're not a human being—you're a marketing rep.

INDWELLING

The critique—of ministry based on influencing individuals toward our interest—is poignant in this rich scene. Yet, to understand the depth of the critique we need to recognize that Phil is calling zealous Bob to be a person, to see personhood by asking people about their kids, about their dreams, about those things that are bound in relationship. Phil calls Bob to be a person, in honesty to be a person to other persons.

What Phil is actually doing in his critique of Bob is inviting him to recognize that to be a person is to indwell another, to *share* deeply in another's life. Phil is pointing to the kind of sharing that has its logic in the indwelling of God's action, indwelling that connects the personhood of our neighbor to the personhood of Jesus himself. Jesus is there with the hungry, homeless and imprisoned because Jesus' person indwells (shares in) them. Jesus indwells them so deeply that to participate in their person is to participate in Jesus; to act for them *is* to act for Jesus.

Because we are our relationships, we have our being in and through each other; we are given our being through indwelt sharing of others in our lives. Of course, we remain permanent centers of consciousness, we are distinct I's. To be our relationships is not to lose this. We are unique, singular, organic bodies with urges, conscious thoughts and reflexes to survive. We have our own brains (as we'll discuss in the following chapters). But even these unique singular brains need and are wired to be drawn into the lives of others—to share (indwell) each other. Phil is calling Bob to indwell others, and to indwell is a deeply spiritual reality that has its heart in the very incarnation and ascension (sending of the Spirit).

So to be in relationship is *not* to seek to influence someone's interest, but to *share* the other's place, by indwelling them through relationship. Phil's driving Bob to ask people about their kids and their dreams is the push to share in others' lives by, *even for a short time*, indwelling them, by taking them into his own person.

To indwell something is to participate in something that is not us. It is to share in something so deeply that what is not us becomes part of us. Human beings, by nature, take in things that are not us, making them part of us. The best example of course is food; an apple is not me, but by taking it in it becomes part of me, using its nutrients to build muscle and other cells. Red Bull is not me, but by taking it in its caffeine becomes part of me, animating my tired body. "You are what you eat," the old

Saturday morning animated public service announcement told us children of the late 1980s. You are what indwells you.

We do this naturally as organic beings; our bodies take in what is not us. But we do this at the social (and spiritual) level as well, and this is the unique reality of being a human person. When we find ourselves in relationships with persons, when we find ourselves becoming *friends*, we indwell each other. Your life becomes part of mine and mine becomes part of yours. I can be greatly affected in my own person to hear that my friend is sick, sad or overflowing with joy. The fact that her experience affects my being witnesses to our mutual indwelling. Our lives are *distinct* but overlapped; we are each our *own person*, but our own unique being has penetrated the being of the other through the relationship itself. Relationships person to person mean indwelling, mean place sharing. Indwelling is the mystical core, the deep origin of place sharing. Place sharing is the outworking of indwelling.

How could there possibly be something called ministry that violates or ignores the dynamic spiritual mystery of personal indwelling? When we really feel ministered to, this is actually what we mean. To be ministered to is to have another person see our own person and indwell it, to share with us as we bury our sister, as we fight for one more day of life, as we celebrate the birth of a long-awaited child. When we say, "The pastor really ministered to me today," we mean that we experienced the pastor sharing in us, giving his person to our own so that we might recognize the presence of God. To minister is to indwell through relationship, to follow the indwelling ministry of God who becomes the God of Israel and the child in a manger to save us by indwelling us.

For persons to encounter persons is to indwell one another, to be drawn into the spiritual through the social. But unlike the organic process, where indwelling means consuming, in the spiritual process to indwell is to *share* in. It is opening your being to be touched (and even transformed) by what is not you, by what you give yourself to in relationship.[1]

LOVE AS INDWELLING

We use a word for this unique spiritual human indwelling that happens at the social level, calling it love. In love parents indwell children, suffering with and for them. In love persons see the heart-break of another and offer an embrace, sharing another's pain by indwelling the other's experience. (And when it is the romantic love of persons, when two have deeply indwelt each other by sharing in each other's place, then they take the next step to indwell each other sexually as they have spiritually.)

Jesus shows his love for us when he states, "Abide in me as I abide in you" (Jn 15:4). The mutual indwelling cannot be missed. It is for Paul the heart of the gospel, which is why for Paul love is greater than faith and hope. Love is greater because love indwells, because love shares completely in persons. Persons indwell others, because to be a person is to love. This is why Phil says to Bob, "Ask them about their kids or their dreams, just to know." In other words, ask them about what they *love*, what they seek to indwell, for *they are what they share in*. Jesus shares in our life, and now we are invited to share in his, to indwell him as he indwells us.

There is something very sacramental here. Taking Communion is to consume the body of Jesus, participating in indwelling organically, spiritually and socially (we don't give ourselves Communion alone). Indwelling is so central that we are to take Jesus' body and blood into our own; his person fully indwelling us.

To answer, then, "What is a person?" is to give more clarity to how a person is his or her relationships. We can state that a person is his or her relationships because persons *always share* in others' lives, a person always indwells other persons (or is tortured by resisting the indwelling). It is indwelling another that gives us our personhood. A brother, mother or friend is called such because each indwells another; their lives dynamically overlap. If they didn't they couldn't be called brother, mother or friend (or the title becomes only a heavy burden that reminds them of the impossibility to indwell). They share so deeply in the life of another that they are what they are, only by sharing in the life of another. A mother is a mother because she mothers, and what we add here is that mothering has no ossified form. Mothering looks different at different times and in different contexts, but what is universal is that a mother mothers by sharing in (by indwelling) her child. *To be a person is to share in the indwelling of another.*

NEARING THE DANGER ZONE

But we should be careful here and avoid misunderstanding by giving preview to a theological point that we will return to later: to indwell is the very action of God in Jesus Christ; in becoming human, Jesus indwells completely our humanity. The divine and human natures indwell each other in the very *person* of Jesus. For us to participate in the life of God, for us to live out of the very image of God, is to be persons who indwell others. But what is important, following this Christological form of indwelling, is for persons to indwell others in a way that avoids confusing one person for another. To indwell another is not to lose ourself in sharing in the life of another. Rather, the divine nature of Christ indwells completely the human nature, but does so without confusion, without mixing one into the other. The two natures indwell but are differentiated.[2]

And this is the heart of persons in relationship. This is the essence of love: to indwell the other, to share deeply in their life, but to do so without confusion, without losing your person in enmeshment, without so identifying that there is no differentiation. It is to indwell the other in and through your person, keeping your person as you share in the personhood of another. *Sharing* as indwelling is the heart of God's own incarnational act.[3]

But we need to push this further. If persons are their relationships of shared indwelling, what does that mean? And what difference does it make for pastoral ministry?

There are four dynamics to personhood as indwelling that we'll explore, four dynamics that further the shape of indwelling and will connect us again with Phil's statements to Bob.

HOW DOES A PERSON INDWELL ANOTHER?

1. A person indwells through action. To indwell another is to act with and for them. Through action human beings relate to what they are not. To be a person is to be an agent; it is to act, to *do* for others by being with them.[4] We reveal our person to others, allowing them to indwell us, through our actions. We overlap our lives through our actions. I know you because you reveal yourself to me in your actions that are with and for me.[5]

Because persons are their relationships, action becomes the way we reveal our very person to others. We know another as he or she acts for us, informing us through action who we are and where we belong. Through action personhood is revealed to us; through dwelling in the action of another I really see him or her. Ray Anderson states, "'The being of a person is being-in-act,' says Karl Barth. . . . If a person does not act, he cannot be known except as an object in an impersonal way."[6]

Someone outside the action may have another perception of it. They may *think* they know the person theoretically. But there is no such thing. We don't *know* people outside the encounter of their action. Thinking I know you before I encounter your action is to refuse the possibility of indwelling; it is to stonewall any sharing by depersonalizing you in an idea I have of you. But for the one acted on, there is a revelation of the other person—"she is so manipulative, with that holier than thou smile"; "I know he seems hard, but he's just shy, his tenderness comes through in his long glances, I can feel them penetrate me."

But the power for indwelling is also shown in the negative; negative actions done to close off *sharing* in the life of the other are deeply painful. The action of throwing sticks and stones may surely break our bones, but because persons are their relationships, the act of name-calling cuts much deeper, shattering the possibility of relationships we need to be persons.

Action is so central to personhood that Jesus promises to indwell those that we act for, "just as you did it to one of the least of these who are members of my family, you did it to me" (Mt 25:39-40). Jesus is with them so unreservedly that to *act* for them is to *do* unto Jesus himself. And this is so because the *person* who acts for another *person* by responding to his or her hunger, nakedness and imprisonment indwells that person. The act of feeding, clothing and hospitality is giving his or her very person; it is taking on the very incarnational action of Jesus himself. The power of this text is the personal encounter; it is the encountering of Jesus' own person through action that mediates the personhood of others. The point of Matthew 25 is not simply to be altruistic and do your duty but to encounter personhood, to give food, clothing and shelter as the actions of personal sharing (indwelling). Food, clothing and shelter offered void of the personal runs the risk of obligation being more important than persons (and when this occurs dehumanization is always a risk).

We participate in the incarnation by acting for others. We cannot share in the life of others if we refuse to act for them. And we are given the gift of our personhood by action done with and for other persons. As the Christ hymn asserts, Christ "did not regard equality with God as something to be exploited, [he] emptied himself, . . . being found in human form, he humbled himself" (Phil 2:5-11). Here the incarnation is the action of indwelling. Jesus acts to indwell humanity completely by acting to take on our very form.

Acting for someone hungry is feeling their hunger and being drawn into their desperation by handing them a bowl of soup. To clothe another is to embrace their nakedness; it is to do the personal act of wrapping a warm jacket around their shivering shoulders. To visit the prisoner is the personal act of sharing in their plight, of acting to offer our own person as the presence that shatters an all-encompassing isolation. To do such personal acts is to indwell the other acted for, and in doing this, Jesus says, we encounter his own person, finding him there as one who indwells the person.

Jesus' call to action is the action of the personal. The individual acts by taking on functions to meet an interest. And this is often where we go wrong in ministry, seeing ministry as the functions of the pastor, instead of seeing ministry as the personal acts done to encounter persons, to indwell others through action as the way of encountering Jesus.

A teacher, for instance, seems to be an active agent—correcting papers, preparing exams and submitting grades. While these functions *are* important, they do not make the teacher a person. Such activities may make her a teacher, but we have known too many who have moved the students from one textbook to the next but could not be a person to students, igniting in them a desire to *indwell* the content of the class by *sharing* in the life and passion of the teacher.

Persons are agents not when they seek a goal but when they take actions to share in the life of others. The point of Matthew 25 is not to end hunger (God will end hunger in the eschaton). The point is to take the more radical action, participating in the life of the hungry. We can feed the hungry in a very impersonal way, in a way that makes them feel less than a person. But the action of personhood, the action that makes us persons, indwells others. We act to share in the life of the hungry, naked and imprisoned. We fight even for structural change, not because they are individuals that deserve the freedom to have their individual wants met. No, we fight for the structures of society to be more humane, asking government to feed the hungry so that life might be preserved, making it possible for us to encounter persons, making the world a place for human beings to be with human beings.

2. A person indwells through communication. Our actions reveal our person because our actions communicate. Ignoring a supposed friend, acting like you never saw him, can be more painful and destructive to the relationship than any harsh words. This is so because to communicate, even in anger and frustration, comes with the intrinsic intention of being with the other, of revealing your person to the other.[7] Even if you use communication to end the relationship, you are doing the personal act of communicating, of entering into (tense) discourse.

Of course it is possible that face-to-face encounter can become destructive, escalating even to violence. But so often it leads here because someone refuses to allow the other to speak and be heard, and instead communicates with fists, either because the other refuses discourse or can't get a word in edgewise. Feeling cornered, the person strikes.

When there is communication, when we hear and respond to another, we've taken on a deeply personal act of sharing in the other's life.[8] This is one reason that it is so bad to break up a romantic relationship with someone over text message or email. It is belittling, because the least you could do is a final personal act of entering into discourse with the other. But when you want to avoid this, you choose the impersonal medium, because to enter into discourse is to reveal your person. And you're done doing that; you're breaking off the relationship. You say to the other, cowardly texting or bravely face-to-face, that you "don't think we should talk anymore." You are saying you no longer want to share your person with him or her, that indwelling this other is no longer for you. We say "I don't think we should talk anymore" because talking most often and most directly is how we share our person. You know me through my actions, sure, but the primary action for the human person is to communicate, to enter into discourse and share their person.

You know me; you indwell me through me communicating my perceptions, tastes and thoughts. These are important; I can glimpse your person through them. But when these perceptions, tastes and thoughts are given to narrative, when I hear the stories behind them, I see you, and in seeing you, your stories become the trail that leads to my indwelling you.[9] I do this by hearing your story and having my own story heard; in the overlap of our narratives we share in a new space; we share each other's place. Your weird perceptions and tastes make more sense (even if they're still weird) now that I see your person through the stories (narratives) that lead you to hold to these perceptions and tastes.[10]

And through my stories, you are with me even before you physically were, even before we knew each other, because you indwell my stories; you hear them as the revelation of my person. In person-to-person relationships of love, time is bent. I've seemed to always be with you, because you have wrapped your being around mine through the communication of my past, through sharing in my past so fully it is like you were there, like I have always been with you. Personal discourse of communicated love does the profound mystery of bringing past and future together. We share in each other's life by listening, by telling, by laughing, by hearing. *Through the act of communication persons indwell other persons.*

Phil says to Bob, "Ask them about their dreams, just to know them." Phil pushes Bob to do the personal act of really communicating with another, to participate in the person by participating in the story of his longing, to indwell him in conversation. To hear stories about his kids is *not* to win leverage but to give full attention to the other's personhood, Phil explains. Just do the human act, the personal act, of hearing, of participating in the story, of sharing in the other's life through the story. Phil knows, I think, that no parents can talk of their children without a story. Parents have overwhelmingly witnessed the personhood of their kids, and the mystery of personhood is best communicated in story. Story is the form of discourse that invites the most direct indwelling. We get lost in stories because they take us to see new things; they share a new world for us to be in.

Discourse is so significant to personhood that the biblical text tells us that the person of Jesus Christ is the *logos*, the *Word* of God (Jn 1). God communicates the fullness of God's Word in the person—in the life story—of Jesus. And we are told that this Word was with God; and so with God, so indwelling God, that he is God. But in grace and truth this Word now indwells us ("tents among us"), taking on the flesh of personhood, so that this Word may find root in our own person.

It becomes an essential piece of pastoral ministry that seeks the personal to provide spaces and opportunities for us to share our stories; the church becomes the place of communication. To see the pastor as the one who facilitates personal encounter is to think deeply about how we can create space and give examples of shared narratives. It is to trust that when narratives are shared, person-to-person relationships of indwelling occur, and that such relationships are to participate in God who indwells humanity, and the human person who indwells God.

3. A person indwells because a person is spirit. The reason indwelling is possible at all, the reason indwelling as sharing is the heart of what makes us persons, is because we are *embodied* spirit. Person-to-person relationship where we share in each other's life to the point of indwelling can only be called a spiritual reality.[11] It is concrete and social (embodied), but as such, it is spiritual, it is the encounter of two spirits. To assert that persons are their relationships is to contend that persons are spirit. It is not the natural, organic process that makes us what we are; you are not just a mother because you've given birth, rather you are mother because in giving birth and then caring for another your spirit connects to your child's. It is spirit indwelling spirit that makes you mother.

Kara gave birth to Owen in the most natural of processes: with blood and primal screams (and to her great pride, no medication), she brought him into the world with one last push. She had spent the nine months of her pregnancy anticipating and even instinctually preparing for the birth, craving certain foods, feeling urges to nest and prepare for him. But with that last scream and the appearance of his body, she said it felt like it was over, like she was done. The natural urges left as mysteriously as they came. She was elated at the moment, but not necessarily in having a squirming baby boy but in surviving the pregnancy. As they put Owen in the warmer, counting his fingers and toes, the other nurses tended to Kara. Kara turned to me and said in surprise, "I feel nothing, I just feel happy to be done, like I've passed some huge evolutionary test and now can go home and keep living my normal life."

She felt no *personal* spirit in the natural process of birth; there were natural instincts and urges, sure, but little person-to-person contact other than the kicks and tosses in utero that kept her awake and gave her heartburn. Sitting in the adrenaline of completing the natural, organic process of giving birth, she said, "I feel nothing. . . . It hasn't hit me that I'm now a mom."

Yet that all changed ten minutes later: after gently washing Owen, they placed him on Kara's chest and asked her to try feeding him.[12] As he took her nipple to his mouth, he opened his eyes slightly and raised his tiny hand, batting it against her, connecting his person with her own, nestling his body against her chest. The organic, natural realities now fused with the personal and the bond between them became iron. His smell, his cry sent her being into action, stemming from hours looking at each other face-to-face. The natural, organic and personal so fused that the indwelling was palpable. It was spiritual; it was embodied spirit encountering embodied spirit, as the tears in her eyes witnessed to, and still appear so often.[13]

After the first breastfeeding session (and then repeated in millions of other actions and forms of communication), it had happened; she was now a mother. Because of the gift of his presence, because through this act of nipple to mouth, face-to-face caring and connecting, his spirit became present to her own. They were now bound forever one to the other. From that moment on she couldn't even think of herself without his person; she had indwelt him and he her. In the personal action of the communication of the breast to the mouth, embodied spirit was bound to embodied spirit through the indwelling of persons. It changed everything about her; his person was the concrete arrival of spirit. And as she acted for him, communicating with him through coos and touch and nurture, their embodied spirits indwelled each other. They were, and continue to be, intractable persons that indwell each other.

To be a person, then, is to be an embodied spirit. The human being is simultaneously spirit and body. The two cannot be separated, and after the incarnation, according to Bonhoeffer, never should. It becomes un-Christian to extract one from the other.[14] We are embodied spirits. Our spirits yearn to indwell another, to be encountered as person. But this encounter, this embracing of our spirit, can only happen within our bodies. This spiritual reality of the personal has even affected our brains; relationships of persons have measurable neurological impact. This shows that spirit can change the organic, that the biological can be adapted by the impact of the spiritual. We act with hands, embracing the other; we communicate with our eyes what we see, and we reveal with our mouths the words of our dreams. To be person is to be embodied spirit through relationship with other embodied spirits.[15]

To define personhood as embodied spirit, then, is to avoid rigid positivist or reductionistic understanding of human existence; it is to see us as more than organic biological beings, while always being organic bodies. The natural organic process too has a form of indwelling, such as in eating an apple. But it is not a spiritual process that makes person-to-person relationships of place sharing possible. There is indwelling in the organic natural process, but it lacks spirit, because it lacks persons.

Any organism consumes what they are not; all living creatures seem to do this at some level—squirrels take in nuts, plants take in soil and sun. But this is not a spiritual act; spirit never consumes. It indwells by sharing in the personal, by being in relationships. We don't imagine that squirrels or plants relate in a personal manner. They relate surely, but through instinct, through the organic and natural. Animals then don't (it appears) possess spirit.[16] The spirit of life may blanket them; they live and there is a kind of spirit to this, and they witness to God as Creator, as the Spirit of life.[17] Life itself is a gift and mystery. It is this spirit of life that aboriginal religions have sensed and worshiped.

But animals (and other living things), while having this life spirit, do not posses the spirit of personal encounter. Therefore, they do not relate to God through speaking and response; their actions are based on the natural, not the personal. Their communication is engendered through instinct, not the desire to share in another (hence animals communicate, but have no language). As Barth has said, the human being is the only creature that can hear God; we are sixth-day creatures like all other animals, but we are uniquely invited into the seventh day by hearing and responding to God's act.[18] The human being is embodied spirit because the human being indwells and is indwelled, even by God, through action and discourse. So we, like other animals, are embodied, but unlike them we are spirit, able to indwell others through action and discourse as the very gift of God, with the very *vocation* of indwelling God and one another.

The organic, natural process most often seeks to consume an other—squirrels consume nuts, plants water. Even in evolutionary theory, the animal cares for its young so that its species may survive and consume its prey or conquer its predators.[19] Consuming what is not us may be the natural process, and it may have some analogy to the indwelling of spirit. But while the natural, organic process *consumes* what it is not, the spiritual *shares* in it. Because we are embodied spirit, spirit must always be respected; it can never be consumed or caged. It must be free to be shared in. The other person as spirit means we are given an ontological priority of never consuming another. We must see the other always as the mystery of spirit, always as other than us, always as a person who is free. To consume another (to oppress, abuse, reject, isolate) is to deny that the other is spirit, and to see the other instead as only organic material to be used. We *are*, to answer Cain's question, our brother's keeper (Gen 4:9). We keep him by remembering that he is our brother, that he *is* and we *are* because we are *together*. I must keep him, care for him, because he is the embodied spirit that gives me my personhood.

To say it again, *spirit always shares in the life of another; it never consumes it.* This is what makes a demon a demon: a demon is a spiritual being that refuses to share; it overtakes a body, making it its own. It binds the strong man and raids the house, as Jesus said (Mk 3:27). But true spirit, spirit that is the essence of the personal, never indwells to consume; rather *spirit indwells to share*, to give, to be in relationships of love. Angels never possess another; they heralded the act of God (Lk

2:8-14). Angels communicate to persons' spirits the coming of God's own Spirit.

Realities like faith, hope and most fully love avoid simple, natural definition (1 Cor 13:13). They are the work of the Spirit. They are realities that only the spirit of persons can share; faith, hope and most fully love are uniquely human, personal realities. They have no foundation in the natural (though dogmatic evolutionists may concoct one).[20] But too much formulating quickly degrades the mystery, beauty and power of a mother nursing her baby for the first time. It reductionistically refuses to admit the phenomenological: that many call this a powerful spiritual reality.[21]

We see then that it is the characteristic of spirit to indwell; spirit possesses the power to cleave to what it is not, making a life as it binds itself to another spirit. It is spirit that can make two into one flesh (Gen 2:24; Mt 19:5; Mk 10:8; 1 Cor 6:16; Eph 5:31). We know when we hear this at a wedding service that after the vows, after the consummation, the two don't actually materially become one, mixing in some kind of strange, sci-fi way. They are embodied spirit and as such remain two bodies. But saying that the two become one witnesses to the indwelling of the two's embodied spirits. The two remain two flesh (when one of their natural bodies gets sick, the other's doesn't),[22] and at a certain level they remain two spirits (they continue to possess their own unique *I*, they remain two distinct centers of consciousness). But now their lives are so bound, their persons so open to being shared, that they indwell each other fully, and as such they are now one spirit. (We will see too how this has neurological impact, that people who live together actually wire their brains together.)

The church is the bride of Christ (Eph 5:21-33). The church remains church; it is not Christ, just as a wife remains wife, not becoming her husband. But the church is called to open its life so fully to Christ that the very Spirit of Christ (the Holy Spirit) indwells the spirit of the church. The church is the community of persons who, as embodied spirit, are indwelled by the Spirit of Christ. The church is the community that shares deeply in the Spirit of Christ, as deeply as a wife shares in the spirit of her husband and vice versa.

It becomes the ministry of the pastor of the church to witness to this indwelling. The pastor's vocation is to help our people participate in this indwelling of spirit to Spirit. But this indwelling of spirit to Spirit happens through the dynamic participation of embodied spirit to embodied spirit in personal relationships of place sharing. In being a community of persons, a community of spirit to spirit, we share in the Spirit of Christ.[23] This is why Bonhoeffer states in *Sanctorum Communio* that "Jesus Christ exists as church community." The road to participate in the Spirit of Christ is the path of the personal. Encountering our neighbor has spirit; trusting that where two or more embodied spirits are gathered in confession of Christ, his Spirit is there (Mt 18:20).

The ministry of the pastor in our time is to make the church the location of the personal, for it to be a community rich in the spirit of personal encounter. The pastor's ministry is to embrace the spiritual, to give language and action to people's spiritual experiences. But we do this not by sending people into themselves, to become self-enclosed addicts of so-called spiritual experiences, but by helping them to participate in each other's life. We are called to help our people see the social, embodied reality of the spiritual and to recognize through proclamation that the fullness of the Spirit seeks to indwell their person through the person of Jesus Christ. To act for one's neighbor (Mt 25) in the community of embodied spirit is to encounter the embodied Spirit of Jesus Christ, who goes through death so all can share in his (Holy) Spirit.

4. A person is indwelled because a person is broken. A person is embodied spirit that shares in the life of others through action and communication (through word and response). To be a person is to indwell others through relationship. But when we say that persons are spirit, we don't avoid the fact that persons are broken. To be embodied is to be broken.[24]

Christian tradition has often held that angels are spirits, but because they have no body they are not broken, whereas demons are fallen spirits. And because they have no body, they have no hope of redemption; they are not broken, because they can never be fixed. Brokenness is the unique reality of being both spirit and body; brokenness is the reality of being person. When we refuse to see another's personhood, we are unwilling to see their brokenness. We resist because to see their brokenness is to see them as the embodied spirits that they are.

Brokenness has its origin in sin. Sin is the *brokenness* of relationship that now all persons must share; no person can avoid this reality (Gen 2:17). We are our relationships, but our relationships are always stressed, fractured and too often severed. Adam sins against God, according to Bonhoeffer, not by eating the fruit; rather fruit symbolizes the more radical sin that Adam commits.[25] When Adam eats the fruit, he refuses to hear God's word (you shall not eat) and acts as if God can be possessed. Adam is deceived by the demon serpent to try the impossible, to act to consume and possess God (Gen 3:1-24).

The serpent does not say, "Hey, are you hungry? Look at that tasty fruit; you should get your needs met." No, the serpent says, "Did God say . . . ?" (Gen 3:1); this is the temptation to violate God's very person by refusing God's communication. But the temptation becomes deeper: the serpent says, "When you eat," when you violate God's person by violating God's communicated word, "you will be like God" (Gen 3:5). In other words, you can consume and possess God. Adam's sin is the sin of attempting to violate God's person, of wanting a goal (to be like God) outside the end of being in relationship with God, walking in the evening breeze of the garden (Gen 3:8), simply being together and sharing in God's person. This, after all, is what Adam was created for, to indwell and be indwelt by God by being a person in relationship.

Adam wanted to be like God, but this can happen only if he consumes God, violating God's Spirit by trying to possess God.[26] Adam violated the relationship between himself and God. And when one relationship is broken by the desire to consume the other, then all other relationships are injected with enmity. Now Adam blames Eve, and Eve the serpent (Gen 3:12-14), hoping that blaming the other will elevate God's anger against the other and preserve their own life.

They have sinned, and as a result they are now alone, and alone there is no personhood. The fullness of brokenness now enters their bodies; they are told they will die. Their person's destiny is to be lost to relationship with others; now death will break their person. They are told that work will now break their backs, and giving birth will bring pain that will threaten to break their will (Gen 3:16-19). To be a human person, now, is to be broken; all embodied spirits must live in this reality.

But even in this dire reality, even in the heaviness of this judgment, comes grace. Now, broken and surely destined for death, God sees their nakedness, their vulnerability. And God sees that Adam and Eve see their nakedness, so God acts to clothe them (Gen 3:21). God's act comes, now, in the communication of love in meeting their need. God's care is engendered from their brokenness; God's heart is moved by the sight of their broken person, by encountering their need. Even in anger for how they have thrust this reality onto themselves, God cannot help but see and respond to their need. Humanity becomes the recipient of the fullness of God's love; their brokenness stirs God's heart. They are broken, but God will give his very person (ultimately in the personhood of Jesus) to love and heal them.[27]

To be broken is to be in need, the need of our daily bread (Lk 11:3). An inextricably embodied request of the spirit to be person is to be at some point in need. And to respond to need is to indwell the other in love. But God's love is poured out to us as God opens God's own person to our need. The need of our embodied spirit reveals our person, propelling the Spirit to share our spirit, propelling the person of God to share God's very life with us.

Later in the day, after Kara and Owen shared their first nursing, a nurse explained that it was time for Owen to be circumcised. The nurse needed to take him into a sterile room, and while parents could come along, it was discouraged. There is little time for childless rest in those first few days, so take it while you can get it was the nurse's suggestion. So Kara gave them Owen and watched them leave the room. As she closed her eyes to rest, she could still feel his person with her, the newness of his person pulsating against her being, making his absence ache.

When he returned, the nurse announced, "He did great!" and handed him back. A few minutes later, with no warning, Owen began screaming in pain. Kara called the nurse, who opened his diaper and explained that it was a bit painful, perhaps, for him to need a diaper change after the procedure. When Kara saw the raw, red circumcision wound, she was filled with a fierce, protective anger, and to the nurse's dismay, she burst into tears. She grabbed Owen, pulling him close to her body, and whispered against his cheek, "I'm so sorry!" The befuddled nurse left, and Kara turned to me, her voice cracking but forceful, "Never again. Never again will I not be with him. If he is going to go through something painful, he won't be alone. I will be right there."

His need, his brokenness, glued her being to his; he was more hers now than ever. His brokenness became steroids to her love for him. Watching him scream in pain, she felt she had violated their indwelling; she had not shared in the suffering of his brokenness. But it empowered her to step into her self-understanding as his mother. His person was naked to her and she could respond by clothing it with her own being, she could only clothe it by indwelling his person with her own.

For the rest of our stay, whenever he needed a procedure, prick or poke, Kara went with him, standing next to him softly whispering to him. The nurse who saw her reaction to the circumcision tried to dissuade her, thinking she was just emotional and reactive to his pain. But they soon discovered that as she stood by him and stroked his cheek, she was calm and comforting. Sharing his place made her indwelling whole.

In and through need and the mutual confession of our brokenness we share in each other's lives. At the end of the scene in *The Big Kahuna*, after turning him to the communication of persons through asking about people's kids and dreams, Phil tells Bob that he will never have character. He will lack personhood until he picks up his regret, those ways he is broken, and lives in and through them. When you do this, he tells Bob, you become a person, because "truth reaches up and tattoos itself all over your face." But until you do that, until you are a person who can admit your brokenness, you can have no relationship.

7

Empathy,
It's a Spirit Thing

Why We're Built for Relationships

The sadness in their eyes was heartbreaking, sure, but the pensive senti-ments on their faces was so cute I couldn't help myself. So I'd exploit it, straining my voice further to make the pathetic sounds and scared pleas of the lost monkey.

Every time I read the children's book *Hug* (by Jez Alborough) to my kids, the emotions were palpable. It is the story, mostly done through illustrations, of a lost monkey looking for a hug. There are only three words in the whole story. And for the first eight of the book's ten or so pages, the only dialogue is "Hug" as the lost monkey moves through the jungle seeing other animals hugging. The little monkey asks snakes, hippos and elephants, "Hug?" walking with his head lowered in sadness, still searching, his desperation mounting. As two-year-old Maisy sat on my lap, I'd raise my voice in anguish with the monkey's plea, "HHH-UUUU-G!" I'd repeat. With every cry her face would fill with worry, her eyes swelling with feelings for the monkey.

After repeated cries of "Hug!" the little monkey breaks down and sobs; the illustration shows tears shooting from his little being. So I began crying myself, adding sound to the pictures. As I did little Maisy (and even Owen when he was two) would get up off my lap to move closer to the picture, pushing her nose toward the monkey's broken need. Often she'd even touch it. I read this story to her no less than two hundred times, but still every time she would react the same way, feeling the poor monkey's pain.

Then, on the next page, a larger monkey comes into the picture, her arms outstretched, and I'd shout with as much excitement as I had read the other pages with pain, "BOBO!" And Maisy's little face would look with shock and anticipation. I'd then read the little monkey's response, his head raised and face alight in joy, "MOMMY!" and Maisy would literally stand and clap, all the worry of missed hugs replaced by the relief and excitement of a reunion with a mommy—what could be more wonderful from a toddler's perspective?

Bobo and Mommy embrace, and now the question becomes an actuality—there is the "hug" of indwelled life. The book ends with Bobo embraced by the hug of his mother and now all the snakes, hippos and elephants who had watched him suffer are hugging in celebration.

As I closed the cover Maisy's little chest would release a breath, signaling the journey that this book had sent her person into. Tired and satisfied, she'd ask me to read it again.

EMPATHY AS THE SPIRITUAL HARKENING TO INDWELL

What was so powerful about reading *Hug* to Maisy was watching her little being be drawn into empathy.[1] Her spirit would spill out, becoming so undeniably present to me when she would experience empathy for Bobo. It was as if Maisy wished to give her very self to Bobo, to bind her person to Bobo. Maisy could imagine nothing worse than not having the hug of a mommy; her face showed that she felt the deep stab of being without the relationship that made you *you*.

And this is empathy; it is the experience of feeling (often involuntarily) the very relationships that make a person.[2] Empathy is a feeling that touches the relationships that make us, a magnet that draws our person to another's. Empathy, as a feeling, is how we experience the ontological relationships that make a person. Because it is the feeling of another's person through their relationships, empathy is the feeling of spirit. Empathy is the spiritual reality that takes us into, that moves us to indwell, another. It is a deep feeling of spirit that pulls us from ourselves to others, which is why some people resent it, punishing those that make them feel, that pull them from their self-enclosed hiding place.

Empathy is the enemy of individualism because such feelings can easily derail our own individual interests, muddying our own individual wants with feelings for others. This is why the heartless individual, the one untriggered by empathy, is often the most successful. Individualists hate emotion. They surely use it, seeking to sell you on their own interest by manipulating *your* emotions. (They rarely use our empathy, however, because it is too powerful, too spiritual; instead they seek to tap into fear—more on this later). But those with the guile to try to fake empathy do something diabolical. For when empathy is discovered to be counterfeit, the violation is deep, because the believed shared indwelling was a lie, leaving one person humiliated for thinking the relationship was something other than it was. The deep violation of faked empathy touches on Bonhoeffer's statement that "it is worse for a liar to tell the truth than for a lover of truth to lie."[3] Too often those who win in the individualist game are those that can reach their goals without being derailed by feelings like true empathy. Those that refuse to see persons, refuse to see with eyes of empathy, which is to see us as our relationships.[4]

When we are drawn into empathy, we see personhood. Empathy is the surest lens of seeing persons, because empathy most often sees the person in stressed or fractured relationships. My heart feels ripped open for the boy across the street when I see him picked on for his learning struggles; my spirit aches within me when my coworker confesses the pain of her marriage. I see them as persons—I see them as their stressed relationships. In so seeing them, through empathy I feel my spirit being pulled toward their own broken person.

Empathy is a human emotional experience that nevertheless is spiritual, for empathy is the surest way we are moved to indwelling (into something theological, even incarnational). At witnessing the brokenness of a person that is his relationships, empathy is the reflex to give your own person to him for a new relationship.

Maisy's eyes filled with empathy because Bobo was cut loose, because Bobo had lost the gift of the relationship that made him a person. Maisy was triggered to see him, overwhelmed with feelings of empathy, ready to act for Bobo. Through empathy she longed to give him another relationship that maybe even in a small way could stabilize his shaken person. Empathy moved her spirit to see Bobo's spirit as a broken relationship, as a shaken person. And in seeing his spirit she was moved to act for him, to share in his life through action and discourse, to indwell him through relationship.

A HUG

Experiencing empathy, witnessing the stressed relationships that are a person, it is no wonder that our impulse is to hug. Seeing the boy across the street I long to run to him and embrace him. I wish to tell him that things will get better, but first, and most primarily, I wish to embrace him. I resist these feelings, knowing they would be socially inappropriate; I barely know the boy. But still, I can't deny that empathy pushes me to his person with such feeling that I want to hug him. Seeing the tears of my coworker roll down her cheeks, I hug her awkwardly, not knowing if it is the right thing to do, not sure if it's company-approved. But the cognitive reflection that makes my action awkward cannot suppress what her being longs for and mine is triggered to give, a hug.

And this desire to hug is born at a deep ontological/existential level of the human spirit's need to be and to indwell. It may be true that in good practice a pastor should never hug (or at least needs to be very reflective when considering it). We need to be aware that bodily given hugs may become a confused text, either confusing the one embraced (for instance, leading him or her to think the hug is "for play") or the one giving the hug (I embrace you because your emotions make me nervous and I use my embrace to shut you up and save myself).

At the level of practice this awareness is essential, but from the level of our ontological state (which practice must attend to), empathy's deepest response is to hug, because empathy is the moving of the human spirit to indwell another human person. Empathy longs to give to the broken human spirit, broken by its stressed relationships, a new relationship, to give my very self—only a hug can represent this indwelling. "If we do live in a participatory world and our very bodily experience is one of continuous engagement with others, then empathy becomes the means by which we enter deeply into each other's lives. It is also the means by which we understand and make our common reality."[5]

Bobo is pleading for a hug, a relationship that can give him his personhood. But there are no hugs for the little monkey at the beginning of the book, because there is no empathy. Even if some of the animals may guess his intention (e.g., the elephant mom helps him search), the other animals and the reader all see Bobo simply as a deranged or imbalanced individual looking to get his interest met (or at the very least, a perplexing oddity as he wanders the jungle pointing out hugs). They are not drawn to hug him themselves until they see his mother, until they see Bobo through the relationship that makes him "him."

When they witness this, the monkey is no longer an oddity or an imbalanced individual looking to have his interest met, but a lost boy, little Bobo, a person with a name, searching for his mommy, needing a hug of indwelling. With the scream "Bobo!" the proclamation of his name, he is undeniably his relationships; he is bound to another who calls him "Bobo." And he responds with "Mommy!" a name that can only *be* because of the gift of a relationship itself. Seeing him as his relationships, the others are moved in empathy; with their arms around one another encircling Bobo and Mommy they all join in a chorus of "HUG!" a testimony of indwelling, of sharing of person to person.

Empathy is the spiritual reality that moves the human embodied spirit to indwell other human spirits at their most basic level, the level of their broken relationships. Empathy is the impetus to share in the personal.

The pastor, in this new era of sharing, need not be the most empathetic person in the church, but should be the one thinking about how to set the space for facilitating these kinds of encounters. And this begins by finding ways for people to tell their stories, to share the relationships that make them *them*.

It is a shame how little we know about each other, how little we know about spouses or children who never make it to church. We so rarely ask people to share about the relationships that make them *them*. But this may be where we need to start, to provide space for people to speak in joy and sorrow about the relationships that make them who they are. (This is what makes funerals so painfully powerful: people speak of the relationship that had made them persons.) When we do, we trust that when others know these relationships, empathy becomes the very blood that fuels the human spirit to indwell, to hug (whether emotionally or physically) other persons, other human spirits. We are embodied spirits. *As spirit we seek indwelling, and as bodies we seek touch.* It is no wonder that the hug is so powerful; it is the act that simultaneously connects bodies and spirits, so often prompted by the feeling of empathy.

EMPATHY AS IMAGINATIVE FEELING

Empathy, *Einfühlung* in German, is "feeling into" another; it is to feel the relationships that make them *them*, that give them their very person. And doing this is a *feeling*. Maisy had no cognitive way of understanding this; she had no logical conceptions that people are their relationships. What triggered her empathy wasn't her knowledge (her intellect), but her feelings. She could indwell Bobo not because she knew something logically, but because she was free to feel something, to feel Bobo. Empathy is not a cognitive reality, but a spiritual one that is embedded in our embodied emotions, in our feelings.

Frans de Waal has made a strong argument that animals, particularly large-brain animals like elephants, are empathetic creatures like us.[6] The debate is still raging. But here I would argue that it is plausible that animals like elephants do feel, as embodied creatures, like us; we feel, and our feelings are deeply bound in our being. We know that elephants feel the death of another elephant. I think de Waal rightly sees emotion, feeling, as bound within embodiedness. All creatures feel, and depending on the size of their brains, these feelings can be more precise. Even sea slugs, we're told, feel pain and learn to avoid it.

Yet what is unique about human persons is that our emotions, our feelings—most particularly our feelings of empathy—are a spiritual reality that allows us to indwell another. We feel, like other embodied creatures, feelings to survive (avoiding pain and seeking sex), but unlike them we also feel for the very purpose of being in relationship.[7] It is beyond instinct and urge; it is the longing of spirit to be indwelled, to be felt and known by another, to *be* through the spirit of the embodied other.

Through her own feelings Maisy could imagine what Bobo felt. And in imagining it, through her emotions she could feel it; she could feel

Bobo.[8] And feeling another—feeling your way into another—is what it means to be a person, to be spirit.[9] "I feel you," the common hip-hop response, denotes not formal knowledge but the triggered imagination.[10] "I feel you" ignites empathy. De Waal states powerfully, "We can't feel anything that happens outside ourselves, but by unconsciously merging self and other, the other's experiences echo within us. We feel them as if they're our own. Such identification . . . cannot be reduced to any other capacities, such as learning, association, or reasoning. Empathy offers direct access to 'the foreign self.'"[11]

Empathy exists on a different plane than formal knowledge. It is true that Maisy was too young, to developmentally fresh, to think the abstract thoughts of rationally seeing the world from another's perspective. But Bobo did not trigger the rational but the imaginative, not the logical but the experiential.[12]

The experience, the all-encompassing experience of sharing in her own mommy's spirit, of having her own being through her relationships, allowed her the feelings to imagine the loss Bobo must have felt. She couldn't rationally name it, but her being felt it. She felt Bobo because she knew the feeling of being indwelled; she was so sensitive to Bobo because she knew the language of indwelling through the mouth and breast.

SYMPATHY

Empathy, because it is the feeling of the relationships that are a person, is fundamentally about subjects, making empathy and sympathy (*as I'm defining them*) different.[13] We have sympathy when someone loses an object—it sucks to lose your iPhone—but empathy is different; it can look similar, but its origin is different. Empathy is fundamentally about subjects, about persons. Empathy reveals that I am a person by giving me the eyes to see the naked personhood of another. By this I mean that empathy is the *experience* of feeling another's vulnerable relationships, of witnessing the beautiful and tenuous strings of spirit that connect one to another.

I feel sympathy for my friend when she loses her passport; I vicariously understand the hassle this will cause her; I can sympathize. When

I discover that losing her passport means she will miss driving her daughter to her first day of college and the final dinner of celebration that was planned, I'm pulled into empathy, because I witness the stress her passport's loss puts on the relationships that makes her "her." I find myself feeling her distress, no longer logically recognizing her hassle but indwelling her person through sharing in her distress.

Sympathy, because it is about objects, is often rational, but empathy, because it is bound in emotions, moves us to share in another's person, to "feel them." I now feel myself doing more then expressing my "too bads." I find myself drawn deeper, sharing her experience, giving my own person as help or at least companion. The most heartbreaking stories our friends or even strangers can tell us are those of lost relationship, the death of a child, the betrayal of spouse, the manipulation of a friend. At hearing these stories, empathy is triggered in us by witnessing the severing of the relationship that gives this other their person. We react because we feel them, and by feeling them we indwell them, even if only for a short time.

Sympathy can stand on the sidelines, recognizing (cognitively) the difficulty of a situation, but sympathy need not share in it. After all, sympathy so often responds to objects, and objects cannot be indwelled: objects lack spirit. But empathy is the witnessing of the personal; it is sharing in broken or beautiful relationships that give us our personhood. Empathy is about spirit, about sharing in the spirit of another by witnessing their tenuous relationships.

A DIGRESSION TO LAUGH

It is true that in all my examples (and I'll even make a stronger case in the next section) empathy is triggered by experiences of brokenness; witnessing persons in need engenders empathy. It is witnessing, feeling, the broken and stressed relationships that are our person which gives the spark to empathy.

Yet these feelings of seeing another, of being near to their person, need not always lead to tears; empathy can also trigger laughter. Often, having experienced the indwelling of another, having truly shared in your person, the only response is to laugh. Soon after the tears that bring forth the hug comes the laughter. Laughter results from the satisfaction of having your person embraced. The broken need most often sends us to another person, but now, indwelling that person, need alone no longer keeps us sharing in their person, but also powerfully, laughter, enjoyment. Sharing is enjoyed, sharing leads to laughter, and laughter connects us deeper. The end of *Hug* is a scene of laughter.[14]

Sometimes laughter isn't just the response to indwelling but is an action that allows for it. A perfectly placed humorous comment can free her from her interests to see you, to recognize the relationships that she is. A child's funny comment can quickly melt dad's interest of hurrying her to school so he can do his own thing. He is frustrated with her because she is keeping him from his interests. Her funny comment breaks through his distracted ambition and reveals his daughter. He now laughs with her. As they stop and laugh, he must see her, putting everything down to just be with her, to share in her by sharing in a laugh. The laughter causes him to feel her, to be with her. The dad cannot help but recognize her person in their laughter; he cannot help but see that they are their relationship one to another. Laughing dad now gently moves her out of the house as a person, no longer as a stopgap to his interest.

Laughter, scientists tell us, has the very purpose of connecting us, of bringing us together. "In a neurological sense, laughing represents the shortest distance between two people because it instantly interlocks limbic systems," says Daniel Goleman.[15] Evolutionary theorists think that laughter serves the purpose of wiring our brains together. It is true that people that "pray together stay together" (see chap. 13), but it is also true that people that *laugh* together stay together, because people that laugh together indwell each other. Laughter is a form of empathy that when done *with* (not at), connects spirit.

This is why the best movies make us laugh *and* cry. These movies are spiritual; they open up our spirit. This is so because need and laughter are so close together; both reside in the relationships that make us persons. The funniest stories are those born from situations, mishaps or miscommunications in our relationships. We laugh because they reveal something—us. They show us to be weak, to be persons, to be in need, but to be beautiful, and as beautiful, worth indwelling, worth sharing in.

Empathy is a feeling, and as spirit we are particularly attuned to persons through need and laughter. It is the feeling of empathy that allows us to laugh and cry with others. Empathy manifested through need and laughter becomes the current that sends us to indwell another. Church communities that indwell each other's need undoubtedly are also the communities that laugh together the most.[16]

NO UTOPIA

Clearly, empathy is no idealistic utopia. Too often talk of feelings makes people (myself included) wary that we've entered the land of *Pollyanna*. Rifkin is known for saying that there will be no empathy in heaven.[17] He means by this that empathy is triggered by witnessing the fragility and brokenness of another; it is through distress that empathy is ignited. If all is perfect, then empathy is dormant. Yet Rifkin is no theologian.[18] His point is a good one; empathy is ignited by seeing another's suffering, by seeing another's most fundamental relationships as stressed or broken, as I would say. But it just might be that the very foundations of heaven are built on empathy, on divine empathy, on the very suffering of the cross.

Paul tells his church in Thessalonica that they participate in the new creation (in heaven) through the cross, through shared suffering one to another.[19] Empathy is no utopia. It is not idealistic but nevertheless unveils something new, something transformative. It reveals personhood and moves us to share in it, to build our very lives around sharing in our persons.[20] And heaven is where we are fully persons, because we are fully our relationship with God and one another, not around or outside our brokenness but through it. God becomes a broken person in the cross of Christ so that we might share in God's person, so death and sin might not keep us from sharing in God's life. Empathy, the very desire to indwell us through relationship, sends God into flesh and into broken flesh, to the cross.

In the passing oil regime, where individualism was essential, empathy had little place. When people are individuals, they are their interests, and empathy is quickly buried under tasks and programs needed to convert people's interests. Here, people are not their relationships; rather they are what their wills are interested in. Relationships are simply the residue of their interest.

We run the risk then of becoming sympathetic to them. We respond to them not for the purpose of sharing in their person—we resist this empathetic pull as inefficient—and rather use sympathy as a strategy to win influence. As self-help entertainer the pastor was actually encouraged to avoid feelings; to be sympathetic, sure, but managing programs and converting people's interest left little time or energy for feeling much of anything else. Feeling, after all, had little purpose in meeting the ends of converting people's interest. But empathy draws us into personhood through feeling. So, it may be that the pastor must be someone who can feel, someone with emotional intelligence.

8

Can I Read Your Mind?

Brain Science &
Relational Ministry

She'll go down in history—at least in our family history—as the best babysitter ever. "Ms. Jess," as my kids called her, was wise, patient and fun. My kids loved being with her, and we loved leaving them with her because we were more than confident that Jess could not only handle emergencies but just as importantly could see our children and respond to them as persons. She had that gift, and that gift now makes her a wonderful pastor.

But according to Owen, her gifts were more mystical, even magical. One day after returning from a hard day of pre-kindergarten, like a teenager Owen began rummaging around the kitchen looking for something to eat. Jess, recognizing it was snack time but knowing he needed to ask before taking anything, questioned him, "Owen what are you doing?"

"Nothing," he returned.

"Are you hungry?" she asked.

No response.

Owen then went to the refrigerator, opened it, and began peering intently, before pulling open the bottom drawer and searching for something.

Ms. Jess then asked more directly, "Owen are you looking for an apple? Are you hungry for an apple?"

Owen froze, his eyes got big. Once uncommunicative, he turned to Jess, looked at her intently and asked in wonder and apprehension, "How did you *know*? Can you read my mind or something?"

As human beings we do have the innate ability to read each other's minds and for each other to be on our minds. It is no magic, but it is mystical. Jess was able to attune herself to Owen, to recognize his need, to observe his actions and to interpret his (limited) discourse. Jess was able to recognize Owen as a person and in so doing was able to read him. (She also knew where we kept the apples.)

Empathy is the spiritual experience of feeling another, as we discovered in chapter seven. Our brains are wired to allow us to read each other's minds, to feel each other's person. Neuroscientists have been looking intently at the brain for decades now, even locating neurological operations of empathy. But before we can get to their findings, we must look at empathy's evil twin.

SCHADENFREUDE

If *empathy* has an opposite, it is the German word *Schadenfreude*, which means "to take joy in another's misfortune." Schadenfreude refuses to imaginatively feel another. Schadenfreude is imaginative, but not for the purpose of feeling another; it doesn't seek to indwell another but rather to be compared with another. Schadenfreude takes joy in the failures or pain of another because these are sure signs that the other is losing, making you the winner. Schadenfreude hopes that the interests of another aren't met, and thus we can feel better about ourself. We take joy in another's misfortune, giving us a stance *over against* them as opposed to *with* them.

Schadenfreude is the ugly outgrowth of individualism, because individualism fundamentally connects people through competition.[1] In the hot glare of competition empathy is wilted, for a person is no longer their relationships but the ability to get their wants. And whoever has more of their wants met wins. Competition has no desire for sharing. And because there is no sharing we cannot see each other as persons; they become objects. Everything becomes an object to compete for. But without sharing, the love of persons is deeply maimed.

As Søren Kierkegaard said, there can be no love in comparison, because comparison breaks the empathic bond of feeling into another, of feeling a person's relationships, and instead defaults into heated competition.[2] Matthew Boulton has beautifully articulated that the first murder, the killing of Abel by Cain (Gen 4:8-10), was motivated by comparison, which led to the competition of worship offerings.[3] When comparison and competition are at their highest, fear becomes the driving feeling that sets the terms for our actions. The great warriors of competition in our time, professional athletes, like the baseball pitcher Jack Morris, often say things like, "in my career I was so good because I was motivated by the fear of failing. I hated losing more than I loved winning. Every time I took the mound I worked so hard because I was terrified of failing."

This may be a good attitude for a professional athlete, but it becomes diabolical in our everyday lives. Comparison that breeds competition becomes just the damp condition necessary for fear to grow like mold on the very material of relationships. And the mold of fear quickly makes relationships uninhabitable to persons. This is so because fear always refuses to indwell another, to be with another; fear pushes away from relationships, deceiving us into even ending relationships so that we might be "safe."[4] Fear believes that the point of human existence is safety, is self-fulfillment, is your own interest. (Anecdotally, this may be why our greatest warriors of competition have been such miserable people and so bad at relationships: think for instance of Ted Williams and Mickey Mantle, beloved ball players that couldn't stay married or ended up estranged from their children.)

Fear inevitably leads to loneliness, to seeking to live outside of relationship. Fear keeps us from allowing others to indwell us and vice versa. Jesus continues to tell his followers to fear not (Jn 14:27), for fear and personhood cannot coexist. Sin serves death; it perpetuates separation and attacks sharing by seeing others as objects of competition and fearing their very presence.[5]

Empathy is to love your neighbor as yourself (Mk 12:31; Lk 10:27). Empathy is the spiritual ability to feel our way into another's place, to feel our way into another's person. It is a spiritual reality with biological/neurological foundations, but nevertheless it is what persons as spirit do. Empathy is the reflex-like jolt that sends us into another's person, to indwell the other, to be our relationships. It has neurological evidence but is spiritual, as our scientists are revealing.

THE MIND

The social and hard sciences have had quite a reunion in the last decade
or so. So often at odds, these siblings have found reason to mutually
engage in a conversation, to put down their opposition and to look, at
least for the moment, at something together. And that something is
"the mind."

Through MRI scans of the brain and psychological case analysis,
these social and hard scientists are exploring how our minds work. A
strong case has been made that human beings, having large brains, are
distinctly wired to read each other's minds. And our minds are not just
large, rational calculators but centers of feelings, where certain stimuli
affect different parts of the brain, releasing different chemicals. But
these releases and effects are the result of encountering other minds.
Our brains are wired for the ability to indwell other's minds, recognizing
their feelings and responding with actions and discourse that connect
one mind to another. Daniel Goleman explains,

> Scientists have begun to [explore] the *open-loop* nature of the limbic
> system, our emotional centers. A closed-loop system such as the circu-
> latory system is self-regulating; what's happening in the circulatory
> system of others around us does not impact our own system. An open-
> loop system depends largely on external sources to manage itself. In
> other words, we rely on connections with other people for our own emo-
> tional stability.[6]

And this is the point of our distinct ability to read each other's minds:
it is for the purpose of putting us in relationships, of giving us the an-
tennas to indwell each other. Daniel Siegel states, "Relationships are
woven into the fabric of our interior world. We come to know our own
minds through our interactions with others."[7] Unlike almost all other
creatures, the human being spends most of life either being a child or
raising children. Not only is our survival dependent on learning, on our
large brains, which give us heads we can't hold up until we grow, but it
also requires us to exist with other minds. Our minds are social organs;
we have a mind when it connects with other minds. Our heads are so big
and our childhood so long because our brains need the nourishment of

other brains.[8] We are to live our lives in relationship.

Evolutionary theorists think that the human strategy to survive is the linking of mind to mind, of person to person.[9] Other creatures thrive in a cutthroat world of natural selection by running, attacking or changing colors. But Homo sapiens survive by using the mind to read the mind of others, to not only discern if other Homo sapiens are friend or foe, but to also bind their lives with others to use their collective brain power to survive the natural world.[10]

Our brains are wired to connect: our brains only work, these scientists tell us, when we are connected. Synapses fire when they encounter the actions and communication of other minds. Science reveals that there is no such thing as an individual, independent mind; our brains are social organisms that only work when we (when our minds) are in relationship.[11]

This natural/organic reality shows the fundamental importance of relationships to our very ontological form. It shows the very embodied reality of personhood, an embodied reality with spiritual ramifications. The hard sciences have shown that the brain adapts to stimuli, and no stimuli more than human relationships. They have discovered that "synopsis that fire together, wire together."[12] In living in relationship our brains literally connect; they wire together, shaping each other. Empathy, these scientists agree, is a particularly powerful feeling, formed in the brain to allow us to connect our minds to others.[13] Empathy may be formed in the brain, but it is nevertheless spiritual because it sends minds to indwell, to literally connect with other minds.

Of course when I say "literally," I don't mean in an objective way. We don't have wires connecting each other's brains. But our synapses, as they fire together, *do* mystically wire together. Just as a computer can "wire together" through an invisible Wi-Fi connection, so our brains wire together as we share in each other's lives. Restak states powerfully, "Think for a moment of the implications of this. You can activate my brain if you can attract my attention enough to get me to watch what you're doing, and vice versa. Thanks to the mirror neurons in each of our brains, a functional link exists between my brain and yours."[14]

This points, I think, to the spiritual dimension in the social, in the neurological findings of both the social and hard scientists. These scientists believe that our brains are created to indwell other brains, and this, I believe, is a spiritual reality, a uniquely human capacity given to us because we are spirit, given to us so that we might be spirit. These scientists believe that the more that we are together the more we share in each other's mind.

I had this experience myself. When Kara and I were newly married we had the great privilege of traveling around the world together for six months. While that sounds exotic, and at times it was, it was also filled with excruciatingly boring days and hours spent with just the two of us, trying to stretch our budget with nothing to do but rest in a hostel room after we could walk the city no longer.

But one of the most interesting things was how often on that trip one of us would say something, something incredibly random, and the other person would respond, "Weird, I was just thinking that." We were sharing so deeply in each other's lives that some of our random thoughts would pop in the other person's head. Through the experience of indwelling each other, of being so deeply our relationship, our minds were wired together.

MIRROR NEURONS

The very neurological location of this ability to mind read, to indwell others, is located in what the hard scientists call *mirror neurons*. These scientists have actually found a group of neurons in our brains that mirror the actions and feelings of others. It seems to start with simple mimicking.[15]

Advanced studies have been done showing that in conversation persons will, almost as a reflex, mimic each other. If one person's hand moves, the other's hand will almost match it, but in reverse, like a mirror. This mimicking is located in these mirror neurons, and scientists think it exists for the purpose of sharing. We begin mimicking each other as a way of sharing, as a way of indwelling each other. We mimic to read each other's minds. We can feel this. We believe that people are really hearing us, feeling us, when they communicate with their actions by mimicking us—nodding as we nod, looking where we look, opening their eyes as we express emotion. "When we listen to others, our motor speech brain areas are activated as if we are talking."[16] Without the simple operation of mimicking, shared action and communication becomes nearly impossible. (Questions about whether social networking triggers our mirror neurons is still up for debate and further study.)

These mirror neurons have their origin in simple operations. A hand in motion gives us the feeling of putting our own hand in motion. (I guess this is the neurological reason that the wave at sporting events seems to overtake the crowd.) But for human beings these mirror neurons do much more—they also allow us to feel, to actually participate in another's feelings. When our mirror neurons are fired by watching another, we are moved to feel what the other feels. Seeing another cry, laugh or yawn, I find myself, if I'm not careful, doing the same.[17] These mirror neurons make it so that we can actually feel what the other is feeling, so we can truly share their place, being affected ourselves by their very reality.[18]

MIRROR NEURONS AND THE SPIRITUAL

The mirror neurons are the embodied location of the spiritual reality of empathy. These mirror neurons give us the ability to feel others, to allow their own experience to impact our own minds, our own being. Cozolino states powerfully,

> Mirror neurons and the neural networks they coordinate work together to allow us to automatically react to, move with, and generate a theory of what is on the mind of others. Thus, mirror neurons not only link networks within us but link us to each other. They appear to be an essential component of the social brain and an important mechanism of communication across the social synapse.[19]

These mirror neurons, these natural materials, nevertheless have the spiritual ramification of allowing us to indwell each other, to give each other relationship. *We are created in body (with mirror neurons) and in spirit for sharing.* Our brains are the social organs, the open-looped system that seeks relationships to give us our person.[20]

And this is the danger of ministry; because our minds are open loops we can indwell each other, feeling each other. But we can also pollute each other, thrusting anxiety and fear into each other. Ministries that seek empathy, that yearn for the sharing of persons, will need to manage toxic emotions or before long an emotional contagion will make the community's air too toxic to breathe, wilting all possibility of shared life.

No one could read Dave, for instance, in the story that this project started with. And without being able to read him, there was no empathy for him. No mirror neurons fired with Dave's. But when he shared, when the space was made and his toxic response was not allowed to produce emotional contagion, Dave revealed himself through his need; he revealed his mind, his very spirit, when he said he saw in Jodi who Donna could be without depression. Revealing his need he became a person. He opened himself to others through his yearning and became an open page. They could read him, they could feel him, and through empathy they sought to be with him.

Dave was changed, transformed, not by his own effort, not because he changed himself, but because others shared in his life; they read his mind and through empathy gave him their own person, changing (transforming) his person by giving him new relationships.[21]

EMPATHY AS THE INCARNATE REALITY OF SHARING

In the last two chapters I asserted that empathy is the catalyst, with neurological foundations, for persons sharing in the life of persons. Chapters nine and ten build on the previous chapters' articulation of personhood, seeking to move pastoral ministry away from individualism and toward the personal.

And now we will take a more distinctive theological turn, seeking to explore how sharing in the place (place sharing) is the very heart of God's own action and communication, how the incarnation gives us God's very person to share in. We'll begin by seeing how classic models of incarnational ministry have missed this significant focus on personhood—both of God and humanity. Throughout this deeply theological exploration of the ministry of sharing, I will seek to uncover how sharing in human relationships becomes the location for sharing in the life of God.

9

New Visions of
Incarnational Ministry

Beyond Our Being Incarnate

Everything changed," Shane, my pastor friend, explained as he finished telling the story of Dave and his confession. We sat in silence for a few seconds before I began sharing my reactions, reactions of ministry bound in personhood, reactions of ministry needing to surround the facilitation of empathic encounters. "Yeah, yeah," he said quickly with his hands in front of him, communicating that I was missing his point.

"Yeah, that's true," he said after a short pause. "But I mean something else." I now sat in silence, realizing that my words weren't helping him communicate his experience. "What I mean," he continued, "is that my whole concept of a theology of ministry changed. This church has had a strong commitment to doing incarnational ministry, the doctrine of the incarnation is a big deal for us—well, I guess for me. But it was so clear that God did something in that moment, and it didn't have to do with us bringing anyone to God. To be honest, we were just trying to survive the awkward tension and weren't thinking at all about "doing" ministry. With Dave's confession he became a person to us, and in seeing him as a person we entered into something holy, a place where God was present. But, honestly, that's not how I've ever thought about ministry or incarnational ministry."

As we talked, Shane explained that the incarnation for him had been imagined as a model for doing ministry that sought to build relationships in order to win people over to God. Pastors do this first and then help their congregation members to do the same with their neighbors and coworkers.

We use language like "ministry is about incarnating ourselves in people's lives" or "the way you impact people is how Jesus did," making a case for faith by living with them, by "being Jesus with skin on." So the incarnation is the doctrinal justification to how ministry is done as a function, for how we use our relationships to influence people toward our values or toward "relationship with God." And we should be clear that this rhetoric of incarnation as justification for using relationships to influence people toward our interest is wed to the passing oil regime, to seeing the pastor as the one who wins religious participation.

But Shane was now in cognitive dissonance because the experience with Dave stood in opposition to this. The good news of the gospel was never spoken out loud, nor did people experience some kind of cognitive conversion. No influence was exerted and no message delivered, no new beliefs were articulated or faith professed. And yet it was so clear to them that it was a holy moment: God was present and they all experienced some kind of inner shift. It surprised all of them; it became a "transforming moment" in which persons were revealed, and that in itself seemed to be sacred.[1] Our conversation ended with Shane's direct question: "How does this experience, that was so significant, have anything to do with the incarnation? I mean that's been my central theme to ministry. Does it connect at all?"

WHAT'S YOUR MODEL?

Shane was in cognitive dissonance because he assumed that the incarnation was a model of ministry meant to win something, that its very purpose was to influence people toward an interest that they wouldn't be concerned with (or at least notice) without the amazing marketing strategy of the Word becoming flesh. In other words, he was struggling to understand the motivation for incarnation, and feared that the ministry model of being incarnational didn't fuse with the personal reality of indwelling he had just experienced.

And in many ways this is our problem in pastoral ministry. It's why I think the incarnation has been such an essential perspective to justify ministry to individuals. I believe we've wrongly understood the motivation of the incarnation, losing the dynamic personal reality and settling for a pattern of ministry that is more embedded in individualism than we notice.

This causes us to see God as an individual who is motivated to meet God's own wants. The incarnation, then, is something God does as a function to meet God's own interest. God uses incarnation to meet some cosmic agenda, to finally and fully get us on God's side by showing us the way to God.

Like the famous Paul Harvey story about the man who refuses to go to Christmas Eve service, not understanding the meaning of Christmas until he frustratingly tries (a function) to get sparrows out of the bitter cold and into his safe, warm barn (an interest). The man's great breakthrough happens when he realizes that he could meet this interest if he could take on the function of being a bird. As the church bells ring, becoming the soundtrack to his frustrated interest, he realizes that the incarnation, Jesus becoming human to show us the way, is the best strategy.

The idea of incarnation makes sense as a strategy to fulfill his and God's interest, to get stubborn or foolish *things* (objects) to change their wants. So the point of the story is that God chooses the incarnation, taking on the function of being human, because of the interest of getting us to heaven, to church, to moral living or to some warm, safe place. The incarnation is the most strategic way for God to meet God's interest. It is assumed that our interest is our motivation. God is interested in saving us, so God uses the strategy of incarnation.

INCARNATIONAL-ISM AS INDIVIDUALISM

Stuck in individualism, this interpretation of the motivation for the incarnation imagines that we (even God) take on actions calculated to meet our goals. We want something, so we do things to get what we want. God wants us saved, so God turns to the strategy of the incarnation. We want people to come to church, want them to become followers of Jesus, so we too turn to the strategy of incarnation, taking on the function of being peoples' friends, believing that if we can be close enough to them to pull the strings that are connected to their wants, we can move them in the direction of our own (and so we think, God's) interest.

Yet it's important to see that when the incarnation stands on the foundation of individualism, then the incarnation itself is caged behind the cold bars of a strategy, an idea, a concept or, as we say so often in pastoral ministry, a model. To seek your interest through functions means entering into a strategic model. If we are competing for peoples' interest, then we are always needing new ideas, concepts and strategies to give us the edge.[2]

Pastors are always (it seems) looking for the next big model they can use to compete for peoples' interest. Strategies and models are so alluring because they give us direction on what we should do to meet our wants. Pastors ask each other what model they use to understand the functions of their church—is it cell model, a seeker model, a missional model, an emergent model, an incarnational model? These models become the strategies that shape our functions as we seek to meet our interest. And when our wants are at our core, we constantly seek new ideas, new models that provide the strategies to get what we want. When individualism is the hidden foundation we stand on, then the incarnation is ultimately a strategy, a model.

The very fact that we say things like *this* ministry is an "incarnational ministry" or even contend that we ourselves are about "incarnation" tends to point to our commitment to the incarnation as strategy, as idea, a model for how ministry is done. One reason the incarnation has been one of the most popular strategies or models in the oil regime might be because it is bound to what appears to be the pragmatic. Incarnational ministry is about *doing*, functions, the entrepreneurial spirit of converting people's wants into new interests, and as a strategy it is wed so nicely with individualism. In this (passing) era we are always looking for the new models to meet our interest, and the ministry model of incarnation becomes compelling in the competition for converting peoples' interest.

LIFELESS MODELS

The problem with a model is that it doesn't *live*, or better, it possesses no reality of its own. It's a mere replica, a scaled-down, less dynamic simulation of the thing itself. Models have their purpose: it is helpful to have a model of a building before constructing it, to produce economic models before investing money. But in the end the model is not the thing itself, just a reproduction.

And this is the problem with making the incarnation a model for ministry; it becomes a reproduction that risks losing the reality. When pastoral ministry is bound to the model of incarnation, of functioning incarnationally, it tragically turns from the real thing. It focuses on details and ideas instead of the life, instead of the person.[3] It focuses on the functions of Jesus (Jesus did it this way; so should we), like a ten-year-old intricately putting decals on a model plane. But just as a sticky-glued plane could never be mistaken for a real jet, so a model of incarnation should not be mistaken as encountering the living Jesus as person.[4] And pastoral ministry, though it is harder, should *always* be about helping persons encounter the dynamic incarnate person, not a cardboard reproduction. And though this is harder, it makes ministry worth doing.

When ministers discuss why they do incarnational ministry, they say things like, "Well, that's how Jesus did it," assuming that the power of the incarnation rests in the idea of functions that can be made into a model, that somehow Jesus' actions can be delineated to the point of easy reproduction.[5] But to make the reproduction of a model the purpose of ministry risks cutting out the very heart of the personal; it threatens to lose the person in the reproduction of the model, to make loyalty to the model the point. When this happens we risk losing the empathetic impulse that draws person to person as embodied spirit. We can miss the other's humanity because our eyes are on reproducing the model, getting the model really humming, which can draw our attention away from the person. Based on the reproduced model, we fall into the trap of ends (of our interest) setting terms for ministry. (This is why almost the first thing pastors ask each other is "So, how big is your church?") Douglas John Hall notes,

> Jesus said "Follow me!" not "Follow a model-for-ministry that I am leaving behind for you." It is not as if the church were a voluntary community of altruistic persons who thought it good to behave in the world as Jesus behaved; rather, it is a community gathered by the Holy Spirit

and made participant in the life and work of the crucified and risen Christ. The church does not "extend" this representative life of the Christ into a world in and to which the Christ himself is no longer present.[6]

Jesus' own actions then become little more than the material to build a functional model from. But as we saw in chapter five, actions are not material to be used to totalize another into a model; actions rather reveal a person. Jesus' action of requesting water from a Samaritan woman (Jn 4) reveal not a model, something we can easily reproduce, but the mystery of Jesus' very person; and *his* very person reveals the being of God. T. F. Torrance says powerfully, "In Christ, what God communicates to man is not something, but his very self. . . . [H]ere in Jesus Christ God acts in such a way that he is himself in his act, and what he acts he is, and what he is he acts."[7]

The action of a person transcend models, because the action is the person and is done to a person. And when some of our action is the communication of our brokenness and need, we reveal the spirit of our person, which seeks indwelling, which yearns for another with whom to share our person.

The incarnation is *not* a model but the fullness of God's action to reveal the Word (the very communication of Godself) as the person of Jesus Christ; to reveal Godself through the personal actions of Jesus Christ, who becomes broken for us (1 Cor 11:24). This personal reality cannot be repetitively reproduced. When it is, we risk that in continued reproduction it loses the dynamic of the personal, becoming generic as we find ourself in the rut of doing functions to reproduce a model. In this rut we miss the mystery of the spirit of the personal; we risk passing over the very place where God's action is encountered. We cleave to a model and lose the relationship—the place of divine encounter—making relationships only a stale, strategic component of the model, like those wooden pegs every Ikea product comes with. The relationship with people becomes disposable when it is no longer needed, or stands in opposition to the functions of the model. The point of ministry becomes successful reproduction of the model, and not encountering divine action.[8]

For example, your wife loves going to the same restaurant every Tuesday night, imagining that you do this repetitive act as an *event* that allows the two of you the space (the place) to continually and personally be with each other. But she becomes angry, propelled by hurt, when she discovers that this Tuesday night dinner only happens because you're too busy and lazy to think of anything else to do. The event she thought was about you encountering her person was instead a function to meet your own interest of keeping her happy and your own life free from the clutter of her complaints. The Tuesday dinner became a functional model to meet your interest. But at the same time, the model blocked your action from seeing her person. She reveals this when she says, "Do you even see me? Do you even care that I'm here? Or is this just some stupid routine?"[9] While practices can open a space, they only become meaningful when in that space they open an encounter with personhood. People in our church wonder if the pastor cares about *them,* or just about them attending worship, or logos, or whatever new program is the flavor of the month.

SO WHAT'S THE MOTIVATION?

Shane was struggling because he had a model of ministry he called "incarnational," but he quickly realized in that holy moment, when Dave's person was revealed, that no model will do. All models melt like the wax idols they so often are when the heat of indwelling persons occurs. Standing in this holy moment, where spirit meets spirit, the model of the "incarnation" is shown to be lifeless. Shane realized that God did *not* become flesh for the purpose of giving us a model. So, then, why did God become incarnate? What is the purpose of God's incarnating act?

What we've missed, due to the blind spots of the passing oil regime and its fetish for individualism, is that the incarnation is fundamentally about sharing in the life of another. The incarnation is for *sharing;* that is the motivation. God takes on flesh because God desires for us to share in God's life, for us to be with God. There is no agenda in the incarnation like the agenda that is often given to us by models. The motivation of the incarnation is the same as the mother-child bond; it is to be together, to share in each other's life. Kathryn Tanner, whose thought I lean on heavily, states, "God does not so much want something of us, as [yearn] to be with us."[10]

The incarnation is about sharing, which is something persons do. We demand that our children share because in sharing they learn to see others. Though they've learned to say "mine," to be a person and not just an individual they must now share as an act of relationship. We tell them to share their things, not just because it is nice but because in learning to share what is important to them, they learn to share themselves with others. Through sharing they learn to indwell others as others indwell them. Sharing is the vehicle that gives us the relationships that make us persons.

And this is the very logic of the incarnation. The incarnation is the ultimate act of sharing as the giving of the relationship that makes us persons.[11] God becomes incarnate so that we, through Jesus' humanity, may share in the relationship of Father to Son, the relationship that makes God *God*. God becomes enfleshed person in the incarnation so that through relationship with the person of Jesus Christ we might share in God's life, and God might share in our life. The point of the incarnation then is the union of indwelling. God indwells us as person through the person of Jesus, and through this relationship of persons we too are invited to share in God's life, to have life, to be loved and known as the person we were created to be.[12] Tanner states, "An incarnation-centered Christology emphasizes the fact that God does not so much require something of us as want to give something to us. Our lives are for nothing in the sense that we are here simply to be the recipients of God's good gifts."[13]

The incarnation is God becoming embodied person, so that we might share in God's life. The incarnation reveals that we share in God's life by being persons, that the personhood of Jesus becomes the doorway into sharing in the life of God (Jn 10:9). The church and ministry then become about being a community of persons that shares in each other's lives as a way of sharing in God's own.[14]

TOWARD THE INCARNATE ONE

This is why we should be careful with how we throw around the word *incarnational* or *incarnation*. When it is a model we're after, we throw around these words to brand our interest and to motivate people to function in loyalty to our branded model. But *incarnation* is only a noun (a word that describes something) because it is first a verb, a word that speaks of an action, and in this case the action of a person. This is why Dietrich Bonhoeffer says, "Strictly speaking, we should not talk of the incarnation, but of the incarnate one."[15] For Bonhoeffer the incarnation is about personhood. It is not a concept that can be caged in the noun but a relational reality that lives only in the action and communication of a verb.

Shane didn't feel like he was functioning incarnationally, that he was operating out of the incarnation model, when Dave made his confession. And this worried him! But through the witness of Dave's broken person, he explained that he felt the action of the incarnate One. It was a holy moment because of the person-to-person act of sharing. *This is the very heart of the incarnation.* In sharing in Dave's person through his need, the church council was indeed on holy ground because they were participating in the indwelling of personhood through the Spirit of the incarnate One. The council was sharing in the life of God through the incarnate act of sharing in the person of Dave. And this was so because Dave's person, his very humanity, was united with Jesus' own person, Jesus' own humanity, through the act of incarnation.

Incarnation in ministry has little to do, then, with cozying up to others to convert their interest; rather it is about sharing in their life as person. It is about following the act of God, who becomes person so we might share in God's life. To follow the incarnate One is to be a person; it is to invite another to be a person with us by sharing in our life. The incarnation, then, isn't a strategy of ministry (a model) but an event, an invitation to experience and participate in God's life. It is about being pulled into God's very presence!

The incarnation reveals that *through personhood we share in God's life and encounter God's presence.* We encounter this God *only* (to follow Bonhoeffer) through being persons ourselves.[16] And we are only persons as we indwell each other; we are persons because we are our relationships. By becoming human person for us God seeks to indwell us, to share in our person by becoming human person. And it is now through these relationships (one to another) that we are taken into the life of

God, because it is here that our spirit of shared indwelling shares in the Spirit of Jesus Christ himself. "Christ is Christ in his social relation with humanity, and by his presence creates a new social community and new social relationships among human beings."[17] *To follow the incarnate One is to be person one to another, trusting that when we indwell each other, when we are human beings one to another, we are sharing in the life of God.*

To participate in this personal act is to participate in the ministry (mission) of the incarnate One, and the ministry of the incarnate One is to give us our humanity by sharing in our life. This is to participate in the new humanity (Rom 5), made new through God's very sharing, God's very indwelling. It is new because it has shared in the life of God. It shares in the life of God because it is Jesus' own person—a person we ourselves are invited to indwell, and through indwelling to share in God's life. We find the new humanity and concretely share in God's life when we share in the life of the person of Jesus through sharing in the personhood of one another (Mt 25).

EMPATHY

This is why I've called empathy an impulse toward incarnational action, because through empathy we find ourselves feeling our way into another's person, sharing in their person. To be empathetic is to indwell another, to encounter his or her person through the doorway of feeling this person's need. Empathy may be the substance of the new humanity; it connects our minds through the natural reality of mirror neurons, which have spiritual significance because these biological tissues give us the spiritual wiring to indwell another at the deepest level (and to allow ourselves to be indwelt by others), to share in their life as God shares in our own.

The incarnation is the act of God becoming person so that we might share in God's life through the doorway of our person. But to truly see our person is to see ourselves in need. To be person is to be broken and needy.

God in Jesus becomes needy, born in the poverty of an animal's feeding trough, raised in the god-forgotten land of Galilee and killed in the godforsakeness of the cross. Taking on and indwelling our need, God invites our person to share in God's life through the broken, placeless, impoverished person of Jesus. It is through relationship that we are made persons, and God desires this relationship that was broken so deeply that God becomes human person, uniting the divine with the human, so that we might share in the life of the divine. So that God might be with and for us.

But the healing of broken relationship, the seeing of those in need, can only happen through the personal act of shared suffering. God desires for us to share in God's life so deeply that God is willing to share in our suffering, to suffer for us. But shared suffering can never happen in a theoretical way (again the problem of a model). For another to share our suffering is for them to share in our person, by being a person with us. God seeks union with us so deeply that God becomes human person to share our suffering all the way to hell, so that even hell and death cannot keep us from sharing in God's life (this is the abundance of the resurrection reality).

The incarnation is nothing more and nothing less amazing than God's act to share in our person by giving us his own person in Jesus ("It is no longer I who live, but it is Christ who lives in me" [Gal 2:20]). The more we scratch this surface the more amazing this gets. Because to share in another person, to encounter a person, is to encounter the relationships that make them such. As I've said, to be a person is to be our relationships. To truly encounter a mother, you have to meet her kids. Encountering her personhood as mother, you feel compelled to encounter the other persons that make her "her." And this very reality, that we are our relationships, has its origin in God's own being. In the Christian tradition God is God's relationship. Yet, God is God, so this relationship that makes God *God* doesn't exist outside Godself, but within Godself.[18] In other words, this is just a convoluted way of saying God is God as the relationship of Father to Son in and through the Holy Spirit.

THE TRINITY

The Trinity is a relationship that exists within Godself. God is a relationship, and we are made in God's image, because we to, as persons, are our relationships (Gen 1:26-27). The incarnation itself makes the Trinity a needed theological concept; the incarnation makes what was hidden revealed, that God is surely a relationship. Once Jesus utters, "If you know me, you will know my Father" (Jn 14:7) because "the Father and I are one" (Jn 10:30) and the church confesses that the once dead but now alive is the Lord, we need a way to conceptually get our arms around this reality. And as any Sunday school or confirmation teacher knows, it is not an easy reality to make conceivable. All analogies of H_2O and the like seem not quite right. How do you illustrate that God is God's relationship? (It is hard enough to understand it now!)

It is so difficult to find the Sunday school analogy because the Trinity claims that God is one, but as one, God is a relationship of three, though as a relationship of three still one (mind spinning yet?). Jesus says he and the Father are one, though he is the Son on earth and his Father is in heaven. But they are one because they so indwell each other that if you see the Son, you can just as well say that you see the Father (Jn 8:19). The Son is not the Father and the Father is not the Son, but through relationship they indwell each other so fully that they are one.

Karl Barth has explained that at the center of it all, the very force that makes existence possible, is the eternal relationship between the Father and Son. And this relationship, according to Barth is one of act and communication. The Son is the Word, and the Son is the fullness of God's act and therefore does only what the Father tells him to. The Father and the Son eternally indwell each other as Word and Response. But Barth explains further that the Holy Spirit is the very substance of this eternal relationship, that the Holy Spirit is the love of the Father to the Son. It is a relationship of Spirit, because it is a relationship of indwelling.

Nevertheless, this relationship of act, communication and Spirit does not escape brokenness. There is no separation, no fracture in the relationship of Father to Son. It is such a full union that the relationship can be called one. But when God takes on the mission of incarnating the Son for the sake of sharing in the life of humanity, for the sake of allowing humanity to share in God's own relational love of Father to Son, God takes on death, and in dying becomes broken. In becoming flesh and taking on death, brokenness is borne within the very relationship of Godself as Father to Son.[19] The Father loses the Son, and the Son is abandoned to death. But this relationship is shown to be more powerful than death; overcoming death, the Spirit of indwelling is so full that even death cannot keep the Son from sharing in the life of the Father. Not for more than three days at least. The Spirit moves, raising the Son, giving him back to the Father, but now having experienced the horror of separation and death. Their love now shares fully in human brokenness, making this brokenness the invitation, the very entrance code, into the life of God.

It is now in this very way, in the way of action and communication through Spirit as broken that the incarnation (crucifixion and resurrection) of Christ opens God's very relationship to us. Our spirit is united with the Spirit (the Holy Spirit) and in our need, in our brokenness, we are brought into the relationship of the Father to Son.[20] Our spirit is connected to the Spirit as we share in the spirit of others, when we share in their lives, by being persons of act and communication one to another.[21] In the personal encounter of spirit to spirit, where the two or three are gathered (Mt 18:20), we participate in the life of God as the Love of the Father to Son.

When we experience this indwelled reality, we can only call it a holy moment, a moment where a rigid Dave, whom all had avoided previously, opens up and is loved and embraced. Where a problem becomes a person as empathy draws us to share in his life. It is holy because when we share in Dave's life we share in God's own. That is our confession, that is ministry—making space for the sharing in each others' lives as the sharing in God's own.

Relational Ministry as Gift

Union, Need & the Pastor

Just the thought of it still shortens my breath and makes my stomach churn with excitement. Just the thought and I'm taken back to being eight years old and I can't help but break a joyful smile. I can still see my eight-year-old self walking into my grandma's living room and witnessing it, the very manifestation of childhood daydreams materialized before me. Wrapped in my winter coat and pulling the hat from my head, the mountain of presents was almost more than I could take. My grandma's Christmas tree was literally dwarfed by the pile of gifts surrounding it; the mound of colorful boxes and bags with bows stretched, with no exaggeration, from floor to ceiling. I understand now why I would overhear my parents on the car ride home saying, "It's just too much; he doesn't need all these toys." But that's how my grown-up, parent self hears these exasperated remarks. Yes, I agree now that it was way too much. (Though now that my mom is the grandma, she doesn't seem to shy away from spoiling my own children.) But to my eight-year-old ears this talk of too many presents was like saying we had just spent the day breathing too much oxygen—it was nonsense.

But truth be told, it wasn't just about the presents; well, a lot of it was, but go with me here. My grandma's living room all other days of the year was stale, filled with knickknacks and antiques. It was an oppressive space for me, where boredom seemed to ooze from her flower-patterned wallpaper. And my grandma herself was often cold, direct with her critique and frequently impossible to connect with beyond the tall walls of sarcasm and dirty looks, which I saw later in life protected her fragile person. For an eight-year-old, sitting in a boring room, eating awful hard candy with a grumpy grandma was anything but a treat.

But this grumpy grandma, who hid herself behind disapproving comments and sarcastic rebuttals, lived for Christmas. The hundreds of crafty Santas she collected over her lifetime were irrefutable proof. But even more so was the fact that she started shopping for next Christmas the day after her tree was finally cleared of boxes. She literally shopped 363 days a year (minus Christmas Eve and Christmas day) for our presents, working a part-time job exclusively to fund her gift buying.

Of course from the outside, it didn't make much sense: a grumpy grandma with exuberant Christmas joy, a boring room turned into a child's dream factory. My grumpy grandma, so out of character, would put on her Santa hat every year, sit on the floor and pass out the presents. Giving each with a smile, a wink and a soft "You're welcome" reply to our parent-urged thank yous.

When all the gifts were opened and the torn paper covered the floor several inches deep, we kids would scramble to find lost toy components unwisely opened among the mess, and my hard and cold-as-a-rock grandma would cry. Standing, she would look over us all and disappear to the kitchen, to begin her inner voyage back to the cold castle she kept her person in, cutting veggies and warming little smokies as the method of her escape.

She lived to give us gifts; it was her obsession, and while it always seemed like a juxtaposition, I really don't think it was. My grandma was cold and closed; that was a fact. But she did with those mountains of presents what she couldn't do any other way. She shared herself with us, for just that one day; those few short hours from 10 a.m. to noon Christmas morning she opened her life to us. We could see her person, and it came through the gifts. Through the plastic toys, socks and skillets, she gave us more than stuff—she gave us her person. It was tragic that she had no other way, that her personal impossibility was too deep to allow her to share her person in any other way. But it *was a* way; her extravagant Christmas morning present giving was the gift of sharing in her person for two hours once a year.

THE GIFT

The philosopher Derrida is known for his assertion that gift giving in an exchange society like ours is an impossibility. He believes that gifts are almost always given for the purpose of winning something in return. We share gifts, he believes, not really to *share* but to consume another, to win their loyalty. And there is something to this; I bring wine to the dinner party as a gift to win the label of being a good and (if it is a good wine) classy guest. I feel obligated to give my sister-in-law a gift card to the Gap for her birthday after she kindly gave me a new iPhone case for mine. Sales reps have expense accounts to take clients to pricey dinners and esteemed golf courses with the hope that the gifts of wining and dining will win them business.

Such gifts have nothing really to do with the person (they actually consume the person); the hope is that by giving the individual his or her wants, this person might help you meet your own interest. Gift giving becomes difficult (or as Derrida would say, impossible) in a consumer culture where individualism reigns. We use the gift as a tool to allow us to consume the others' interest. The gift helps us to win in meeting our individual interest. And in this logic our relationships in ministry become the pseudo-gifts that win us peoples' obligated loyalty.

A true gift. But there is another kind of gift, the kind my grandma sought with her Christmas bonanza.[1] We've all had experiences in which we have given a gift that offered us little in exchange, that quite honestly cost us more than we'd ever receive back. Yet we still felt the desire to give it. So often we refuse to even calculate the exchange; we are happy to just give with no strings or expectations. These are true, blessed gifts!

These gifts (whether given or received) become so important to us because in them we wrap our person around another; we give another a gift, but really only as a way of sharing in each others' lives, as giving each other to each other. Philip Rolnick beautifully says, "Every gift is thus in some sense a celebration of the personal, a festive recognition of the other's personhood."[2] Gifts are for sharing ourselves; gifts are often simply tokens of the experience of our indwelling. I give my wife a new sweater, but it is not the sweater that matters as much as that the sweater represents that I have thought of her, that I have heard her say she needed new clothes for work. The gift is treasured because it is a witness that I have embraced her person, revealing mine in my giving.

We feel compelled to share something with another when we see this other. We share in this life by encountering another not as some thing with wants but someone with needs. Lovers keep the oddest tokens of their relationship; in the breakup you give back the jewelry but keep the emails, give back the iPad bought on your birthday but keep the receipt from when you first met at Subway. These things mediate his or her person, and are now gifts worth keeping, especially now that he or she is gone.

Encountering a person leads to an impulse to give a gift as a way to share in this person's life. Mothers love to give good gifts to their children and are overjoyed when given gifts by them. Scribbled pictures and glued popsicle sticks have no exchange value, but to a mother they are gold, not because they are excellent (objectively she would agree they are not bound for a museum). She treasures them more than any Van Gogh, her heart skipping when she sees these gifts, because the gift opens up her child's person to her. It becomes a witness that they share in each other's person.

Ministry as gift. If God's own ministry is the action of giving the gift of God's very self, then for us too, ministry is a gift. Oh, how our pastoral complaints keep us from recognizing this! Ministry so often feels like a busy burden, and it is a burden when we evaluate our ministries by the results of our meetings, by getting our (or we assume God's) interests met. It is very tiring to keep pushing for your wants.

But this isn't ministry; ministry isn't necessarily about building or maintaining something. Ministry is the gift given to us by God to share in God's life, to participate in God's action as we share in the person of others. Ministry is the gift of being a person, to dwell in doubt, fear and need, inviting others to indwell us as we indwell them. Ministry is God's gift to us, the gift of leading others in sharing in the life of God. It is such a gift that even council meetings can turn mundane business into holy moments.

But then ministry should also be a gift to others as well; it should be the very place where they are given the gift of their personhood through the proclamation of the Word and the empathy of human encounter. There should never be the feeling that they are being coerced, that we only seek to influence them toward the ends we want for them. Ministry is the gift to others of finding their personhood by sharing in the life of God. At its core, ministry is the gift of participating in God's life by participating in God's action. We concretely participate in this act by being persons one to another, by sharing in each other's lives as a gift, and thus are drawn into sharing in God's own life.

THE GIFT OF UNION

The act of the Word become flesh in the incarnation is the *gift* of God given to us to share in God's own life. The motivation of the incarnation is to take us into the relationship of the Father to Son through the humanity of Jesus. The incarnation is the *gift* of sharing in the life of God so deeply that we find ourselves bound within the very union of Godself. Tanner says, "In Jesus, unity with God takes a perfect form; here humanity has become God's own. That is the fundamental meaning of incarnation, of God's becoming human. . . . [U]nity with God is the means of gift-giving to what is other than God."[3]

When gifts are given as a reflex of encountering personhood, when we give them because we have shared in another's life, we find ourselves in union, we find ourselves bound one to another. The wrapped present becomes an important token, but in the end it isn't the point; it is only a sign that a person has become the gift. We give gifts to communicate our union one to another, to testify that we indwell each other's lives. My grandma's explosion of presents sought to communicate her yearning for union with us, even if she couldn't say it. She shared herself with her gifts as a way of opening her closed being to us, so we might, for at least two hours, have union with her.

Jesus' own personhood is the gift given to humanity. (Hence the reason, before it became a consumer/consuming blitz, that we gave gifts on Christmas.) And this gift of Jesus' person in the incarnation does the two things that gifts do. First, it offers something to the receiver; the gift of Jesus' personhood gives us our own personhood, freeing us from sin and death so that we might be persons who are our relationships. And this then is the second thing that the gift of Jesus' personhood provides us with. The gift of his person gives us union with God; it gives us the fullness of relationship with God and neighbor. And it gives us this relationship with God not outside of but through our personhood, within our humanity.

Sharing in personhood is the act of God seen in the incarnation, and the disciple witnesses to this union with God that gives the gift of personhood, signaling the person's union with God by sharing in the personhood of his or her neighbor.

OUR NEED

The very impulse for God giving us the gift of the incarnate One is our need; God's own compassion is stirred to give the gift of God's very self to us.[4] I once had two friends whose dads gave them gas cards for Christmas. Upon opening his, one friend's dad said, "Now you have gas money to go find a job." The gift was given in anger because of his son's perceived laziness. Needless to say it was no gift; it was a resource for the dad to get the son to do want he wanted him to do. It wasn't given from the empathy of seeing his son's person and therefore never revealed the father's own person. The gift provided no union, but salt in the wounds that separated them.

The other friend got the same gas card, but when opening it his dad said, "Now you can go visit Cammy [his girlfriend] on me; I hate seeing you moping around missing her." *That* was a gift. Seeing his son's person, seeing his need and brokenness, the dad responded by giving a gift that not only addressed his son's sorrow but in so doing mediated the dad's own person to his son.

Seeing our need, how exposed our personhood is to fear, loss and death, God acts. The best gifts are given to those in need and by those empathically drawn into another's personhood by this need. God gives us the gift of sharing in God's life because God desires to be with us; in seeing our need God longs to embrace us as persons. The incarnation is not a transaction that gets God what God wants (like getting Jesus to find a job). The incarnation is the gift of Jesus' person given in response to our yearning humanity.

It then makes little sense to contend that God's raging justice is what moves God to send Jesus. No good gifts are given in raging anger. If the point of the incarnation is to share in God's life, it makes little sense to view Jesus as the blood sacrifice that must be paid to avenge God's wrath.[5] God's wrath is not the anger of frustrated wants; this is to make God operate as an individual.

LOST GIFTS AND LOST SONS

Rather, God's pathos, according to Jesus' own life in the Gospels, is that of a father who grieves for his child to come home from the far country (Lk 15). It is the heartbreak of a father whose gift that reveals his person is spit upon. The son wants his inheritance and wants it now. This son consumes the gift, taking little stock of the person who gave it to him. Denying union, he leaves. This God, like this father, seeks union with his son, and grieves that he is now lost. God, like this father, has every right to be enraged and seek retribution, but that is not what he wishes; it is not what motivates his action. This God takes the empathic move; this God sees need and seeks to feel God's way into broken personhood so that God might give Godself to this brokenness.

Jesus tells us, through the story of the prodigal son, that his Father longs for us to share in God's own life. God longs for us to come home and find union with God again. The son in the parable wants the gift of his inheritance so he can meet his own wants. He has one interest, leaving for fun and freedom. The gift is taken and squandered, and to squander the gift is to dismiss the person who gave it. The parable is so tragic because the gift leads to separation, not union. Gifts are meant to unite us, but the son takes what he wants and wishes the father dead— lost forever from union with the son.

But when the money is gone, when the wrapped gift is lost, the son assumes he too has lost the personhood of his father. He'll return home prepared for his father's wrath (a wrath that is justified). The son assumes that his father will never treat him like a person again; he'll have to settle for being a slave.

Yet the son returns to find an altogether new gift. Coming home beaten and ready to face the anger of his father, he finds instead the gift of his father's embrace, joy that his son is back. The father is overjoyed that the son is alive, that union is possible. It is a sure gift that he is back; the son was lost but now is found. Even though the son has cursed the father and wasted his gifts, he is still offered union with the father, a new union, a stronger union constructed out of need and brokenness. The son is given the more extravagant gift of sharing in the life of his father again. (This is a witness to a resurrection reality.) The father throws himself around his son; with the laughter and tears of a fool he indwells his son in his embrace. The son is given the great gift of the grace of sharing in the union of father and son through brokenness and need that leads to new life. Thus, the son's return is the father's gift, and the father's embrace is the son's gift—meeting one another's person in the connection of empathic openness.

Out of compassion, tenderness and longing, God sends God's own Son into the far country, into flesh, into our world. To indwell another through empathy means to feel our way into another's experience, to share in the other's life as the gift of union. The incarnation itself is the divine move to indwell the human. It is the gift of sharing in God's life, walking with God in the cool of the garden (Gen 3:8), the gift so squandered that may still be restored. It is so that we might no longer be consumed by sin and death, but find ourselves in union with Godself.

We participate in the incarnate life of God by also taking on empathy, by feeling our way into each other's lives, sharing each other's place, living in the union of sharing in each other's person.[6] As we saw in chapter seven, empathy is the expressway to indwell each other, to share in each other's lives. To find ourselves in the embrace that transforms us from slave to son or daughter.

THE FACILITATION OF EMPATHIC ENCOUNTER

In chapter nine I took away (maybe for some, rudely) all models of ministry. I can imagine that a few of you wrote in your margins, "Give me something to do since you took away all models!" I won't reverse field, taking away all models with the right hand only to give you my own (that you can buy for $99.95) with the left.

If ministry isn't about models but sharing in each other's lives as a way to share in God's own, what do pastors do? What is the shape of our action? Does this not radically change the nurture of pastoral ministry? It may be that our job as pastor shifts from being the one who builds or protects the church to being the one who creates space that allows for sharing in each other's lives. It can never be the pastor's job to share in everyone's life, rather it is the pastor's job to set the table, to create space through story and activity for people to share their person with each other through their experience.

The pastor becomes the one—and this is not easy—who invites each person to be vulnerable with others, to be loved and known through their vulnerability. As individuals with interest, we're often unwilling to even admit our vulnerability, believing that to be vulnerable will keep us from getting what we want. But there is a mystery of vulnerability, seen in the Christ in a manger and the father losing a son to the far country; and that mystery is that when we are seen as vulnerable we are seen as *person* and given the connection and union for which we so yearn. The pastor's job is to offer his people the gift of union by opening the space for people to be vulnerable with one another.

But we should be careful here, because *the great enemy of vulnerability is sentimentality*. Vulnerability cannot be fabricated; we resent sentimentality's manipulation of our feeling. We swear when the Hallmark Channel movies make us cry through their sentimentality. The pastor, then, as the facilitator of sharing, sets space for people to share but at the same time must also be the guardian against sentimentality. She or he must be able to feel enough to know when an experience is "real." And what is "real" is what opens up for the indwelling of others.

Yet there is a further mystery to this experience that I shouldn't neglect to share. Hearing my call for the pastor to take on the disposition of facilitating sharing through vulnerability (need) could lead someone to think that I'm calling the church to be a community in sackcloth and sorrow. A community of bummers! Yet the truth is that to cut off feeling, to refuse to feel fear, loss or yearning, to refuse to be a broken person is to also cut off the feelings of joy and celebration. Strangle one feeling and you strangle all. One who cannot admit need also cannot allow him- or herself to celebrate. Pastoral ministry that sets the table for encounter also celebrates with joy. When we enter into the heaviness of life, sharing each other's person, we are free to celebrate with them as well. Embracing them in tears, we can let loose in laughter.

A gift indeed!

Sharing Is More
Than What You Learned
in Kindergarten

Relational Ministry & the Hypostatic Union

It was an honor to be invited to lunch with the old professor. It was a kind lunch, a generous offer of hospitality to me as the invited guest on his campus. We engaged in small talk for a while, discussing old friends of his that I now worked with. But soon it became clear that he was after more than just easy conversation. Kindly but directly, he asked me why I keep talking about the incarnation when discussing ministry; why did I think that there was some connection between pastoral ministry and the doctrine of the incarnation? He explained that he believed that incarnation had little to do with what human ministers might do and has everything to do with what God does. He explained that no human being can be incarnate; this is God's own work. So why use it as a way to talk about ministry?

I thought about how incarnational ministry needed to shift to seeking the incarnate One, as opposed to conforming to a frozen model or pattern of ministry.

So I agreed with the professor. It is true that I personally couldn't become incarnate myself; this was God's own work. And I agreed with him that when we use this language, when we say that ministry is about incarnating ourselves in people's lives, we usually succumb to a model which tends to use incarnation as a means to influence people toward our own interest. "The incarnation just becomes a way of coercion," I said forcefully.

But I soon discovered that though I had thought we were on the same page, we were clearly on different chapters, maybe even in different libraries altogether. He explained himself further, recognizing that I wasn't getting his point. "No, see," he said, "the incarnation is God's work of saving us, the incarnation is about soteriology, it is about what God does to take away our sin."

He paused, grabbed another piece of bread from the basket and said with a direct tone that communicated that he had the upper hand, "Don't make it about ministry! Of course, all ministry really is proclaiming to people that their sins are forgiven, right?"

I should have punted, nodded, said thank you, ordered my BLT and changed the subject. It was clear that the professor was right; the incarnation is much more than a model of ministry, but to say that it had little to do with directing our own ministerial actions seemed to undercut its significance.

So I cleared my throat and explained, "I agree that we're not called to be incarnate, that we as human beings can't do what God did in taking on flesh. And I think when the incarnation becomes a model of ministry it becomes about converting individuals to our own interests. But I do think the incarnation has a ton to do with ministry. While I might not be able to incarnate myself as Jesus did, I am called to encounter Jesus as the incarnate person Jesus is, to share in God's life by sharing in Jesus' person. And I think what the incarnation does is give me the gift of sharing in God's life by sharing in the personhood of others. I think that the incarnation, the revealing of God's person in Jesus, makes personhood the very structure within which we encounter God. So to claim the incarnation for ministry is to claim that we share in God's life, that we have union with God, through sharing in the personhood of our neighbor."

The professor paused midchew, looked at me with a dramatic sigh, and said, "Boy, that's a mouthful. And one I disagree with." I now became certain that our nice lunch was in peril. But he then breathed in and said, as if to release me from the hook I'd swallowed, "So, what's your school's sabbatical policy?"

MINISTRY AS SHARING

Saying that the incarnation is formative to ministry is not to make it into a model of how we use relationships to meet our interests. Rather, turning toward the incarnation is to turn toward the person of Jesus Christ, who shares our humanity fully. But Jesus shares it fully while at the same time sharing fully in the life of God.

Jesus is the God-man, as Kierkegaard liked to say. Jesus is the fullness of God, because Jesus fully shares in the life of God. Jesus has complete union with God, indwelling the Father as the Father indwells him ("I and the Father are one").

But while Jesus fully indwells the Father, he also fully shares our place. Jesus shares completely in the person of God; he is the Son of God. By taking on flesh and it's finitude Jesus also shares completely in our humanity, he is the Son of man, indwelling our brokenness, becoming broken, so that through his person we might find our own person in union with God's person.[1]

I'm claiming that at the heart of the Christian confession is *sharing*, meaning that ministry at its core is about sharing. And this *sharing* includes material things like money, clothing and food (see Mt 25). The church must share these things. But not because they are the right things to do. Instead, we share material things because they rest in an even deeper form of *sharing*, the sharing of personhood, the sharing that leads to union of persons. The incarnation is about the *sharing* of personhood.

This is why, I think, Jesus rebukes Judas for his harsh moralistic words directed toward the woman who pours the perfume on Jesus' feet (Jn 12). Judas saw this as a waste of money better spent on feeding the poor, but Jesus calls her blessed, because to him the act was personal. As she embraced Jesus' person, she exposed her own. She became vulnerable; her person unveiled before him. She sought to join Jesus' person through the brokenness of his coming death.

We must give to the poor, but not in a way that makes them objects of consumption, objects of our good work. They must be persons, seen as brothers, sisters and mothers. Not just individuals we help. We care for the poor when we are able to give them food *while calling them* brother and sister. One without the other is to miss their personhood. Church food shelves are important, but the congregation is *sharing* when the gift of food or shelter is not an exchange for feeling better about themselves (it is no longer a gift), but for hope of sharing in the person of the hungry by encountering their need.

In the horrifying story of Ananias and Sapphira in Acts 5, the husband and wife are struck by the Holy Spirit not necessarily because they refused to share all the money made from the sale of their land, but because they said they did, hiding their person, refusing to share in the life of the community through honesty and struggle. Their gift was no gift because it hid the vulnerability of their person. *Sharing* is the core of the church of Acts; the members share their things as the more fundamental sharing of their person. Refusing to share is one thing; Ananias and Sapphira are free to refuse, but fake sharing damages the community.

People are free to *not share* themselves in our churches. But what can't be stood for is the feigning of openness. To fake sharing is a very different thing, and far worse, than to refuse to share, because fake sharing makes our own interests and wants more important than persons. It is to hide our person. To allow for personal encounter, to see the pastor as the one who sets the table for the sharing of persons, encourages the freedom of honesty. When the pastor has to win program participation, he or she must push and cajole participants—"butts in seats" is what matters. But when ministry is about the sharing of persons, then freedom and honesty must be central. Then getting butts does not constitute the heavy lifting, but the difficult and beautiful task of creating an environment that allows people to share, to refuse to fake it.

THE INCARNATION AS SHARING

Incarnation is the *sharing* of union in personhood. If we want our ministries to be shaped by the incarnation, we have to recognize that it has nothing to do with *us incarnating ourselves* in others' lives to win the necessary leverage. When we think it does, we become like Ananias and Sapphira, only sharing enough of ourselves to get what we want. Rather, serving the incarnate One means following Jesus in finding union with our neighbors through their need; giving ourselves to truly share in their life. As Jesus shares in personhood for the sake of union, so too ministry becomes about sharing in the personhood of others for the sake of union. It is setting the table for personal encounters as the way of sharing in God's life by sharing in each other's. It is union one to another in and through our brokenness.

This union with our neighbor isn't just a nice thing to do, but the very way we participate in God's presence, the way we share in God's own life. And this is so because the incarnate Christ has given himself to our neighbor, standing with and for our neighbor, giving Christ's own personhood so they too might be persons free of sin and death.

We participate in God's life when we find union with Christ, and we can only share in Jesus' life where Jesus can be found, with and for our neighbor (Mt 25). Jesus is with and for our neighbors, calling us to share in their lives as a way of sharing in God's, because this Jesus bears the union of Godself in his person. This Jesus can draw humanity into union with God because this Jesus (to take us back to where we started) is simultaneously the Son of God and the Son of man. Both the divine and human are bound in his person.[2] So to share in his person is to be a person that shares in the life of others. And to do this is to be taken into the relationship of the Father to Son through the Spirit that is the relationship of God's own person.

A HYPOSTATIC UNION

How can Jesus be at the same time Son of God and Son of man? This is a radical claim, maybe even an absurd one, to follow Kierkegaard's language again. Coming to some understanding of how this is possible was one task of the church fathers; they somehow had to articulate the very mystery of how Jesus' person could be simultaneously divine and human.

The church fathers pulled their hair out trying to solve the problem of how Jesus of Nazareth was both bone of human bone and nevertheless the Son of God. How can the human Jesus say that if we know him we know the Father (Jn 14:7), that he and the Father are one (Jn 10:30), because he and the Father are so fully indwelling each other? Is it possible for the differing natures of humanity and divinity to come together in Jesus?

The relevance of these questions still confronts us. I know they feel like old essay questions you answered your second semester of seminary, but these very questions have everything to do with ministry. How is Jesus to be confessed? How do people encounter this Jesus in our ministries? What is really happening (following my thesis) when people share in each other's lives? After all, ministry is the privilege, the gift, of witnessing to divine and human encounter.

To answer these questions the church fathers wrestled with the biblical text, seeking to explain this double union of Jesus as the sharing of two natures in one person (Cappadocian Fathers). This sharing of two natures in one person they called the "hypostatic union."[3]

We can break down the hypostatic union into two components. First is the attention to union of natures; how is it that divine and human come together? This is the heart of ministry. So how do humans encounter the divine presence? The second component asserts that while there is the union of two natures, these two natures find union in *one person*. The church fathers attended to the reality that God had somehow brought the divine and human together in personhood, that the very location of divine and human encounter was in a person.[4]

COMPONENT 1: BRINGING UNION BETWEEN THE DIVINE AND HUMAN

To focus on this first component, the hypostatic union claims that Jesus uniquely was one single person with two natures. There is *not* a divine Jesus and a human Jesus, but one single person. Jesus' divine person did not, as some heresies claimed, magically leave his human person when he was suffering on the cross. No, the church fathers asserted, there is only one person. But this one person possesses two inseparable natures that can be neither confused nor blended.

Union of sharing in personhood is the heart of this hypostatic union. It is a union, but not the union of ingredients—like mangos, bananas and yogurt—blended into one smoothie. Rather than the union of blending one into the other, this is complete sharing, where the divine remains divine and the human remains human (even in suffering). Jesus' natures indwell each other, but never in a way that loses one for other. Blending them would lose the need for sharing.

Through the hypostatic union we also are to share in God's divine life, but never outside our humanity, for we can *only* share in God's life through the humanity Jesus shares with us. We participate in God's life through the sharing of the divine and human in the hypostatic union. We are to be human persons with God. The purpose of God's mission is to be in relationship with us, to make persons who are the relationship with God and neighbor. And there is no relationship when sharing is replaced by consuming. Jesus stands as the one whose two natures share in but never consume each other. *Jesus is the unique human whose very being* shares *fully in divinity and humanity.*[5]

Running right through Jesus' single person is the relationship of the *sharing* of two natures. Jesus is like no other, because no other can claim the sharing of these two distinct natures in one person. Jesus' person becomes the location, the stage, of the union of the divine and human. And this union of divine and human in the one person of Jesus gives us the greatest of gifts: the very union of the divine to our own humanity. When Jesus' person is bound to our person, we are taken into union with God; we are given Jesus' life as our own. He takes our brokenness so that through sharing in our broken person we might find ourselves in the union of the Father to the Son.

Yet this union does even more. Because Jesus is the single person with two natures, he not only takes us into his person by sharing in our humanity, placing us in union with God, but Jesus also gives a gift to the Father. As the one person in union with both divine and human natures, Jesus gives to the Father the gift of complete union with humanity. "In the hypostatic union, God remains God and man remains man, and yet in Christ, God who remains God is forever joined to man."[6]

It would be easy to miss this point, and I fear we often do in ministry. The hypostatic union means not only the *sharing* of humanity in divinity, but also the *sharing* of divinity in humanity. God is not a disconnected royal monarch waiting for humanity to come and kiss God's ring; the hypostatic union does more than give us an invitation into God's court. As a gift to God, the hypostatic union sends God on a search for humanity. Like the father running wildly to his lost son in the parable of the prodigal (Lk 15), so the hypostatic union opens God's heart to us, allowing us to share in God's life as children and no longer as servants (Jn 15:15). The hypostatic union places our own persons so near God's own that God refuses to be without us. God seeks to share deeply in our lives.

Our ministries then should proclaim in word and deed a God who joyfully seeks us, who yearns to allow us to share in God's own life. Our ministries must communicate that our people are *a gift to God*, and that their brokenness is the very jolt that sends God running to share in our lives. We, you and I, participate in God's life when we follow God's lead, running to embrace the other, our neighbor—not because it is a good work but because we seek God. And this God who shares in the brokenness of persons through the person of Jesus is found with and for our neighbor. To love this God is to love our neighbor; to share in this God's life is to share in the person of our neighbor. Jesus' two natures in one person place the hand of humanity into the hand of God, so that we again may share in each others' lives.

COMPONENT 2: THROUGH THE PERSONAL TO GOD

So confessing the hypostatic union is to claim *union* as its first component, but it also claims a second component. Through its confession of Jesus having two natures in one single *person*, the hypostatic union reveals that *personhood*, that the personal, is the core of God's act. It is at the location of personhood that God most fully reveals Godself. Torrance states, "Hypostatic union is also known as 'personal union.'"[7]

The church fathers held to the *person* of Jesus; Jesus was no magical illusion, no demigod, no hologram; Jesus was human person, his personhood was not simply a Gnostic covering to be done away with. Jesus was human person. *And because his person brings the union through sharing of the divine and human, personhood becomes the form God takes.* The Word becomes flesh (Jn 1:1-3). The union of the divine and human come together only in the *person* of Jesus, and we can encounter Jesus only by being human.

Too often in ministry we seek to make our people into some form other than they are, to make them "holy" by pushing them to transcend their humanity. We seek to use our relationships to get them into this new, holy form. We tell ourselves that we need butts in the pews so lives can be changed. We need to use our relationships to get them to come, because if they come, we tell ourselves, they'll be changed. And this change is too often into some form other than our *shared humanity*. But this second component of the hypostatic union makes it clear that human personhood is the very form in which we encounter God. We are called to be human, the new humanity that seeks to encounter God as the person we were created to be. The sign of the new is manifest in the willingness to share in personhood.

We live into this new humanity by seeking to encounter all others as human persons themselves. We can only be holy by sharing in God's life, and God chooses to take on the form of human person as a way to share in God's life. We, then, are holy when we are human; *holiness is not an individual state, but a reality shared.* We are holy when we share in God's life, but we can share in God's life only by being human persons. And as persons (remember, we are our relationships) we participate in the holy by sharing the personhood of our neighbor whom God is for.

The hypostatic union not only makes human personhood the form we should take to encounter God, but it even more dramatically makes human personhood the form God takes. *Because God becomes human, we cannot seek to share in God's life outside of human personhood.* This is why sharing in another's life is a holy moment of revealed personhood. It is holy because it is sharing person to person; it is the experience of participating in God's life through sharing in personhood.

Through Jesus' humanity, God is found sharing in the life of broken persons. "Lord, Lord when did we see you?" You saw me, Jesus tells us, when you shared in broken humanity (Mt 25). You did *unto the Lord* because this God has made personhood the form of God's presence. Sharing in personhood is being swept up into union.

This hypostatic union makes all encounters of divine and human happen at the location of personhood. In the relationship of sharing in each other's person our human nature is united to God's. Empathy, feeling our way into another's life, which breaks the competition of individualism, takes on the form of this union. Empathy is sharing in the life of God by sharing in the life of each other. Pastoral ministry is helping such sharing to happen. Ministry is relational, but relational in a personal sense—not in an individualistic sense! Relationships are for sharing in each other's lives as the way to share in God's. Relationships in ministry must always uphold persons, seeing persons as their relationships of indwelled sharing.

CHRISTIANS AND NON-CHRISTIANS

What makes Christians different from non-Christians? Christians are not different ontologically; their form hasn't changed. All people are *persons*, not just Christians. Our unbelieving brothers and sisters take the same personal form we do, and by this shared form God yearns to embrace them too. What is distinctive about Christians is not the form itself but *embracing* the form. Christians seek personhood; Christians should seek to live only as persons, acting to encounter other persons in the world as the overflow of the gift given to them by Jesus' person with two natures.

In other words, Christians together seek not to transcend their humanity or the personhood of each one, but to celebrate it as the gift of God. Individualism is idolatry because individualism seeks to transcend humanity by making us all gods with our own interests and wants. Individualism is idolatry because it denies that we are our relationships. But as our relationships, we are first and foremost wired to share in personhood, to encounter God in the form of sharing in broken humanity. As Christians we are to embrace our humanity, to live in and celebrate personhood.[8] Christians are not more than persons in form, but are those who celebrate this form, who embrace all those with this form, and who worship God in this form. Those who are holy are fully human, and to be fully human is to be those persons who share in the life of God through sharing in the broken and needy persons of our neighbors (Mt 22:37-39).

THE WORK OF THE SPIRIT

But there is more to this. We are already in the form we need to be to participate in God's life. It's God's work in the hypostatic union to take on humanity, making humanity the form of sharing in God's life through the personhood Jesus shares with us. So Christians are not separate from or better than those in the world, but rather are those who more fully embrace their own broken humanity by being persons who share in the life of others through our own broken persons. Christians are those who know we are our relationships. We then embrace persons, whether they are believers or not, whether they are enemy or friend (as Jesus ups the ante [Mt 5:44]).

But there is another layer to add to this. Christians are free to share in their neighbors' lives because we are empowered, we are animated by the Holy Spirit. [9]

After all, this hypostatic union of divine and human natures in the one person of Jesus is a spiritual reality; it is the act of the Holy Spirit that binds one nature to the other, without confusion or consumption. The Spirit is the bond of love of the Father to the Son; the Spirit is the tangible manifestation of the union of Son to Father. And as such the Spirit is also the bond that unites the divine and human natures in the person of Jesus. It is the work of the Spirit to indwell. *The Spirit is the indwelling love*, the very manifestation of the relationship of Father and Son.[10] The Spirit then acts in the person of Jesus, allowing one person to be indwelled by two natures.

The very glue that holds Jesus' own divine and human natures together in his one person is the Holy Spirit. The Holy Spirit descends at Jesus' baptism to give witness to what has already occurred in the virgin birth, that the divine and human natures are bound (but not confused) in Jesus' person. The heavens are opened and God speaks at Jesus' baptism as the witness that Jesus' very person connects heaven and earth, that in his person God is with humanity and humanity is with God.

Jesus is the one with the Spirit, and with the Holy Spirit the divine and human are in union in his person. In his person the divine and human natures indwell each other through the work of the Spirit. It is the work of the Spirit to unite—to unite Father to Son, to unite divine nature and human nature in Jesus, to unite Christ, the head, with the church, to unite human to human in personal encounter.[11] Tanner discusses further the Spirit's work of union,

> The Holy Spirit could be said to be what unites Son and Father in bringing about and sustaining a conformity of wills between the one and the other; the Holy Spirit is the power by which their oneness of heart and action

for us is manifested. In much the same fashion, the Spirit brings about our unity with Christ in establishing a conformity of life and purpose between ourselves and the Father.[12]

Where there is indwelling union there is the work of the Holy Spirit. A relational ministry that is about influence has little need to discuss the Spirit; it has little imagination for how the Spirit works in relationships themselves. But when relationships are about persons sharing each other's place, then the Holy Spirit moves to allow one to indwell the other, for persons created for relationships to find themselves bound one to the other in love. The relationship itself becomes the point of ministry, because in the relationship, in the mystical wonder of sharing in each other's lives, the Spirit moves. Moving us together, person to person, in union, the Spirit takes us into the life of God. Where the Spirit is there is union, which is why Paul calls his young church to live in union, not for political reasons, not for the church growth results it brings, but because union is the sure sign of the Holy Spirit's presence.

There is a tangible spirit when we are united. There is nothing better than being united with others; feeling connected and known is good. The Holy Spirit's work is to bring union in and through persons, connecting us to Jesus' person through our relationships with the person of our neighbor. Our relationships in ministry then cannot be means to other ends; rather, our relationships in ministry are for shared union. And the experience of this shared union through person-to-person relationships is to be "in" Christ through the work of the Holy Spirit. Relationships in ministry are not for other objectives. Relationships are for experiencing the Holy Spirit.

THE ASCENSION

The presence of the Holy Spirit, which gives us the gift of union with God and one another, is the promise that Jesus makes to his followers, a promise that is fulfilled in the ascension (Acts 1).[13] Jesus promises to overcome death, the great enemy of union. And when his person has overcome death he will depart so that the Holy Spirit might descend on us, doing the Spirit's work of bringing union, moving in us so that we might be indwelled by God and participate in God's life (Jn 14:26).

The Spirit makes it possible in Jesus' ascension for all persons to share in Jesus' person and therefore share in God's life as God shares in theirs. Tanner says, "Christian experience hereby takes on its own Trinitarian form: in the Spirit, who is given to us by the Son, we gain the Son, and through the Son, by the same power of the Spirit, we have a relationship with the Father."[14]

The Holy Spirit is the gift given to humans so that we too might share through Jesus' person in the love of the Father to the Son.[15] After all, the Holy Spirit *is* the union of Father and Son; the Holy Spirit is the tangible reality of the sharing of Father and Son. And this tangible reality, the union of Jesus to his Father, is given to us. Tanner notes, "United with Christ by the Holy Spirit we go with Christ to the Father, from whom we receive, as the humanity of Christ did, gifts from the Father."[16]

So Christians are indwelled by Christ through the Holy Spirit. But saying that we are given the Spirit to unite us with God is not to turn us from embracing human personhood as our form. To be in the Holy Spirit is not to be other than human. The Holy Spirit is no strange substance, like some kind of spiritual steroid, allowing us the power to be something other than human persons, taking on some kind of super-spiritual form.

We too often think this in ministry. We wrongly imagine that for a church or a person to be in the Spirit is to be something beyond their humanity. Too often we've validated an action in the church because it was thought to be "the leading of the Holy Spirit." People often justify saying hurtful things, comments that threaten union, because of "the Spirit's leading." I know a young person whose mother pushed and mocked her about her weight gain because the mother believed the Holy Spirit told her not to spare the rod.

But the Holy Spirit's work is union, allowing the sharing of divine and human and of sharing human person to human person. The Holy Spirit can take no other form among us than personhood, for the Holy Spirit is the gift given to us to share in the life of God, by sharing in Jesus' person that is two natures.

So where persons are dehumanized, the Holy Spirit is not at work. For dehumanization hates the form that God has given us. It hates being human, and to hate our form is to worship division. Where the Holy Spirit is at work, there is fullness of human life, sharing of love, patience and kindness (these are the Spirit's fruit [Gal 5:22-23], personal acts that give us the gift of relationships in union).

SPIRIT TO SPIRIT

To be a person is to be spirit. Embodied spirit is the form God gives us. The person is spirit because all persons are their relationships, and all relationships are the mystical indwelling of two or more. A newborn baby is given the form of being human, because the newborn baby is given the relationship of its mother to indwell her or him. (We know that the newborn's humanity is lost if it is locked in a closet and never touched; we are given our humanity through the touch of our mother and caregivers, through the relationships we are.) The newborn is human because its mother indwells him or her, touching the baby's spirit with her own. All persons are embodied spirit, and spirit allows us to read each other's minds. Empathy itself is a spiritual reality.

What makes Christians unique is not that we are spirit and unbelievers are not. All children that are not dehumanized by being neglected in relationship reveal that they are spirit. Unbelievers, then, also are spirit, for unbelievers are persons. What makes believers different is that we have accepted the gift of our spirit being indwelled by the Spirit of Christ, by the Holy Spirit.[17] The Holy Spirit is the gift given to all humanity; it is the door that has been opened for all persons to share in God's life through God's own reconciling work. Believers have simply walked through this open door, allowing our spirits to be empowered by the Holy Spirit to share in the life of our neighbors as the way to share in the life of God. By participating in the gift of being indwelled by the Spirit of Christ, by the Holy Spirit, we are given our humanity. It frees us to be the embodied persons we are, but now free to be persons, to be in relationship, without the threat of sin and death.

What makes us different is not that we are human or that we are spirit; humanity and spirit cannot be disconnected. To be human is to be embodied spirit. What makes us different is that we have witnessed the depth of our union. Like a picture inside a picture, inside a picture, we come to recognize that our embodied spirits are bound in union with Jesus' two natures, and through his two natures, bound in the union of Father to Son. Recognizing the gift of multiple layers of our union, of the depth that we share in Jesus' person and God's life, we seek to participate in the form we have been given by giving our lives over to sharing in union ourselves, to loving our neighbors.

But the very recognition of this union starts at the concrete level of our relationships; it starts with another sharing our place, indwelling our brokenness as the confession and ministry of Christ. When this happens—and this is our ministry—we see layers of the union given to us as gift.

UNION AS THE VOCATION OF THE CHRISTIAN

When the Spirit indwells Peter while napping, he is told to eat, to participate in an embodied reality as a spiritual witness to God's uniting work of obliterating the division of Jew and Greek, slave and free, male and female (Acts 10; Gal 3:28). All are persons, and as persons all are embodied spirit, which the Holy Spirit unites with God through the person of Jesus. We are spirit, but due to sin and death, we exist in the tragic state of yearning for union but finding only division. The amazing gift of the hypostatic union that we share in through the Holy Spirit is that *this division is healed by the person of Jesus*. Our relationships in ministry are the palpable witness that divisions are healed and union is possible. Tanner says wonderfully, "We are to be for one another as God the Father is for us through Christ in the power of the Spirit."[18]

So what makes Christians unique is not that we are spirit, but that we live from the gift that our person as spirit is indwelled by the Holy Spirit, that our very person, through our spirit, is drawn into God's life. Our vocation is to go into the world and serve God by sharing in the life of others for the sake of union (reconciliation).

As those who have experienced this reality, our job is not to manage the Spirit's work of giving union of person to person in the world. Our vocation, our calling, is to witness to it. As those bound in union with Christ, through the reality of our own spirits, we are to herald the work of Christ through the Holy Spirit uniting person to person. With childlike faith (Mt 18:1-4) our vocation is to play I Spy, pointing to those places where persons meet persons as God's act of sharing. Even if the people "spied" don't claim their acts as participating in God's life, we can and must. The Holy Spirit is not something individually possessed but the tangible reality of shared life. When we see shared life we proclaim, "Here is the work of the Lord."

The Holy Spirit is *holy* because it is the Spirit of the Father sharing in the life of the Son, of the divine and human sharing fully in union in Jesus' person. A holy moment is an occurrence where the Holy Spirit moves, connecting person to person through sharing in brokenness, leading to the new life of union.

Empathy, the road to persons sharing in another person's life, is the act the Holy Spirit uses to move us simultaneously in the direction of sharing God's life as we share in each other's. This is why the fruit of the Spirit is love, patience, kindness (Gal 5:22-23); these are the relational realities of shared life. They are actions empowered by the Holy Spirit that direct our sharing in each other's lives. The fruits of the Spirit are the outward realities of our shared life, how empathy has drawn persons into persons to share in the life of God.

HOLDING CHRISTOLOGY AND
SOTERIOLOGY TOGETHER

So we find ourselves in this shared union when we are moved toward the other by empathy. We can only share in each other's lives as human beings by indwelling each other, and this indwelling happens by sharing in the other's need (the need that leads to sorrow and celebration). We see our neighbor's need and share in this person's life by empathically feeling our way into it.

Jesus brings forth the divine act at the graveside of Lazarus (Jn 11:1-46) when he feels his way into Martha's need, when he sees her sorrow. Sharing in her tears he is bound in union with her suffering; he is found sharing her suffering as indwelling her person. Through her need Jesus is in union with her, and in union with her he cannot help but invite her into the union he has with his Father. This union makes his very person the resurrection and the life (Jn 11:25), this union that even death cannot overcome. Sharing in the grieving person of Martha, Jesus is in union with her, and in union with her he gives to her the union he shares with the God of life.

As Jesus calls Lazarus and the dead man walks forth (Jn 11:43), he is given back to his sister alive. Lazarus and Martha are back in union; the separation of death that ends all our sharing in each others' lives is overcome because Jesus *is* the resurrection. His person *is* the life because his person is in complete union with the Father. Now found in union again, Martha and Lazarus can only celebrate, for separation has given way to shared union.

This is what the incarnation is for; this is what the hypostatic union does. The incarnation gives us the person of Jesus, who invites us to share in his life as the only way to have union with God. And in union with God we are saved, for all that stands against sharing in union—all sin and death—is overcome in Jesus' own person. In the incarnation, crucifixion, resurrection and ascension we are given Jesus' own person; we are "in" Christ through the Spirit (Rom 8:1-2); our person is hidden with his person (Col 3:3); his life becomes our life because he has shared in our death.

And this is where soteriology and Christology are held together. My lunchtime professor believed the incarnation had nothing to do with practical ministry because it had everything to do with soteriology. In other words, God becomes incarnate only to become the sacrifice to take away our sin and save us. But this has only a forensic or functional understanding of the incarnation and misses the wonder of the hypostatic union, ignoring the work of the Spirit. Torrance adds powerfully,

> This is why the New Testament speaks of the penal substitutionary aspect of atonement, not in the detached forensic categories that have developed in the Latin west, Roman or Protestant, but in terms of the intimacy of the Father-Son relation, in which the Son submits himself to the Father's judgment and is answered through the Father's good pleasure . . . the New Testament nowhere uses the word *kolazo,* punish, of the relation between the Father and the Son.[19]

Making the incarnation only about the function of salvation is to make God an individual that functions to get what God wants—sin taken away and us saved.[20] But this undercuts the very person of Jesus; it makes Christology as tough as a cheap steak. My lunchtime professor diminished Christology by his soteriology.

Yet the way to avoid this is not to do what so many pastoral theologies do: they separate Christology and soteriology as if they are tools to use at different times in dealing with different problems. The incarnation reveals Jesus entering into our world, so we are told to enter into others' lives. But it is rarely discussed how this entering into, this being incarnational, participates in soteriology, other than using the relationship to convert people's interest.

When we see the incarnation as the revealing of Jesus' person—the one who is both fully in union with God and fully in union with us—we see that what he does (soteriology) unites his person with our own, overcoming all that separates us from sharing in God's and each other's lives. This person, this Jesus, saves us (soteriology) by giving us his person (Christology) so that we might have union with God. God in Jesus shares in our lives as we in Jesus share in God's own. Torrance explains further,

> It is the hypostatic union or hypostatic at-onement, therefore, which lies embedded in the very heart of atonement. All that is done in the judgment of sin, in expiation of guilt, in the oblation of obedience to the Father is in order to bring humanity back to union with God, and to anchor that union within the eternal union of the Son and the Father, and the Father and the Son, through the communion of the Holy Spirit.[21]

We are made new; we are new creations, new human beings, because we are now claimed by this union; we are participating with the Spirit in living for this union by being persons in relationship—this holds Christology and soteriology together. We are our relationships, and Jesus now becomes our friend (Jn 15:15), our brother (all personal realities), to bind us in union with God, to make us new because we now are the relationship of ourselves to God. What more could salvation be than to be the persons who *are* in union with God through sharing of the divine and human natures of Jesus, who are given his Spirit so that we might participate in this union by sharing in the lives of our neighbors.[22]

The Place Between

*How We Encounter Christ
in Relationships*

Shane said "everything changed" with Dave's confession; he had become a person—the council members had shared in his life. But I have to admit I was skeptical. Not skeptical that they had shared in his life, but skeptical that things had changed. We so often have significant experiences, but it is harder for these significant experiences to really change things. "You can't teach an old dog new tricks," and Dave was an old dog.

So I asked Shane, "What changed?" I was hoping to hear stories that Dave was now humble, never again the know-it-all, that sensitivity had replaced his brash exterior.

Shane laughed, "No, Dave is the same Dave in some ways, just last week he cornered a mother of a two-year-old to give her unsolicited advice on her child's hesitancy around new people. Dave launched into all the things she could do, but worse, he brashly told her all the things he saw she was doing wrong."

"So what's changed?" I interrupted, skeptical and confused. "Everything," Shane returned as quickly as I interrupted him. He offered nothing else to my question, just an "everything" and a grin.

I sat in the silence for a few seconds, trying to make sense of this seeming contradiction. Finally, all I could do was plead, "Help me understand. I really don't get it. Everything has changed, but Dave, as you said, is in many ways the same Dave? So?"

"I don't know if I can," Shane returned. "Dave has changed. I mean his personality is the same: he still is brash and sometimes harsh. But two beautiful things have happened." Holding up one finger Shane said, "Dave has become more aware of people; I think he now sees people as persons. Even with the mother with the two-year-old, Dave stopped himself, recognizing her uncomfortable disposition. He said, 'I'm sorry, I shouldn't be telling it to you like this. I guess in my odd way, I'm just trying to help. My problem is when I try to help, I always try to fix things. I guess what I want to say is that I've been there.'" Shane paused, shook his head and said, "And I think that is really the point. Maybe the very point of ministry is to help people be 'there' for each other."

He paused again, staring off into the distance as if he were putting the pieces of his experience, his theology and his passion together, finding the words to articulate the core of his ministry.

He then continued, holding up two fingers, "And this is the second thing that happened; Dave changed because he knew that people were 'there' for him. Dave knew that those of us at the council retreat had shared his place, we had walked into his life, we had been there for him. Dave changed not only because he knew that he was no longer alone but also because *we* saw Dave differently. I personally now saw him not as a know-it-all jerk but as a broken guy trying to control everything because so many things in his life were impossibly uncontrollable. Before the retreat I couldn't stand Dave, and now I saw him and began to love Dave. Dave changed because others were with him, and when we were with him he changed, because he wasn't afraid to *be*. I also think Dave changed because we too took on new dispositions toward Dave. We now shared his place. In this new place he looked different; he looked human. He looked like a man who was his relationships, and the beauty and fragility of those relationships, seen from the angle of sharing his place, made him beautiful."

Shane than paused for one last time, and looking directly in my eyes with intensity and friendship he stated, "Yeah, everything changed!"

PLACE

In chapters nine through eleven I've asserted that the heart of ministry is sharing, that God's life is offered to us through the incarnate person of Jesus Christ, who unites God and humanity in his one person with two natures (the hypostatic union). Through the Holy Spirit we are invited into sharing in God's union of Father to Son by sharing in the person of our neighbor. Shared personhood becomes the structure, the gift, given to us to participate in God's life. Ministry then is sharing in persons' lives as the way to share in God's own life.

This emphasis on *sharing* assumes, though I have not explicitly stated it, that *all sharing happens in a place*. Because we are embodied spirits, because God has taken on flesh in the person of Jesus, *place* becomes essential. Persons are always in *places*, whether those places are physical, psychological or spiritual.

Christianity is not a transcendental state that seeks to move past concrete places or spaces (I'll be using these words synonymously) as the location for God's presence. Christianity is bound in *place*; it is inextricably connected to the *place* where God reveals Godself. Revelation always happens in a place, because revelation is an encounter. In the Old Testament these *places* became sacred, mounds of rocks placed on top of each other as a witness that this *place* (like Bethel [Gen 28]) was where someone shared in God's life. *Places* are essential when God reveals Godself; revealing can only happen in a place.

But places are also dangerous. Places can easily become more important than the people encountered there; we can worship the place more than the one revealed in the place. Places are only holy and meaningful because of who was encountered in that space. Places become significant, even holy, when they mediate persons, when they are created by relationships. Places have both the potential and peril of revealing persons or concealing them.

So often pastoral ministry feels like the maintenance of buildings, of places of exchange that we are called to attend to. Our jobs can feel judged by how nice or expansive our buildings are, by how these places we're called to maintain meet peoples' individual needs. (Have you seen the gym? The fellowship hall? The amazing Sunday school rooms?)

Church buildings are important, but only as *places* (holy spaces) where human beings have *shared* in God's life. These places, even those of tradition and beauty that must be respected, are honored as the *place* where persons shared in each other's lives as a way of sharing in God's life. These places become holy spaces, because though they are built with stone and wood, they are formed through spirit, through encounter with the Holy Spirit, through indwelling spirit of persons. These places, in Christian history, are almost all gathering places of persons. Even those European cathedrals now only museums, or those churches in urban America converted to pubs, have their origin in communities of persons. These *places* are not transcendental locales, rocks where individuals had an out-of-body experience. Rather they are *places* where people met to worship, pray and break bread as the way of sharing in God's life as they shared in each other's in this concrete *place*, dwelling in the space between them.

PERSONHOOD AS A PLACE, AS A FACE

The incarnate One makes *place* essential, but it is a new place where God meets us. It is not necessarily in structures of stone and wood that the God of the incarnate One meets us. Rather, the primary *place* where God meets us is in the structure of bone and spirit, in the *place* of human personhood. God no longer encounters us in a temple, for our bodies now are the temple (1 Cor 6:19-20).

The incarnate one makes *shared personhood* the *place* of God's presence. After all, the hypostatic union is the confession that the divine is bound within the human in the concrete *place* of the personal, in the *place* of the one person Jesus Christ. Sharing creates a *place*, a new space, by calling each person to share in the other's person. In sharing the other's place, a new place *between* us is born.

Personhood is unique because personhood is a *place*. Persons are firmly in the world, but in the world they are more than the world. In the *place* of human personhood, God takes up residence somewhere concrete, but somewhere concrete that cannot be owned or bought, somewhere tangible—a place in time and space—but one that is nevertheless a mystery; while near at hand it is always other than us. Personhood always overspills the categories of being, it is always more than you can say, understand or even experience.[1] Personhood is concrete because it is embodied, but at the same time it is transcendent because persons are spirit.[2]

This concrete but transcendent reality is encompassed in what Jewish philosopher Emanuel Levinas calls "the face of the other." The face of the person encounters us as an event of revealing (revelation—it is not *the* revelation; that only happens in the person of Jesus, but it is a revelation of personhood).

Neuroscience tells us that mirror neurons are most fully engaged when we find ourselves drawn to another's face. Like a reflex, empathy is engaged as our faces (our spirits) begin to mimic the other's face. It is now believed that autism is a deficiency where the person struggles to read another's mind, to indwell another.[3] Some breakthroughs have occurred by getting those with autism to mimic another's facial expression. As they deliberately do what comes natural to many of us, they make strides in connecting with others. Their mirror neurons begin to fire, wiring their person to the person of others, creating a new place that through facial mimicking welcomes them.

If we had taken a movie of Dave's confession at the council retreat, many of the council members' facial expressions would have matched Dave's own. The face of another is a revelation to us; it reveals the inner life of another to us. It is hard, nearly impossible, to hide the state of our being on our face. Research even shows that the facial muscles used in fake smiles and true smiles are distinct.[4] In a true response of joy, laughter or appreciation, the edges of our eyebrows go up as we smile. This is not the case in the feigned smiles of social niceties; we use different facial muscles.[5] We don't think about this, but our face communicates it, just as we don't try, but automatically mimic each other's faces in conversation; we do this tacitly as a way indwelling each other, of sharing in each other's *place*.

The mimicking of the face draws persons to persons, creating a new (spiritual) place of indwelling that exists between persons. Empathy triggered by seeing another's face creates a new space between us. It is a place we nevertheless fully share through our person. The face of the other both draws me to the person but also reminds me that this person is other than me and can never be possessed. The other's face is tangible and also transcendent. (It is more than and always escapes my own being.) And because of this his or her face creates a new space of our shared relationship, of love, of trust and appreciation of shared life. Empathy draws me into the other's place, to share his or her place, to stand in the other's shoes. But as I do, empathy becomes spiritual, creating a space between us that belongs to each of us, but is more than us. The space between us is the relationship that makes us *us*. This between is a spiritual reality where tangible faces encounter each other.

THE LIE TO THE PLACE

This reality is why the con man or the professional liar is so hurtful and dangerous. The professional liar can use our tacit personal responses to manipulate us or to fool us into thinking that he shares our place, that we are together in our sharing in a new space, only to use this new space against us. It is deeply painful to have a sacred *place* created by the indwelling of persons used for someone's individual interest. It violates the personal; it pollutes the holy place created by the sharing. It's a shock to our being to realize this person never wanted to share at all, but to use us, stealing our person by making our relationship about his or her own wants. The liar offers to share our place, to be with us in a new space of sharing, only to enter this space to rob us. It is dramatic to say it like this, but when relationships are tools for ministry they lean dangerously close to being lies as they pollute our shared place with individual wants.

Only human beings can lie to each other, because to lie is to violate a place created by the sharing of each other's person. This is why lying to a stranger may make you feel bad, but you quickly forget your transgression. But lying to a loved one lives on and on. It weighs heavier because lying to a loved one not only to violates her or his person (lying to a stranger violates the person, making it wrong), but it does more. The lie to a loved one throws into question the place, the space, your persons have created through your relationship. The lie is heavy because the lie threatens the place in which your personhood rests. When the loved one finds out you have lied she or he says, "I don't know what to trust now." The person questions the very space between you, the place between you this person thought was filled with love and trust.

Adam and Eve lied to God as they hid from God, seeking to run from the shared place created in their relationship (Gen 3:8). Having violated the relationship between them and God, they hid, they ran from the place of their shared life. "Come out," God calls, *come back from your hiding and face the violation of our place.*

Human beings can lie, because human beings uniquely can share in each other's place. Human beings not only can share each other's place, empathically standing in another's shoes, but in so doing create a new place, a sacred place bound in concrete persons, but more than them individually. We can lie because this place is created through the relationship itself. In relationship we assume we are in a new space that we share in each other's place as the substance of this new place.

To lie is to threaten the place we share, the space between us that allows us to share in each other's person. Encountering each other's face is a catalyst for the creation of this place we share in, this space between us. Adam and Even are given this place as they walk with God in the cool of the garden, seeing God face-to-face. Your wife is furious, questioning the place created in the space between you, because you lied, but didn't just lie, but lied to her face. "Right to my face you lied!" she screams.[6] Her face is created in the encounter with this place; to lie to her face is to threaten this place, this place in which she has rested her being. To lie to her face is to violate the space between you—it feels spiritual.

THE FACE AS OUR SPIRITUAL CENTER

It may be that the spiritual center of a person is not some invisible soul but the face; our face is the instrument that mediates our spirit; encountering our face is to encounter our person. We say to someone we want to see us, to know us as person, "Look at me," and we mean, "look at my face," see the mystery of my personhood. Women feel dehumanized when in conversation men look other than at their face. The man *is* looking at her, perceiving her body, but she rightly feels that he is not seeing *her*, not seeing her person, her spirit, because his eyes wander from her face to somewhere else.

The face is common (every *person* has a face), but also each face is unique. All persons have faces, but every face that has ever been is one of a kind. Neuroscientists tell us we mimic each other's faces in conversation (in action and language). They tell us that the brain has an uncanny ability to remember faces, and that we remember these faces not in parts ("I've seen that nose before") but as a whole.[7] As a matter of fact, if shown just a part of the face, even a familiar part, like the mouth of my wife, I'll have a hard time determining it is her. The brain grasps faces as one, a full experience of the other, as a spiritual whole.[8] This neuroscientific reality has a spiritual corollary. We remember faces, we mimic faces, because the face reveals a place, a person, whose face draws our spirit into their own. Through the other's face we create a place between us, for us.[9]

Human beings uniquely use their faces to connect and communicate with each other. Our faces are uniquely our own. We may have a doppelganger, but this is only fun and humorous because it is always up for interpretation; our faces are so unique that it becomes fun to compare them. The face, then, is the *place*, the locale of experiencing spirit, of indwelling the spirit of the other. But this face that invites indwelling, resists capture. I *indwell* you, but can never *be* you. So in our indwelling, we can through empathy share each other's place, but once we do, we create a space between us that binds us. One person cannot live inside another. The face will not allow it. Rather, through face-to-face encounter a new space is created between us that we both share. We remain two distinct persons, but through empathy we have now entered a shared space between us.

To understand why, we need to turn back to the incarnate One.

JESUS AND THE SPACE BETWEEN

Jesus' human face is the face of God; "whoever has seen me has seen the Father" (Jn 14:9). God takes up a place, tenting among us, in personhood, in the person of Jesus (Jn 1:14). Where is God? Where is the place God is found? God is found in the person with two natures, in Christ, Jesus from Nazareth, born in a barn, who promises, after his ascension, to be present in the *place* where the face of two or three are gathered. In this *place*, where we share in the humanity of our neighbor, where we give them our person, revealing our face, as the gifts of food, shelter and hospitality (Mt 25).

This is the *place* where Jesus is present, in the space between persons. Jesus is in between us, sharing in the place created by our persons, through the Holy Spirit creating this spiritual space between us for us. Jesus is in the place between persons sharing in persons' lives. This is how what we do for our neighbor is done for Christ (Mt 25). The text is about the concrete presence of Jesus, not some moralistic imperative. Loving our neighbor, providing food, shelter and hospitality, means inviting them into a place of shared life, to create a space between us that Jesus through the Spirit is in.

Human beings are spirit (as I've argued in previous chapters), but what makes us spirit is that we are persons with faces, and persons are their relationships. We are embodied spirits because we are our relationships. Being a mother, sister or brother is as spiritual as it is concrete. As embodied, what makes us spirit is not something in us, like an invisible soul, but something shared. We share our faces with each other as the way to share our persons. As persons we are spirit because we are social. Something outside of us makes us spirit; when we share in each other's lives through action and language that reveals our brokenness, we share in spirit and are spirit. Our brains are the gift that allows us to socially indwell other brains, entering a reality deeper than the biological, moving into the spiritual. There is little doubt that the first time a person holds his or her infant, it is a spiritual experience, but it is spiritual because it is social, because it is the deep indwelling of persons.

We then are spirit because we are persons that share. The very spiritual center of us is not inside us but in a new place created by the space between us. And it is in this between that Jesus, after the ascension, gives his own Spirit to us, the Holy Spirit. In the encounter of persons that share with each other (food, shelter, hospitality), the Spirit of Jesus is there in that in-between space giving the Holy Spirit to our spirit. *Relationships then in ministry are the place, the very space created, to encounter the living Jesus.*

RELATIONSHIP VERSUS CONTAINER

But this is hard to get our minds around because we are making a major shift here. I am asserting that Jesus encounters our spirit with the Holy

Spirit not inside of us but in the social reality of our personhood, in the in-between space of shared place. This is a shift in thinking because so often we've assumed that a place is a container. We ask, "Where is the *place* I left my keys?" assuming that they are in some contained location.

In other words, thinking of God's presence we so often feel the urge to locate God's presence in a container. Or, uncomfortable with locking God in a container like a church building or program, some of us have simply refused to talk at all about God's presence. Having little idea of how to discuss God's presence beyond a container, we've starved our people of any way of tasting God's action and presence in their lives. (Anecdotally this is part of the divide between conservatives and liberals. Conservatives wrongly imagine God's presence as a container, and liberals, uncomfortable with this, but nevertheless philosophically wed to it, can't imagine another way to conceive of God's presence, so they just don't talk about it!)

But a place can be thought of not just as a container but also as a relationship. This is what I'm advocating. There is no container in which you can put your marriage or friendship. You can't jar it, only to take it out when you need it. Your marriage has a place; there is a space in which you indwell each other. There is something about your marriage that is bigger than you or your husband. We call it our "marriage" because it is a space that fully includes our person, but is also more than this. We say things like "My marriage is great" or "is in trouble" or "is dead," showing that the marriage is its own space, but its own space not as container but as a relationship. The relationship of persons is what creates the space of marriage. But created through the relationship, it nevertheless becomes a space bigger than our own individual wills. It is a space with a life of its own.

And this reality is why we often try to teach Sunday school or confirmation children that *the church* is not a building but a people. The church is a *place*, but not so much with an address; it is the space where people share in each other's lives as the way to share in God's own life. The church is not a building but the *place* where two or three are gathered (Mt 18:20) as persons in the name of the person Jesus Christ.

The church may have a building, but that is not its *place*. The building may be the church's location, but its *space* is in the shared humanity of its persons. We so often think of the church building as its place, because individualism encourages this. Individuals use places as containers that meet their interests, that can provide their wants. Things like the parking lot and the youth room are important, but they cannot become the heart of our ministry or the center of our missional outreach—using our facilities as the carrot that gets new members to commit.

Jesus is *the relationship* of the divine and human natures in one person, which allows the human to share in the divine and divine to share in the human. Jesus' humanity becomes the place of God's presence, not as a container but a relationship. You have seen the Father if you have seen Jesus (Jn 14), not because Jesus holds God in his pocket but because Jesus lives only from the relationship of his Father. And his humanity is given to us so that we might have the gift of making our shared life, the life we share in relationship with our neighbor, as the *place* of God's presence. Seeing the other's face, seeing the hunger, loneliness and ' omelessness (Mt 25), seeing the need of this person becomes the place of God's presence, because it becomes a shared space, a new place where food, shelter and hospitality are offered as the gift of personhood in relationship. Torrance explains,

> Thus it came about that in seeking to articulate its understanding of God's activity in creation and Incarnation, Patristic theology rejected a notion of space as that which receives and contains material bodies, and developed instead a notion of space as the seat of relations or the place of meeting and activity in the interaction between God and the world. It was brought to its sharpest focus in Jesus Christ as the place where God has made room for Himself in the midst of our human existence and as the place where man on earth and in history may meet and have communion with the heavenly Father.[10]

This place of God's presence then is a relationship; it is relationship that creates a space of person meeting person, of the divine and human coming together in one person who is the relationship of the Son to the Father. This place of God's presence is no longer a container (if it ever was) like a building, but has become a relationship.[11] Jesus can be both divine and human simultaneously because relationship makes this so. He doesn't have to choose one or the other, deciding to be in one container over the other.[12] Rather, the relationship is the very force that allows his unique person to be both divine and human, that allows his humanity to become *the place* of God's presence. Jesus is divine because his full humanity is the place, the relationship, where the divine and human share in each other. God is present in Jesus through the relationship of the Father to the Son.

Jesus' divine and human natures are in relationship; they are not boards glued together but are two natures in relationship in one person. This makes relationship of persons through Jesus the place of God's presence. Relationships in ministry are so significant not for what they get us but because they become the concrete yet mysterious places where the divine and human come together. Jesus is not the substance that fills empty containers but the person who is the relationship between the divine and human. Jesus is *the* place sharer. And place sharing becomes the relationship that creates the space to encounter God's presence.

JESUS AS THE PLACE SHARER

Place sharing is the very state of Jesus' being. He is, according to Bonhoeffer, ontologically *pro me*, for me, for you, sharing your place.[13] As the person with two natures, Jesus is fundamentally a *Stellvertreter*, the state of his being is *Stellvertretung*; he is the place sharer and is about place sharing.

Jesus is fundamentally a place sharer because he simultaneously shares in the place of God and humanity, because his person is the *place* of divine and human union. Jesus place shares God and humanity. Jesus creates a new place in his person, a place through his person for humanity and God to share in each other's lives.[14] Jesus takes residence in the space between God and humanity, making in-between spaces the place of his presence.[15]

But his presence is not in just any in-between space: it is in the spiritual space between persons, for Jesus is *the person* with the two natures, making the state of his being in-between, creating a space/place for sharing. So the location of God's presence is in the *place* of one person in two natures, in the one person that shares in the divine and human. Jesus' body is the temple of God; his body is the shared place of God's presence, the place of the divine and human relationship.

And Jesus has given his body to us to share in (Lk 22:19). Communion is the tangible act of taking Jesus' body into our own, of participating through our bodies in the divine and human union. Having been given Jesus' body, we now, through the Holy Spirit, share in his person in our person. Our body too becomes the temple of God's presence (1 Cor 6:19-20). As temples of the Holy Spirit we are a new creation; we are now the location of God's presence in the world. We are the place where God is through this relationship.

It is not *I* in the singular that is the *place* of God's presence. It is not *I* as an individual container. (This is where all this "you are the temple" talk becomes dangerous and weird.) Communion itself is a social reality of shared personhood.[16] We cannot take Communion without a brother or sister (a person) giving us the gift of the elements, giving us a place between persons to encounter Jesus in the bread and wine.

We don't possess God somewhere inside of us as container; Jesus is not necessarily in our contained hearts, as our Sunday school curriculum taught us. So often when we say "Jesus is in our hearts," we mean our individual heart (container and individual go together). This moves us too close to the idol of individualism, allowing me to individually possess Jesus as a charm. God is present not in individualism but to persons who are their relationships. Jesus is present in the *heart*, at the center of our persons. And because persons are their relationships, the center of the person, the heart of the person, is the others with whom he or she shares life. To say we have "Jesus in our heart" is to say Jesus is present in the space between the relationships that make me a person.

We are the temple; *we* as a shared, communal reality are this temple. No one person is a temple; our shared body—the sharing of persons that make us the body of Christ (1 Cor 12)—is the temple of God's presence.[17] Again, it is in relationships, not containers, that God is present. It is therefore persons who are their relationships, who share in each other's lives, who are the temple of God's presence, because God is a relationship of three in one, and Jesus is a relationship of one person with two natures. It is here that we are truly human, witnesses to the new creation, as we participate in the new Adam (1 Cor 15).

CURATING A PLACE

Dave is changed because Dave is in a new place, a shared place of person meeting persons. Dave is changed not because the experience was some kind of self-help charge to be the best person he could be. This is to be deceived into imagining change (transformation) as an individual process. Rather, Dave is changed because he is no longer alone. He is bound in a place with others that have seen him, that have empathically encountered him, creating a new space where Dave is seen and known in a new way. In this tangible place between persons, in the reality of relationship itself, Jesus is found through his Spirit taking our deaths and needs so that we might have life, so that we might have union with God experienced palpably in the place of persons' shared life.

Ministry is the curating of these places, these in-between spaces, through facilitation of locales that allow people to share in each other's needs, to see each other as persons. No pastor has the power to create these places. They are spiritual; they are outgrowths of the work of the Holy Spirit manifest in the mystery of persons seeing each other face to face, of wiring their brains together by encountering each other.

We cannot force these places, but we can curate them. When people indwell each other through relationship a new place is created between them. A family has a space, material space (containers) like a house and backyard that they live in. Yet what makes them a family is not the material space but the relationship. Close families almost always (or do) have a substantive place about them. Wherever they are, there is a place, a shared life, bigger than a single member, out of which they live and into which they invite others. Ministry, much like good family life, is about providing the spaces for people to share each other's place, confessing that in sharing each other's place, Jesus is present between us, allowing us to love him as we love our neighbor.

We as pastors are not called to be incarnate, to do the work only Jesus as the second person of the Trinity can do. But we are called to be place sharers, to be attentive to curating places where the sharing of persons can happen, and in all of this to confess the presence of Christ—the person who is the relationship of the sharing of two natures.[18] Luther says it this way, "Everyone should 'put on' his neighbor and so conduct himself towards him as if he were in the other's place. From Christ the good things have flowed and are flowing to us."[19]

How to curate this space for place sharing in pastoral ministry is the subject of the final three chapters (with further examples in the appendix), which examine three core pastoral practices of teaching/ preaching, prayer and leadership. But before we can get there, a little more is needed. We have already looked at evangelism in the periods of pastoral transition. So what would evangelism look like through this vision of place sharing?

EVANGELISM AS SHARING OF PLACE

The heart of our ministry, evangelism, is the *sharing* in the *place* of personhood. Our mission to the world is to share the place of those in the world.[20] Ministry is uniting with those in the world for the sake of being human, for the sake of being together—trusting that when we are together as persons we encounter the living God. This means that evangelism is not the competitive battle of one interest over another. Evangelism isn't about fighting or coercing individuals to *want* to come to church or follow the idea of Jesus.

Rather, evangelism is the invitation to come and share in our place (Jn 1:38-39), to share in the place God has given us, the place of persons sharing in each other's lives. But it is not just coming but also going. The church also goes to share in the life of those in the world. It does so trusting that because we are our relationships and in those relationships of spirit the Spirit moves, the church shares in the life of persons in the world.

Evangelism is living out the good news of the gospel by uniting with our neighbors in the confession of Christ, for the sake of being human one to another. Even in the passing oil regime we've often said that evangelism was about sharing, sharing the truth of the gospel, sharing the benefits of being individually converted toward the church's interests. We used our relationships as the sound system of this individualistic sharing. We used relationships to get people into one container called "Jesus" rather than the other container called "the world."

But this kind of sharing to convert to a container had little to do with persons. Evangelism, in the theological stream we've been riding, asserts that *sharing* is about persons, making evangelism about uniting with our neighbors for the sake of sharing in their lives through the power of Holy Spirit, sharing our neighbors' spirits by empathically seeing their faces. We call them to a particular *place*, we call them to a *particular person*, we invite them to come and participate in the *place* of shared persons as the participation in the person of the resurrected Lord.

Evangelism is loving the world enough to seek the person of Jesus in the sharing of the person of our nonbelieving neighbor. Evangelism is not trying to convert our neighbor into a new form, a new container, but embracing him or her through relationship. Through relationship, then, our neighbor might have the eyes to see that God has shared in his or her life so deeply that this God has taken on this neighbor's form, giving the neighbor union with God, a union that the persons of the church have witnessed to in their sharing of the neighbor's person, in the invitation to have a place in their community of persons. Evangelism is place sharing, because we confess that in the place of our shared person, in being spirit to spirit, the presence of Jesus through the Holy Spirit is there, binding us in union with one another and God.

A Quick Pauline Excursion

Sharing and Place in Paul—
It's All About the In

The theological threads we've been working in the last few chapters are grounded in the apostle Paul's thought. Paul has had an experience that has radically transformed him. Moving along the road to Damascus, the zealous Saul was ready to kill and destroy the young church (Acts 9). His passion drove him. But on this road he is encountered by a person, by the living and ascended person of Jesus Christ. "I am Jesus, whom you are persecuting" (Act 9:5). It isn't a strange force that encounters him, but a person, an *I*, that confronts Paul. But this *I*, this person Jesus, equates his very self with the church Saul is trying to destroy. Jesus does not say to Saul, "You have been persecuting my church. Stop!" Rather, Jesus gives his person to Saul, "It is I," and in doing so Saul is judged, but the judgment of personhood is also a grace. It is a judgment that says, *No further. See my person? You can no longer violate my face. See me.* But it is also grace because it gives us the person to be in relationship with, to be found sharing in his life, if we will see him and stop.

But there is more to this. When Jesus says, "It is I whom you persecute," it is clear that Jesus equates his very person with the person of the church. To persecute this church is to persecute Jesus himself. There is a sharing of persons. The persons of the church are *in* Christ and so much so that to persecute them is to persecute Jesus himself.

From this experience for Paul, sharing becomes the key to ministry. Paul, on that fateful day, on that dusty road to Damascus, is taken into union with Christ. Paul finds his own person bound to the person of

Jesus. Everything changes for Paul (so greatly that he is no longer Saul) because he is now *in* Christ. Paul now recognizes that he is taken into union with Jesus, sharing in his death, he shares also in his life (2 Cor 1:5).

There has been a mystical interchange, a sharing so deep for Paul that he now exists *in* Christ. The church is so *in* Christ that to persecute them is to persecute Jesus. It is more than just an *exchange*, a simple consumptive transaction of one thing for another, Jesus dying so we have the coins to pay for our salvation. It is not an exchange that Paul believes he participates in, but an interchange, such a mystical indwelling that Jesus' very life is given to us. It is the mystical indwelling of spirit, an interchange between our spirit and the very Spirit (the Holy Spirit) of Jesus.

A highway interchange is the place where one road shares in the other. For Paul, interchange becomes the metaphor, the very reality, of what it means to be *in* Christ. It means that through the humanity of Jesus we share in Christ's divine life. We are given the gift of Jesus' life, as Jesus takes our own, sharing in our brokenness, so that it might become the expressway to share in his presence as we share in the brokenness of our neighbor.[1]

And brokenness, or shared suffering (2 Cor 1:5), becomes the way *in*, the very road to interchange. All can be *in* Christ because all have suffered, and Jesus is with all who suffer, seeking to take them, through their suffering, *into* his own life. Saul is knocked from his horse, he is exposed, he is left blind. But this Jesus who confronts him does not leave him maimed. Rather, Jesus calls the persons of his church (Ananias [Acts 9:17]) to join Paul's person, to share his suffering of body and mind. He calls his body to come and share Paul's place, hear his confession and pray that his sight might be returned. Paul chooses to know only Christ and him crucified (1 Cor 2:2) because he had the experience of being taken into the person of Jesus, finding union with God through Jesus. But this union was lived out by the church that came to him and shared his place. In fear and trembling, they nevertheless joined his suffering. Even abandoned in Jerusalem, Barnabas came to his side, sharing his place (Acts 15). Paul has had the experience of being taken *into* the person of Jesus, but this interchange, this *in* Christ, this union, is lived out by his brothers and sisters who join him, nurse him and pray for him. Paul is *in* Christ, and as actualized witnesses to it Ananias and Barnabas have lived out their own *in*-ness, their own participation in this union, by sharing Paul's place as sharing in Jesus' own person.

So the church is the community that is *in* each other's place as the way of sharing *in* the union of Father to Son.[2] From his own conversion experience, from this mystical union of being *in* Christ through Ananias and Barnabas standing *in* Paul's place, sharing in Christ as they share in Paul's person, Paul wants his church to recognize this. He wants them to see that they are *in*, so *in* Christ that they share in his life. But they do this by sharing in each other's suffering, just as Ananias and Barnabas did for Paul, just as Jesus did for all humanity by being crucified. Through the cross Jesus shares in our life as the Son of God and Son of man, providing an interchange wherein our old Adam gives way to the new Adam, to sharing in the new life given by the union of the Father and the Son. Or as Morna Hooker says, "Christ became what we are—Adam—in order that we might share in what he is—namely the true image of God."[3] Paul's church, our church, shares in this union by sharing in each other's place, by joining our persons one to another as Christ joins his person to us, by humbling ourselves (Phil 2:3) as Ananias and Barnabas did and giving our person to share in each other's place.

When it comes to Paul's churches, it is in embracing our need that we are bound together, that we witness to the union of being bound to the new Adam. And this is so in the context of ministry, I think, because seeing need and brokenness is the spark that ignites empathy, and empathy is the human impulse to share in each other's life, to seek the union of shared humanity. Empathy draws us to the other's face, to share in the other's place, by encountering his or her face. Empathy creates a space between. Empathy becomes the work of the Spirit to bind us to our neighbor as the way of sharing in the life of God.

The point of ministry, the very point of evangelism, for Paul is to share *in* the life of God by sharing *in* Christ, and this happens by being in union with our neighbor, by sharing our neighbor's place. Evangelism as well as day-to-day ministry in the church is the call to share the place of other as the pathway into sharing in the life of God.

Will You Pray for Me?

Prayer as the Essential Practice
for Relational Ministry

I stood in the gravel parking lot surrounded by cars as planes from Newark flew above. It felt like I was in a scene from *The Sopranos;* I'm actually pretty confident that this offsite airport parking lot had seen its share of drug deals and that at least a few bodies were stuffed in those car trunks. It was a shady, scary place, making it an odd locale for a prayer meeting.

Our prayer meeting started with a phone call. I was told to call this number when I had returned to the airport and the offsite airport parking lot van would pick up me, Kara and seven month-old Owen, and take us back to our car.

Returning from our trip I called the number and got no answer. After retrieving our luggage, I called again, still getting no answer. Waiting five minutes I tried again. This time, on the seventh ring I got someone. Sounding flustered he said he'd be there in five minutes.

As the van arrived the flustered voice emerged in bodily form, now seeming more flustered than even his voice had revealed over the phone. He threw our bags in the back only to drive away without closing the back doors. Now, his flustered disposition turned frantic. He apologized, explaining that he had been working for the last twenty-two hours straight and had done so because his boss was taking advantage of him, exploiting him, paying him nearly nothing and forcing him to work or lose his job.

We responded to his story with empathy, feeling him, sure, but also hoping that our signs of compassion would keep him awake and engaged and get us back to our car safely. But empathy, signs of sharing, have a way of inviting others to share their story, so he continued. For the next five minutes he explained that he was a recovering addict, that he'd been clean for months, but the temptation was fierce. He couldn't lose this job or he'd not only violate his parole but have no chance of seeing his children, whom the state had already taken away because of his addictions. He had just been allowed to see them again once a week, but a violation of his parole, like the loss of his job, would end the visits. He was a broken man.

As we entered the lot, we dropped Kara and Owen off at the car, and I followed the driver into the office to pay. While he ran my credit card, I told him that I felt him, that I could feel how hard this was. He nodded with appreciation, cracking a half smile. I then told him that my wife was a pastor and that we would pray for him. I almost couldn't believe the words were coming from my mouth; they felt so trite in the shadow of his story, like a religious placebo that would allow me to leave this man in his hell guilt-free.

Ashamed, I felt like my "We'll pray for you" rested on seeing him as his interest, meaning "I'll pray for you that you get your interest met. And as I pray for you, who can't get what you want, I will thank God that I've reached at least many of my own desired wants, that I've seen my interest met."

Prayer is a deadly religious farce, used for manipulation, when we imagine that we pray as individuals. When individuals pray, prayer can be a cosmic wish list or metaphysical magic that we think forces God to meet our individual interest. Then prayer functions to get what we want (like in the popular book *The Prayer of Jabez*).

As I stood there sheepishly wondering what I'd just said, the driver paused for a few beats with his mouth open and eyes widened. He said, "Wait, what? Your wife is a pastor?" "Yes," I said, almost ready to apologize. To my shock he started to cry. Grabbing my hand, tears running down his cheeks, he said, "Will you pray for me *now*? Right now could you please, please pray for me!" He wanted prayer, but more than knowing someone was out there praying for him. He sought, he yearned for, the personal sharing that praying together brings. The power of prayer is that it is the sharing of the personal. We pray together ("let us pray"), and in praying we share in each other's lives as we share in God's ("Our Father," we say, using the relational name, "who art in heaven" [Mt 6:9; Lk 11:2]). Prayer is sharing in the place where God is present; it brings heaven and earth together.

We walked out of the office to meet Kara waiting in the car. I opened her door and explained quickly what was happening. She got out and the three of us grabbed hands and prayed for him; in a godforsaken parking lot a stone's throw from the New Jersey turnpike we prayed for our driver. But grabbing hands, he no longer was our driver; his function gave way to his person. Prayer is done with *persons*. When we pray with others we admit that we are our relationship; this brother or sister that prays for us gives us the gift of our person. We are with them, and with them, as we pray, we are with God. We may pray for functional things like computers to work or weather to be good, but these only become more than wants when they are articulated within the field of the personal. Prayer is the concrete way (the concrete practice) that moves persons into sharing in each other's lives as they share in God's own.

Preparing to pray with our driver, we needed his name. Mike was not an individual to us now that we would pray together; he was a person. And when we prayed for him, we prayed for the relationships that made him *him*, the relationships that gave him his humanity or threatened it. We prayed for his boss, who caused stress in their relationship; we prayed for his children, whom he'd sinned against, breaking their relationship; we prayed that the God who is the relationship of the Father to the Son might indwell Mike's person, touching his spirit with the Spirit. In prayer we shared in each other's person; in prayer we confessed that we shared in the person of God. Mike wanted to be prayed for *now* because he needed to share his person, because he needed to be found in a relationship of spirit that might draw his broken spirit into the very relationship that is God.

We said "Amen" and hugged Mike, and Mike shouted "Thank you! Thank you!" partly saying it to us, and more so shouting it to God as he pumped his fists in unison and looked to the heavens. As we got in the car, he hadn't stopped, still shouting "Thank you! Thank you!" in the gratitude of a broken heart touched. We drove off, with Mike still visibly shouting his thanks in the rearview mirror.

WHAT DOES IT LOOK LIKE?

There is quite a temptation in pastoral ministry, a temptation that I'm sure many of us have battled throughout reading this book. That temptation is to want to know how to do this. In other words, we want to know how this would look or how it could be implemented in our church.

I don't think this is bad, and in many ways it is my job to give you some hints—and I'll try. But we should remind each other that this is a temptation because our desire to know how it works is often a knee-jerk desire for the how-to. And yearning for the how-to runs the risk of cutting off or derailing our ability to imagine, because the how-to is often overly committed to data, to information. The pastor is looking for the new data, the new info that can make ministry successful. Pastors read books too often not to ignite their imagination to see God's act, to help them bend ministry toward the action of God, but to know what works, to have the data that can bring success. So often we find ourselves wanting the how-to, the data, because we want to avoid the hard work of imagination, of thinking and discerning as the core of pastoral ministry.[1]

After all, the heavy desire for the how-to in pastoral ministry is bound to the passing energy regime. In the era of the pastor as self-help entertainer who manages programs, we want the how-to because we want to know how to convert peoples' interest toward what we want for them. (It is interesting that the heavy *how-to* was not bound to pastoral ministry in pre-oil regime periods.) Edwin Friedman says, "As long as leaders—parents, healers, managers—base their confidence on how much data they have acquired, they are doomed to feeling inadequate forever. They will never catch up. The situation can only get worse."[2]

But this period is coming to an end, and a new era of sharing is coming. It may be then that the task of the pastor is no longer to find the cutting-edge programs or strategies to implement, which will free the pastor from the idol of how-to. Rather, it may be that the pastor's task now is forming communities of persons that can share in each other's lives as the way to share in God's own.

But here it comes again—the temptation—so what does this look like? And this is the right question as long as we're willing to seek visions, pictures or vistas for this living and then do the hard work, the artistic work, of mixing and crafting these pictures and vistas for our own communities. This is the right question as long as we're not seeking step-by-step directions like those found in a Lego box.

PRAYER AS A RELATIONSHIP

What then does a community of persons who share in each other's lives as a way to share in God's own life look like? My simple answer is that *such a community is one that prays.*

The central mark of the sharing church will not be full calendars and large buildings with coffee shops, but places of prayer where persons share in each others' lives as they share in God's by praying with and for each other as persons.

Only persons who are their relationships can pray. Prayer is action and language; prayer is done by broken people who pray in the Spirit, people whose groans of spirit are interpreted and prayed by the Holy Spirit (Rom 8:26-28). Prayer is action and language done in brokenness by our spirit, through the Spirit; these are the very realities of personhood as we saw earlier. Prayer is not cosmic leverage that gets individuals what they want, that aligns their luck so their interest will be met and never tarnished.

Rather, prayer itself is a relationship; it is an action and language that articulates that we are persons who are our relationships. Prayer is a relationship because prayer *cannot* be done alone. As Bonhoeffer has said, no one prays alone.[3] Even when alone in our prayer closet, we never pray alone. We pray with our brothers and sisters; we pray with the persons who are the church. And this church has its foundation not in buildings and structures, but in relationships of persons that share in each other's lives.

Our voice in prayer is simply but beautifully one voice in a chorus of the continually praying church. Praying for Mike that night in

Newark was an act of the church, *not* because my ordained wife was there to preside. No, it was an act of the church, a prayer of the church, a relationship, because our prayer joined the prayers of others. Our prayer for Mike that night joined a chorus of persons who pray, those persons called the church. Our prayer for Mike shared in the church's continued prayer.[4]

PRAYER AS INDWELLING

But there is more to this. Prayer is a relationship because prayer is sharing in the other's person; prayer is indwelling. Even alone we pray for our relationships; we bring our mother, our friend, our child before God in prayer. We prayed for Mike's children, we prayed that his boss might see Mike as a person. There is always a social reality to prayer, even when done alone. When we teach children to pray we often, rightly, start by teaching them to pray for others, to pray with us for others like grandmas and friends. The very fact that we feel compelled to pray for these others shows that we are our relationships and that prayer itself seeks them, to be moved to indwell deeper these very relationships.

This is why praying alone is fine and good, but something in us desires the prayer of others. I said to Mike "We'll pray for you," not "You should pray more." We need others to pray for us. In a panic, hit by the wave of brokenness, rarely do people say "Leave me alone so I can pray." (Jesus pleads with his disciples to stay with him, to stay awake in the Garden of Gethsemane [Lk 22:39-46].) Rather, in the plea of a broken heart they often ask, as Mike did, for someone, anyone, to be with them, to share in them by praying for them, through prayer to give them a relationship to stabilize their shaken being.

To pray with another is to receive the gift of the other, the gift of shared indwelling. In need of prayer what we long for is not a strategy to help us be more successful ("you should pray more") but others who will do it, who will see us, and be with us by praying for us. Mike wanted to be prayed for *now*; he needed us to pray for him. We need others to pray for us, because we need others to share in our person, to indwell us and be with us. *The way this looks, the way a church looks that shares in each others' lives, is as a community of people that pray for one another. It looks like a community that needs, that asks, others to pray for them. A community of sharing is a humble community that seeks to pray and be prayed for by each other.*

PRAYER AND PERSONHOOD

Prayer forces us to see others as persons; it unleashes the metal claw of individualism to see personhood. In prayer we confess that we've violated the relationship between our friend and us by lying or gossiping; we intercede where our friend's relationships are at risk; we plead in prayer where cancer threatens to end the relationship with our friend in death.

Jesus tells us to pray for our enemies (Mt 5:44), to pray even for those that would celebrate our death, because even our enemy is a person. And when we pray for them they are transformed from a blockage or threat to our own interest into a person who is her or his relationships. In prayer even our enemy is made into a person, for prayer moves us to indwell, to share in another's life, to have eyes to see even the relationships that make our enemy a person. Praying for our enemy is a dangerous move because to pray for our enemy is to share in his or her person. It ties us together; it gives us a relationship.

It is hard to kill my enemy when I'm praying for him or her. To pray for my enemy is to indwell him or her by praying for the relationships that are this person. And when I pray for my enemy, we have a relationship; our persons are now defined (at least in part) together. I now, having prayed for this person, cannot kill him or her without killing part of myself. When I pray for my enemy's children, parents and spouse, it becomes nearly impossible to exterminate this person like I can when he or she is an individual who is only his or her interests (and whose interests are a threat to me). Prayer then becomes the heart, the core activity of facilitating personal encounters.

No one prays alone, because prayer moves us, by the Spirit, to indwell, to share the person of those we pray for. Mike wanted to be prayed for now, because Mike needed a relationship, because Mike needed others to share in his broken person.

Prayer moves us to indwell those for whom we pray. Because prayer is done by our spirit, there is a mystical (even neurological) way that praying for another connects our spirit to the other's spirit. In prayer we may join hands, but so often we also join faces, seeing our brother, sister and enemy as we pray with them spirit to spirit. There is something important about on-line prayer chains or text message prayer requests, but it still seems that when we really find ourselves in need, we yearn for the face of others; we yearn to be with others so they can pray for us.

This impulse is bound in the very fact that we as persons are spirit. And as spirit we yearn for the spirit of others, which is located in their face, to encounter us and join with us, so that together we might become the two or three where Jesus, through his Spirit, joins us (Mt 18:20). Prayer is a relationship of spirit connecting to spirit, and this connection is so fused because this spirit-to-spirit encounter in prayer draws us by the Holy Spirit into the relationship that is God, into the life of the Father to the Son.

PRAYER AND THE HYPOSTATIC UNION

But how is this? How is it that prayer draws us into the very life of God? How is it that prayer is not only an action and language that moves us to indwell each other, but also sweeps us up into the relationship that is God, into the continued word and response of the Father to the Son?

John Calvin beautifully said that we pray only with Jesus' mouth.[5] Bonhoeffer articulated that we never pray alone because the church is always praying, but this church is always praying because its Lord has promised to pray its prayers.[6] In a theological sense no person prays directly to God; no human words and actions can penetrate the very relationship that is God. But in the mystery of the hypostatic union, the mystery where Jesus is *the* person who shares completely in the divine and human, this Jesus prays our prayers.[7] Fully sharing in our person through his own person, indwelling us through his Spirit, Jesus takes our prayers, takes our words spoken for Mike, our words and actions that connect us to Mike's person, and prays them for us.

Standing in the dirty parking lot, our prayers become Jesus' own.[8] As we pray and share in Mike's person, Jesus becomes present as the one who shares in humanity, as the one who is human and prays for humanity. As one who shares through his humanity in our prayers, this very one also fully shares in God. Sharing in God, Jesus takes our broken human prayers and shares them with God, praying them to God. It is through the sharing of prayer, through sharing in Mike's person by praying for him, that he is taken by Jesus into the very life of God. God has heard our prayers for Mike, not because of us, but because Jesus prays for us. And Jesus prays for us because Jesus is the person who shares, and praying is the sharing in one another that we confess brings us into the sharing of God's very life.

RESPONSE

This then means that the concrete practice of these communities of sharing, of a church of persons in relationship, is prayer. It is praying with and for each other. As pastors our job is to teach people to pray, to form the community around praying with and for each other. We pray as a way to share and share as a way to pray. Praying is for sharing in the person of God by sharing in the person of one another. To form communities of sharing is to form communities of prayer.

Something had happened to Mike that night we shared in his life by praying for him. After our "amen," in joy and appreciation, all Mike could say in response was "Thank you, thank you, thank you." And in some ways his "thank you" was to us, but more so it was said through us to God. If prayer is the core practice of communities of sharing, *then the central disposition of these communities is one of gratitude.*

As people who share, as people who have shared in the lives of each other, we are praying people of gratitude. The very heart of witness and evangelism is to share in the lives of others, finding union, making all others brother and sisters. This is our openness to the world. But our particularity, our very *difference* is that we share in others' lives (even our enemies) by praying and being grateful, by praying and saying thank you.

Matthew Boulton, following Karl Barth, has made a persuasive argument that the way of the Christian life is gratitude.[9] The Christian, the disciple, is not called to do anything to earn his or her salvation; there is nothing to be done; it is given as a gift. There is no lever that our behavior or piety can pull to make God look on us with favor. God chooses to act for us, to give us God's very self by giving us the man Jesus, who shares in our humanity for the sake of us sharing in God's own life. God acts for us, Boulton asserts, because God desires to be our friend, because God wants us to share in God's life. Knowing this, seeing this done for us, our only response is to say "Thank you, thank you, thank you."

So our response to this reality of a God who shares in our lives is to live in gratitude. Gratitude is the thankful feeling that others are in our life who give us the gift of our person. Often parents can only describe the experience of sharing in the person of their children, of being with their children, as a feeling of gratitude, a feeling of being thankful to be with them, to share in them.

The response to the reality of our brother or sister sharing in our lives is to say thank you. This is the mystery of faith, the hidden logic of personhood. The more we share in each other's brokenness—the more we indwell even each other's experience of death—the more we are bound together. And the more we are bound together, the more we are compelled to say thank you for our shared life. Our prayer witnesses to life breaking through our death. Prayer is an act of friendship; we pray to God because God has made a way for us to be friends, to walk again (eschatologically) in the cool of the Garden. Prayer with our brothers and sisters too is an action of friendship. It is sharing each others' persons, loving each other as we indwell each other by connecting spirit to spirit through the moving of the Holy Spirit.

Prayer then is *not* a religious exercise but the communing of friendship with God through the praying friendship of person to person. And there can only be one response to the sharing of friendship, the joy of gratitude. Gratitude itself is different than happiness. The church is not a place of happiness; we are too scared to share in each other's lives for fear that another's pain might dampen the mood. Happiness is the feeling of getting your interest met, and Christianity has little to say about happiness. But gratitude is the response to shared life, to finding your life indwelled by others. Gratitude then is the only appropriate response to shared life. The church is no place of happiness, but it should be a place of overspilling gratitude, a place of laughter and tears, a place of deep sharing that shouts thank you.

Gratitude is the only response to the gift of another sharing in our life. When another is with and for us, seeing us, feeling us, we respond with a thank you, with gratitude that another shares our place. Communities of sharing are those that indwell each other by praying for each other, by saying thank you to each other and to God by sharing in our neighbors' lives as God shares in ours.

The pastor should measure the church not primarily by membership or giving (not by the numbers—this is the old regime), but by the level of gratitude. For the higher the level of gratitude, the higher the level of appreciation, the more persons are sharing in each other's lives. Denominations would do better to spend money on instruments that can measure gratitude (if such a thing is possible).

SHARING AS PRAYING, PRAYING AS SHARING

It's worth saying again that gratitude is ignited by sharing. You are stuck on the side of the road and a passerby stops to share his jumper cables; your only response is the thank you of gratitude. Hungry for a meal, needing a place to rest, excluded from hospitality (Mt 25), the *sharing* of food, bed and company cannot be repaid but only met with humble gratitude, thanks for an act of friendship, even to a stranger. To expand gratitude in our churches we need to expand the space for prayer, because gratitude is the response to sharing, and all sharing has its origin in prayer itself.

Gratitude happens at places where our personhood is shared, where we are known and embraced. And shared personhood bears the theological DNA of prayer itself, for prayer is the primary practice given to us to share in each other's person as the way to share in God's life. So all sharing that leads to gratitude takes the form of prayer. Gratitude, it seems, can happen outside prayer itself, because sharing, it appears, can happen outside prayer. It seems like sharing jumper cables, food or hospitality is simply a favor or a response of altruism. But theologically it is more; all sharing in personhood wears the marks of prayer itself. These experiences of giving and sharing, though maybe not prayer proper, *feel like prayer* because they are the sharing of personhood. They feel and smell like prayer because they are the experience of spirit.

This is why we've seen such an uptick in people volunteering, because though many can't or refuse to pray, they seek such experiences of sharing. So they give or volunteer with the hope that they'll have a spiritual experience of sharing, an experience of spirit, that, although they cannot name it, feels like the sharing of prayer, leaving their being coated in gratitude.

Gratitude is the visible sign of a community that shares in each other's person. Gratitude is the tangible experience of people that pray with and for each other. Prayer is a language and action that gives us eyes to see a new reality, the fuller reality of the hypostatic union, of the sharing of God in persons, of the sharing of personhood in God. Prayer is an action and language of a new reality because it is fundamentally done by embodied spirits, touching the spiritual realm of spirit sharing in Spirit. The new reality that prayer itself reveals is the indwelling of divine in the human through the one who continually prays, Jesus the Christ. Prayer is spiritual, not in the weird New Age way, but in a personal way, in the way that it touches our embodied spirit, moving us to indwell each other as we share in God's life, giving us eyes to see a new reality of the sharing of the divine and human.

All acts of sharing are proto-prayer. That's why they often feel transcendent: they are actions and language that point toward God's life. Even those who share without confessing Christ participate in this new reality. Their actions and language may be muffled, lacking full sound, like Apollos's message before Priscilla and Aquila told him the fullness of the gospel (Acts 18:24-27). But just like Apollos, the lack does not negate the sharing. To share in personhood is to take on the action and language of a new world, of the reality of God's very self. Even in Matthew 25 those that actively share have no idea that they've taken on the action and language of a new reality, a reality of sharing in God's very presence, the very disposition of prayer. But they have. They have prayed, creating a space for sharing in personhood and therefore sharing in God's life.

PRAYER AS A SPACE, GRATITUDE AS A PLACE

I've said throughout this book that the task of the pastor in this time is to create places of sharing, to help people be place sharers. Prayer is the gift that opens this space for sharing; prayer is the concrete practice that allows for this encounter of person to person, and person to God, to occur.

These spaces of sharing are always revelatory; they just happen as an event. They can't be controlled—council retreats or airport parking lots can become the spaces where sharing in each others' lives happens. Praying for and with the world (Jn 17) is not an internal religious act that insulates the church, but rather calls us to join those in the world, to share in persons' lives in the world as an act of prayer, with the very language (thanks, petition, supplication) of prayer.

So while these spaces cannot be coerced and controlled, they can be sought. Thus the very shape of prayer—the articulation of our need with others in gratitude—becomes the disposition that allows for the potential of these holy spaces of place sharing to occur.

The pastor can't force or coerce sharing. To force sharing is to strangle it. Rather, seeking sharing, the pastor sets up a space of prayer, a place where people can pray, where they can share their person (their story) and be prayed for. The pastor uses the anchors of church programs—Sunday worship, midweek Bible study, education hour—as the spaces to create a reality of sharing by creating a space for prayer.

The pastor also teaches people how to pray beyond the walls of the church. How can we pray for our coworkers and neighbors? We do this *not* by giving them strategies or bracelets or tracts; these are the (annoying) methods of the old regime. Rather, we teach our people to pray for others by sharing in the lives of others. By being with and for them, by sharing their place, by sharing their own brokenness, helping them to see this new reality that sharing is praying and praying is sharing.

People live out their vocation as disciples in their world by being place sharers, by sharing in the personhood of others. They are continual pray-ers, because they continually seek to share in the personhood of their neighbor as the tangible space of sharing in God's life—of being swept up in prayer.

THE PASTOR'S CORE JOB DESCRIPTION

What happens in this space made for prayer can't be controlled by the pastor. It is the idol of the pastor as self-help entertainer that must control everything, getting the sought-after results. Rather, the pastor as facilitator of personal encounters can only open the space, articulating that this space is a place where we share in each other's lives as the way to share in God. The pastor can only be one who prays, inviting and teaching others to pray as the way of sharing.

All the pastor can do is articulate this new reality of God's sharing in humanity and invite people to pray by sharing their story, to pray as the way to glimpse this world the pastor speaks of. And when we do, when we pray, we'll be found in gratitude. The pastor then says and encourages others to say thank you to the God who acts for them and thank you to their brothers and sisters that have indwelled them. Gratitude is the tangible sign of the freedom of the Christian. But to push a little further than Luther, we are thankful for the freedom of being justified by God's act alone, *and* grateful that this act of God is concretized in the persons in this community who share in our lives.

We have hit then on the two core movements of the pastor, and these movements rest on the core practice of facilitating personal encounter by making space for prayer. *These then become the core movements of the pastor: he or she articulates reality and says thank you.* Leadership guru Max De Pree says this is true leadership.[10] The difficulty of these two elements, defining reality and saying thank you, seems varied. Defining reality seems hard, and saying thank you so easy. But I think De Pree's definition of leadership is a good one for the pastor seeking to lead communities of sharing.

The pastor's job description is to lead in articulating (proclaiming) a new reality of sharing, proclaiming the good news of the hypostatic union. The pastor teaches people to see this new reality, not through the force of intellect, parsing verbs and reading Torrance's lectures to the congregation; rather, the kerygma goes deeper than speaking: the pastor articulates this new reality by helping people feel it and experience it. They experience it by praying and feel it when they articulate their own narrative of when and how others have shared in their lives, when and how others have embraced their brokenness. The pastor articulates this reality through sharing prayer.

Our job as the pastor is to continue to remind and proclaim, through

Word (Scripture) and deed, that God seeks to share in our lives, that God invites us to share in God's own, by opening the very reality of our own person to another. Our job as pastor is to proclaim the reality of personhood; that we are our relationships and the God who is a relationship has acted for us, has promised to indwell us as we indwell each other.[11] The pastor's job is to sketch out this reality, to proclaim it (the gospel) without pause. The whole point of seminary education, the whole point of reading books like this one, is to provide us with vision, vision of the reality to which we bear witness.

And seeing what is, seeing God's act for us, hearing of others who have shared in our lives as witness to God's own sharing, we can only respond with a beautiful thank-you, the very thank-you that Mike proclaimed from the parking lot in the shadow of the New Jersey turnpike.

So the pastor then does the second element of his job description, saying thank you, thank you to the people who have shared, thank you to God who loves from death to life. The pastor then should spend a good amount of time finding ways to say thank you to people, expressing gratitude to people. Where people feel appreciated, where the ethos of the community is one of thanks, people feel free to share. Where people feel valued, they feel safe enough to not only see this new reality of God's action but to take the step of participating in it by opening their person by praying and being prayed for in and through their brokenness.

The pastor, then, facilitates personal encounters by creating spaces for people to pray, and this creating of these spaces for prayer happens by continually proclaiming the new reality of God's sharing and always saying thank you, always living in honest gratitude. Eugene Peterson beautifully sums up the direction I've taken in this chapter:

> This is my basic work: on the one hand to proclaim the word of God that is personal—God addressing us in love, inviting us into a life of trust in him; on the other hand I guide and encourage an answering word that is likewise personal—to speak in the first person to the second person, I to Thou, and avoid third-person commentary as much as possible. This is my essential educational task: to develop and draw out into articulateness this personal word, to teach people to pray. Prayer is language. It is not

language about God or the faith; it is not language in the service of God and the faith; it is language to and with God in faith.[12]

But . . .

I know what you're thinking, *You promised us vistas! You promised us pictures of what this looks like!* I've tried to provide some handles for the practice of pastoral ministry in this chapter. But I do recognize that handles and pictures are two very different things. I hope my handles have been helpful as I've sought to spin us into these ideas. But you're right; it is time for a picture. So I promise to start chapter fourteen with a vista of what this all looks like.

14

What This Looks Like

*How Story, Teaching
& Preaching Fit*

The following is a vista of what being a relational pastor might look like, but first let me offer an embarrassing confession, especially after going on about prayer in chapter thirteen. During the "prayers of the people," during the time where the pastor prays peoples' prayer requests, I almost always catch my mind wandering. To say it crassly, during this time I actually find myself *not caring*. I really hope it doesn't sound as harsh as it feels writing it. But it's true; as the pastor prays for people, as he or she gets three or four prayer requests in, I feel numb.

Those prayer requests become like the CNN ticker, telling of significant news, but soon I couldn't care less because these bottom-of-the-screen news stories come at me contextless, ironically not as stories at all. They confront me as information, as data, with no narrative, meaning I either need to fill in the narrative or not care. And if I'm too tired, distracted or saturated to create my own story (or simply feel like I don't have enough context to do so), this information becomes meaningless.

Without story, without narrative, it is impersonal. Its lack of story does not draw me into a personal reality that I might indwell. Often, when people are moved emotionally by a story, they rarely quote statistics or facts, but will say things like, "Those children, I just can't get over how they must be feeling." It is the *personhood, mediated through the narrative*, that connects us and draws us through our emotions to share (to care), moving our spirits to seek spirit.

As with the news ticker, so it is with the pastor's prayers. I find myself disconnected, and we often describe this disconnected feeling as boredom. I'm bored because there is only information and nothing to indwell, nothing that stirs my spirit. When I hear prayers for people with cancer, the elderly who are lonely and children who are hungry, it's mere information. It may even be fact, but these prayers lack the personal quality that leads me to search for meaning, to seek to indwell. Without a context, I more often opt for daydreaming about another Vikings loss.

If my own story connects to this information, however, if *my mother* has cancer, then the prayer for those with cancer becomes more than information. It takes on the shape of story; it becomes personal and means something to me because it is part of me. It touches my spirit. I am (in part) my relationship with my mother; my being is locked in our story of sharing in each other's lives, spirit to spirit. Because we are our relationships, her cancer means our relationship (something inside me) has cancer as well. *We are our relationships, which means that my mother's cancer is part of me, though it is apart from me.*[1] I don't literally have cancer, but now that my mother does, because we are our relationships, because we indwell each other so much that we are fundamental to each other's story, when she has cancer physically, I too bear its reality.

But if I can't—if I can't create a story for the information—then my mind wanders and I find myself grossly bored in prayer. I have no story to put the information in context, so I either resent it or am apathetic toward it. It is meaningless.

For prayer to create a space for sharing, then, it must be done in narrative shape. It's time for our vista, a view of what this looks like.

NOW FOR A VISTA

My mind-wandering prayer boredom changed one day at my little church in south Minneapolis. For our vistas, I'll be drawing heavily from the case of this little church. While this doesn't constitute representative research, Danish sociologist Bent Flyvbjerg has made a strong case for the power of reflection. A single case like this church and Shane's experience with Dave, Flyvbjerg believes, can be more generative for reflection (and construction) than a large sample set.[2]

In our little church Kara decided to move the "prayers of the people" to a more central location in the worship order, giving more space for prayer so it was not rushed but actually participated in. She then also decided to invite people in this small church to share their own prayer requests as opposed to harvesting these requests either before or within the service itself and then praying them *for* people. So now people came forward, lit a candle or dropped a stone into a clear font, and shared their prayer request. (Anywhere from six to twelve people shared for less than a minute, making the practice last no longer than ten to twelve minutes.)

Something happened very early in the tweaking of this practice of opening up space for prayer. As people came forward they began to actually share their person, by telling the story of their prayer request. I noticed that when someone came up, lit their candle and said, "I'd like to pray for people who've lost their jobs," I'd nod my head and wait for this religious exercise to be over. But it was radically different when someone would stand, come to the front, drop their rock into the font and say, "I'd like to pray for people who have lost their jobs, because this Saturday night we went over to my brother's house for dinner and he has worked for General Mills for twenty years, and just Thursday they laid him off. When his daughter answered the door, I could see the fear in her eyes and then after dinner my brother shared how lost and depressed he feels. So, I don't know, I guess I'm praying for my brother and like him all those others that have lost jobs."

This changed everything. Prayer was no longer the *relaying of information*—people need jobs—but the *story of persons*, persons feeling lost and betrayed, persons with daughters nervous and scared, persons like me who need others to be with them, who need a God who comes near to share in our need. Now we were praying for a *person*, this woman's brother, not just an *issue*. We were praying for a person with a name. Praying for *him*, the church was now acting and speaking (praying) as persons too, because the narrative gave us a person to pray for, to seek to share in, as opposed to an issue to feel bad about or morally indignant toward.

This prayer request not only gave me a story to connect to my person, it not only revealed the personhood of the brother I was called to pray for, but also revealed the humanity, the personhood, of the woman sharing it. As she opened her person by telling this story, we felt her. We shared in her humanity; connecting spirit to spirit we were drawn into the life of God through the Holy Spirit as we prayed for her relationships.

We all now yearned to pray for her, to embrace her, to make her story part of us. Our hearts broke with hers. But they also rejoiced, for her story of her brother revealed *her*, and in praying for her we were together. Her narrative prayer request gave us the gift of her person. Praying for her by praying for the relationships that are her, we gratefully embraced the gift of her person. "Thanks for sharing," as we so often say, means *thank you for giving us/me the gift of your person that I share in through your story.*

Even more interesting is that objectively the prayer request of the woman for her jobless brother had nothing to do with her; from the perspective of individualism this is true. It was her brother alone who was kept from meeting his interest, and from an individualistic perspective we prayed for him so that he might individually be strengthened to find a new interest. But from the perspective of the personal, praying for *him* meant praying for *her*. And knowing that her person was revealed to us in her story, praying for *her* was to pray for *us*, for we are our relationships and her story connected us to her, her to her brother and her brother to us. He was now with us, he mattered to us because he mattered to her, because he was her brother. His joblessness was now part of the church's story. We joined our spirit to hers through her face, which told the story that sought to pray as a way to share and share as a way to pray.

The ripple effect of personhood went even further. When this sister saw her brother in his job loss, it opened up in her awareness of all other persons in the same situation, with similar fears and nervous daughters. And this led her to want to pray not just for him but for all those who had lost jobs. For us, hearing her prayer "for those who have lost jobs" stopped being an issue, a nameless, faceless collection of individuals (e.g., the poor, the military, the homeless, etc.) and brought to mind persons we were connected to through the shared experience of her brother. God is God for all. And the prayer became holding these—even nameless, faceless *persons*—in God's care, through the connection of spirit to Spirit, shared in her story.

MORE OF THE VISTA:
♪ IN YOUR LOVING MERCY . . . ♪

But this is only part of the practice of prayer at our little church in south Minneapolis. After a person has shared a prayer request, offering his or her need or thanks in the shape of a story, together we sing a refrain: "God, in your loving mercy hear our prayer." The person returns to the pew and another comes and shares a story of prayer. We pray by singing, and so it continues.

We pray together, in worship, by telling the stories of our personhood, by offering them as the avenue to share in each others' lives, as the mysterious path into God's own life. And then hearing these stories of need and thanks, these stories that reveal persons—who grieve broken relationship, yearn for their healing or celebrate their sustenance—we, with one voice, sing. Sharing voice to voice we sing as witness; we sing as a manifestation that we have union in Christ as we dwell in one another.

We sing our prayer as an act of gratitude. We speak our narratives in fear, pain and need, but we sing as a sign of hope. We sing as the manifestation that all our prayers join the chorus of the church's prayer, that Jesus himself prays for us by sharing in our person, which is revealed in our stories. We sing because in sharing in prayer we trust that Jesus shares our prayer with the Father, hiding our lives in the life of God (Col 3:1-4).

We indwell each other by feeling each other. Music itself is a feeling; it's the uniting of sound, sure, but more so it is the uniting of voices in a personal sound that stirs our spirit. Music indwells us. People sentimentally say that "everyone has a song inside them to sing," and while the sugary sentimentality makes me gag, there is some truth to it. Music, singing, touches the depth of our being, rushing it to the surface, putting it to song that others might join, not only hearing it but singing it with us, uniting with us in the song of our being. Singing witnesses to the reality that we are embodied spirits who yearn for union with each other. And prayer is the song of the church. Prayer and song cannot be separated; the psalms are songs of prayer. Our prayers are the rhythms that join the hosts of heaven, that fill God's very life with the songs of love and union.

The practice at our little church in south Minneapolis closes with Kara praying for the whole church. She often prays again for what was shared, sketching out in her own prayer this reality of the hypostatic union, this divine reality of sharing, reminding the community that in this place of prayer we have shared in each other's lives, and as such, have shared in God's life. She recaps these narratives as a way of linking them, as a way of showing our church that these narrative prayers now are the story of our little congregation, the story of people who share in each other's lives as a way of sharing in God's.

STORY AS TEACHING, TEACHING AS PRAYER

Stepping from the vista, an important question is, How does this little church do it? How do we get people to offer their prayer requests in narrative shape?

We so often forget this, but prayer is something that must be taught. It actually might be that the core of the teaching office of the church, the teaching ministry of the pastor, is to teach people to pray. Jesus' disciples asked him, "Lord, teach us to pray" (Lk 11:1). Eugene Peterson said he realized in his own ministry that his "primary educational task as pastor was to teach people to pray."[3]

Teaching people to pray in narrative shape begins by teaching them how to tell a story.[4] And the way we learn to tell a story is by hearing a lot of stories. So the pastor's job is to tell stories in a manner that he or she desires for people to tell their own, guarding against long-winded, self-involved tales that seek to reveal how great he or she is.

If the pastor tells stories that are succinct, to the point and explore his or her own person by articulating the stress, beauty or brokenness of personal relationships, then the people will tell stories in the same shape. Hearing stories told, we often tacitly tell our own in the shape of the stories heard (this is the power of a genre).

So teaching people to pray is teaching them to tell their story. In our cultural context this task is both easier and more difficult. In this coming energy regime, with its already-in-place communication system, story is actually everywhere, or so it seems. Every fifteen-year-old boy has a YouTube channel and every Facebook status update opens a window to a story. (Most are not worth sharing, because they are pointless data and information, making them either not a narrative or just very poorly told ones.)

People *yearn* to tell their story, yearn to share their person with anyone who might listen. The question we face is whether the technology itself allows people to tell their story or just clutters our lives with information.

We are challenged with helping people understand, through hearing good stories, that *narrative* and *information* are different things. Just because we have exposed ourself, giving others information, doesn't mean we have told a story. Indiscriminate sharing of information can repel people, leading us to avoid the person, shut down or protect ourself.

Imagine shaking hands with someone you meet for the first time and saying, "Hi, I'm Josh. I have a terrible relationship with my mom; she said terrible things to us when we were young, and we witnessed her sleeping with so many different guys." This isn't a story, but the spewing of indiscriminate information. It steamrolls the power of story, which is to connect us with others. Story calls others to link their experience with our own, to open a space for sharing. Information dumps leave the hearer no connections to link their person to.

STORY AS HOOKS OF PERSONAL CONNECTION

Teaching people how to *tell* a story rests on the same foundation as teaching people how to *hear* a story. It is teaching them how to make connections by being *specific* and *self-aware*.

What makes a story (or even a song for that matter) powerful is its hooks. We are moved by stories that draw out our person by connecting our own story with the story being told.[5] A story has hooks when it is *specific*, particularly about events or, even more powerfully, feelings. Narrative praying prays *specifically;* it prays for persons and their relationships. But all of this is moot without self-awareness, without the story itself articulating our own experience, opening that experience to be shared by others. The earlier example of information dump happened because Josh lacked self-awareness.

We become more self-aware and specific when others comment on our story.[6] This means that teaching people to pray means providing the space not only for people to share their story but to receive comment on it, to hear people make connections to their stories, or struggle to do so. Inviting people to tell their stories in education hour, new members' classes and confirmation is essential to teaching people to pray.

It is hard to know now if our communication system, the Internet, makes people better or worse storytellers—the jury is still out. But it's clear that story has changed from what others have called command/ control to sense/response.[7] For most of history stories, because of their power and their expense in creating, were controlled by religious, tribal or political leaders, and the rest of us were *told the meaning* as well as our part in the story. Story was most often linear, both in expression and in control, moving from top to bottom, from beginning to end.

But in a sense/response world things are different. People seek to be active in *making meaning* by responding to stories. We want to place our own stories in connection with others' by reworking stories to express our own experience. Story becomes more fluid as each of us adds to it, and story itself becomes much more serialized than linear. We now tell stories much more like hyperlinks, where one experience opens us to others, and one experience takes us to another.[8] Story becomes the linking of discursive narrative into a shared experience. And when there is linking—when others can connect to our stories—propelling others to tell their own stories, we are sharing in each other's person by indwelling each other through the linking of our stories.

STORIES AS TEACHING AN ESCHATOLOGICAL IMAGINATION

We indwell stories because they mediate persons; we seek stories because as persons we yearn to share relationships. Movie characters become real to us in a good story because we indwell them, opening our persons to them as we make connections between their experience and our own. The Bible becomes the Word of God to us when it speaks to our person, when its narrative wraps itself around our own.[9]

We feel our way into persons through story, but as such we also feel our way into new realities, new worlds—into the new world (the strange world, as Barth said) that the Bible speaks of. But even these new worlds are not compelling without the personal. The Bible without mediating the personal God is just stale data. And even sci-fi stories like *Lost* and *The Walking Dead* work so well not only because they present a new imaginative world, helping us to think in a new/different way about our own, but because they powerfully show how even this new world is mediated through personal relationships, through the viewer connecting to the persons in the story as the persons struggle with their relationships.[10]

The island in *Lost* is cool, but just as compelling is all the yearning and brokenness around fathers—Jake, Kate, Locke and Sawyer all have to deal with the stressed and broken relationship that has defined them. Next to the person's broken relationships, the power of island to heal or punish them becomes captivating, because it is the imagination of a new reality that is born and lived out in the personal.

Shows like *Lost* and *The Walking Dead* use flashbacks to make connections between persons and their stories. These connections cause us to see that there is something mysterious about our lives, that there is something spiritual, something that connects us, that yearns for connection, and that there is mystery in the connections themselves. Stories with personal connection are mysterious, hearing another's story and connecting to it points beyond to something new, to a world of indwelling, to the mystery of sharing. It is powerful when we say, "What? Wait! That happened to you? Me too!" "Really? I know him! My dad went to school with him!" We respond to these connections with words like *weird*, *wild* and *amazing*, words of the eschatological.

Teaching as prayer, and praying as being taught to tell our stories, has an eschatological element. We need teaching in this ministry of place sharing because we need to teach people how to pray by telling their stories. But in telling them, we need to help them connect with the new reality of sharing, the mystery of the hypostatic union.

Sharing our stories as prayer, finding connections, links them to the mystery of the coming world, where the first are last and last are first, a world where from death comes life, a backward world where persons are healed and made whole by sharing their brokenness. These backward realities that are tackled in narrative prayer must nevertheless be taught because they stand in opposition the logic of the natural, because they exist in the logic of spirit, because they are experiences of the eschatological.

Evangelism itself happens through shared story. We confess the faith and share it with other persons *not* by sharing the gospel as data or information to which to assimilate (e.g., the Four Spiritual Laws) but as *intentionally* telling our story. How we were once lost but now found. How we once did not know we had union with God, but now we share in it. We tell our story by giving testimony to how we are now sharing in the life of God by sharing with these people. I share the faith by sharing my story, by sharing *the* story of this new reality that is coming and is already tasted in these people that pray together.

Prayer itself is the sharing in one another and the sharing of God that opens our eyes to see this eschatological reality, where the mystery of the hypostatic union will one day become all there is, where the full sharing of the human in the divine life will be complete.

This new reality, this new reality which Max De Pree told us the leader points to, is seen through the window of prayer. The Lord's Prayer points to this new reality when it says, "thy kingdom come . . . on earth as it is in heaven" (Mt 6). But this narrative praying does more than articulate reality. By hearing each others' stories and connecting to them, praying them, we also say thank you, living in gratitude. After connecting to another's story, which prompts the telling of our own story, the response that arises is thank you, thank you for sharing. For the one that has shared and been prayed for, likewise, the response is "thank you for praying with me."

ANOTHER VISTA

But again, what does this teaching as praying look like?

Starting in the education hour or small groups, the pastor invites people to share stories, helping, drawing out their hooks and links, giving people openings to share a story that comes to mind as they hear this other person's story.

Neuroscience is now telling us that memory doesn't work like information kept in a database that can be retrieved and used when needed (making my juxtaposition between story and information all the more relevant).[11] Scientists are telling us that when we remember something, we actually reconstruct the memory, not from some storage disc but from our feelings. We still feel those experiences, and when triggered, most often by hearing another's story, we bring it back to memory by remaking it in our brain.[12]

This has powerful ramifications for telling stories together. When we tell stories together, we not only connect to each other's person, but so fully connect with each other's person because we share memory. We reconstruct the experiences of the past with others. Inviting them to share in our experience we now share in a story, which uniquely, now that it is shared, exists simultaneously in each of our brains. When I tell you my story I recreate it; I remember it anew to now remember it with you.[13] You become present in my old experience as I reconstruct my memories with you. (This is why tribal people believed that by remembering their ancestors, the ancestors became present, because to remember them is actually to reconstruct our memory of them in the now of our cognition.)

This is why long-married couples have such a hard time imagining a past without their spouse's presence: "You were there, weren't you? It just feels like you were." They say this because it is true; they were there in a sense, because now that they have told and retold the story, they have given new memory to old feelings, to old experiences. But they remember it now, with their spouse, who, as they tell it, indwells them spouse, sharing in their person.

Siegel explains the importance of story for the bond of children and parents, but this can just as well be applied to other human relationships, though maybe not with the same intensity.

> A profound finding from attachment research is that the most robust predictor of a child's attachment to parents is the way in which the parents narrate their own recollections of their childhood experiences. This implies that the structure of an adult's narrative process—not merely what

the adult recalls, but how it is recalled—is process—not merely *what* the adult recalls, but *how* it is recalled—is the most powerful feature in predicting how an adult will relate to a child.[14]

But how do you do this? There are many ways to do this and education hour, small groups and new members' classes are places to start. When the pastor first tells stories, when the pastor first makes a connection, when the pastor first says thank you, room is made for stories to be told.

Why not create nondirective small groups. (I'm sure you could think of a better name.) A nondirective small group would consist of a handful of people who gather to do nothing more than share stories. (This contrasts with how we usually do small groups. We tend to bring people together to do something or accomplish something.) This might feel like an overwhelming task. So maybe you could start by bringing these people together around a specific situation (not a task or function) that connects to their narratives, that they all face. For instance, in most churches parents raising children at times feel lost and confused. Too often, in response, the church creates events that bring in parenting experts to give parents more information (parent your child like this or that). But more information sometimes makes parents feel even more overwhelmed or defeated. (Or if they're smart, knowing this will be the case, they don't attend the meeting.)

It might be more helpful to form groups with broad child-raising experience, from parents with infants to great-grandparents, and to invite them to tell stories about parenting. This group would not focus on the content of help and insight but rather on the stories themselves, the invitation to share in each other's lives. It is a transformative experience for a young parent who says, "We just don't know what to do with Billy; he just won't walk! He is so behind and he seems to have no motivation," to hear someone respond, "Oh, the same happened with our Jenny. She didn't walk until four, but in tenth grade she won the state high hurdle competition. Hang in there." The connection made is transforming. It's the sharing of life; mutual indwelling. This is why twelve-step programs are so powerful; they are simply but profoundly the telling of story.

PREACHING

If there is a core practice that defines a pastor, it is preaching, the act of mounting the pulpit and sharing an eight to twenty-eight minute monologue. This practice is so central to the identity of the pastor that it has become the pastor's label. Just as a firefighter is labeled by the function of fighting fires, so a pastor is a preacher.

The pastor as preacher has its strongest connection to the energy regime of steam/coal. Born much earlier from the theological commitments of the Reformation, in this period of ideological consciousness in which the pastor was the protector or perpetuator of a tradition, preaching stood as the task *sine qua non* of the pastor. And to be a good preacher the pastor needed to be learned, studious, spending time in a bookcase-filled study crafting a sermon monologue.

In the following period, the oil energy regime, the pastoral task of preaching remained strong; the pastor still was a preacher. But as the central definition of the pastor changed, so too did the heart of the preaching task. As opposed to writing rich theological, biblical or political sermons, as in the steam regime, in the oil regime the pastor was a self-help entertainer, meaning sermons were now judged not by their (wooden) depth but by their ability to engage, to entertain. Who cared about intellectual depth? People wanted to be engaged, to laugh and cry, while learning a few things (three!) along the way. And those few things should give pseudo-therapeutic help to individuals; so sermon monologues were about improving your marriage, your devotional life or even your sex life.

In the transition from the steam to oil regime preaching remained a monologue.

THE MONOLOGUE

In the present energy regime, in which sharing is central, it is no surprise that the monologue is being questioned.[15] The idea that one person dumps information on passive listeners has begun to be questioned. And neuroscience gives us reason to wonder if this critique is more than just iconoclastic. Marco Iacoboni has written convincingly on the neurological difference between conversation and monologue—he actually shows that brain activity during each is radically different. He wondered why it is easier for most people to have a conversation with someone than to give a speech. After all, a speech, a sermon, is prepared; the speaker doesn't have to respond to someone else and is free from the interaction that a conversation demands. In a speech, the speaker simply works through a manuscript, notes or memorized points. But in a conversation none of that is possible. Those involved have no idea what will be said next, no way to control the setting. They have to jump into the stream of conversation itself.

Almost everyone talking in the coffee hour after church would be scared to death to preach a sermon, but they have no problem chitchatting about any number of topics they have neither rehearsed nor prepared. Why?

Iacoboni argues that in a conversation our brains are more engaged. In a conversation we read each other's minds, picking up cues as our conversation wires our brains to one another. In good conversations we actually *think together*. The conversation is easy because we are sharing thoughts, lifting them together, feeling each other as we do. The conversation is easier and more energizing because in it we indwell each other. The conversation, more than monologue, leads to indwelling; it leads to us sharing in each other's person. The person delivering a monologue is alone. It is up to the speaker to make a connection or impact; no one's brain is joining the speaker's (at least in the way it is in a conversation). As a matter of fact, during a monologue most brains are idle. They need someone, the individual standing before them, to thrust them into drive, either through content or style. But they are idling, waiting for someone to move them. But in a conversation they are already moving; they are committed to move. They have joined the one speaking. In Eden God delivers no sermons to Adam; in friendship they share in each other's life by walking and talking, by being in conversation.

WAIT!

I'm sure this makes some of you uncomfortable, and in many ways I'd count myself in that group. In many traditions (Lutheran and Presbyterian to name the two that I live in) the preaching moment has significant theological meaning; it is not simply a practice that you can take or leave when and if it is relevant. The thought of replacing the sermon with coffee-shop conversation feels like anathema.

And this is so because in these theological traditions the preacher is called to proclaim the Word of God, to point to God's action in Jesus Christ. Karl Barth used Matthias Grünewald's classic 1515 painting of Jesus' crucifixion (the Isenheim Altarpiece) as his central illustration. Barth loved the picture (a print hung above his desk) because in it he saw a paradigm for the theologian, a paradigm for the pastor.

In the picture, on the right side, John the Baptist holds the Scriptures, pointing with an extremely long and boney finger at the crucified Christ. Barth asserted that this holding and reading of Scripture and pointing toward (proclaiming) Jesus is the action of the Christian, is the work of the pastor. We point to Christ by reading Scripture and witnessing to God's action; that is, we preach.

And there is no doubt that this is the job of the pastor. We must delve into the Scripture to point our boney fingers, proclaiming Jesus Christ and him crucified. But Barth has ignored the other side (the left side) of Grünewald's painting. On that side are three people, two women and a man.

The man is looking away from the crucifixion, not because he is denying it but because he embraces another, because he has been called by Christ to participate in the life of another. The disciple Jesus loved, John, is holding the grieved mother Mary, embracing her, hearing her, empathically sharing in her pain as he gives his very person to her in embrace. John, the beloved disciple, is also participating in crucifixion, participating in God's act; he is proclaiming the gospel by sharing in the brokenness of this mother. He too preaches Christ crucified by sharing in the life of another under the cross of the One who in death is sharing in all humanity.

And while the Baptizer stands confident, pointing on the right side, on the left with John and the mother Mary is Mary Magdalene, on her knees, hands folded in prayer. Just as the Baptizer's hands are directed toward the Christ, so are hers, not with a pointed finger but with folded interlocking fingers. Mary Magdalene stands with John the beloved and Mary the mother and prays; with her eyes on the cross, she prays. The

Baptizer looks to us, but Mary Magdalene looks to the cross, pointing to it by opening herself to it, by praying. She too is preaching, but with hands in prayer.

It may be, in this time of sharing, that our stance of proclamation, of preaching, may look more like Mary Magdalene's proclamation than it does the Baptizer's.[16] Of course, there is always an element of the Baptizer in our preaching; it is a must to speak boldly and from the heart of Scripture. But ministry as personal encounter in prayer may mean *preaching as prayer*. It may mean embracing our stories, the stories that have become the prayers of the congregation, as John the Beloved does the mother. Preaching may mean pointing to Christ with hands folded in prayer for one another, by embracing each other, as the Beloved does, and pointing our fingers folded in prayer toward the cross.

If prayer and story are so central to a ministry of place sharing, then preaching too will need to be prayer as the pointing to Christ while embracing each other, while indwelling each other as we witness to God who indwells us by fully sharing our place on the cross.

FINAL VISTAS (ONE A DREAM AND ONE REAL)

To preach like Mary Magdalene puts preaching and praying together, *not* blending one into the other but to do them together. And by this I don't simply mean praying before and after starting a monologue, as though prayer were the emcee of your sermon. Rather, I literally mean to do them together. Here's an example: as the parishioners come forward and share their narratives during the prayers of the people, it might be that *now* is the time to preach. After the woman prays for her brother, after the persons of the church sing their prayer, the pastor could preach a two to three minute sermon launched from the prayer itself.

Connecting to the woman's narrative prayer, the pastor could open up the Scripture and connect her story to the Bible. Connecting her story to others' stories, the pastor might say, "In our Old Testament reading today we heard the story of Moses, who was an outcast, ninety years old; he got fired from everything, even being Israelite. They wanted nothing to do with him. He was lost, feeling old and beaten, feeling a failure in a far away country. Yet, it was right in the middle of his personal failure that God found him, that God called to him, to come and see a bush that burns but is not consumed, to come and share in the very person of God. It was right in the middle of Moses feeling lost that God called out. In the middle of not knowing what is next, we hear God calling our broken person to come and receive. And what Moses receives is God's very name, God's very person. Moses is invited to join God, to live and act with God. We pray for people who have lost their jobs, people not only like Janet's brother but like my sister, like Jerry's friend whom we prayed for last week. We pray that the God who calls, the God who searches when we are lost, might move in them and in us, that we might find our very persons bound in God's own."

The Word has been proclaimed, but it has been proclaimed as prayer itself. It has connected like flashbacks in a good narrative, stories within stories, drawing the narrative of the pray-er, the narrative of Scripture and the narrative of the whole community's story into one. The pastor then might do two or three more short sermons off other people's narrative prayers.[17]

This vista no doubt is a paradigm shift. However, it does not mean that the pastor no longer needs to prepare for the week's sermon. Rather, it means he or she needs to prepare differently, needs to actually read, needs to indwell both the texts of Scripture and the stories of his community. The pastor may very well write something, but this something may be three to four vignettes the text draws out. With this preparation the pastor will trust that these vignettes will find their connection with the prayers of the congregation.

And truth be told, if the pastor is praying with them, teaching them to tell stories, hearing their stories, the ground is already fertile for the connections of the vignettes and the parishioners' lives. Even unconsciously these connections will be made.[18]

Of course this changes the way we think about educating pastors. Seminaries and other training centers would need to focus more on actually teaching their students to *think* theologically, to do theology on their feet, to live their very theology next to real people's lives. But then maybe instead of having preaching labs where students hear each other's monologues and then comment, we would have experiences where students are asked to take questions, to make connections, to draw out the text and link it to their fellow students' lives. (This may be closer to formation, in the end, than the preaching lab allows.)

But the very beauty of this approach is that preaching, prayer and story share in each other, making a place, even in the preaching moment, for a conversation of sharing, for a place where people indwell each other as they indwell the Word of God.

Another vista is something Kara has done in our little congregation. She weaves people's stories from our own community into the sermon. She will ask a few people if they would share with her, in person or email, their experience of a situation the Scripture raises for the upcoming week (e.g., "Where have you found yourself, like Joseph, the soon-to-be husband of Mary, to be somewhere you never chose or imagined you would be? What did it feel like? How did you feel God's presence or absence in that experience?"). Then she'll preach their stories alongside the Scripture text.

Every year, the week after Easter, in lieu of a sermon, three different individuals share their own "stories of resurrection." Kara asks a few members several weeks in advance if they would be willing to share places in their life where life came from death, where despair gave way to hope. Sometimes they need to get together with her over coffee or lunch to talk through their story and find ways to speak of those places. Every year this experience is a powerful one; people diverse in age and life experience share their places of loss and redemption, and we all hear within them places our own lives and experiences connect.

Both of these ways of pulling people's stories into the sermon open up rich times of prayer. Being both specific and self-aware, sharing stories within the congregation leads to parishioners upholding in prayer not only the people whose lives they've just entered but their own lives, and also the connections made with others in their neighborhoods or jobs who share similar experiences and feelings.

15

I've Got to Run the Church Don't I?

Leadership as Letting Relationships Flow

One of my favorite clips from *Everybody Loves Raymond* starts with the MacDougalls, whose daughter Amy is engaged to Robert and who are in conflict with Robert and Ray's parents, the Barones. The MacDougalls are very religious and find the Barones not only uncouth but un-Christian at that. As they try to get to know each other for the sake of Robert and Amy, it becomes too much. Frank (Robert and Ray's father) is sure that Mr. MacDougall is lying about never having eaten a muffin, and Mr. MacDougall can just take no more of Frank's company.

But before they can leave in conflict, Debra, Ray's wife, pleads one last time for them to stay, to give the Barones another chance. Mrs. MacDougall says, "We'll pray about it."

Debra returns, "Why don't we pray together, that's a value we share, right? Let's pray together to work out our difference, right?"

Ray says in the background with cynicism, "Oh, God."

Debra shoots Ray a dirty look.

"What?" Ray says, "I'm starting things off."

"It is a nice thought, but I'm not sure this is the environment," rebuts Mr. MacDougall.

Frank then jumps in, "See, I bet all his stuff about church is a load of crap too. He probably doesn't even go to church but spends all Sunday watching TV in a muffin shop!"

Mr. MacDougall then says, "You know what, I will pray. I'll pray for *you*," pointing to Frank.

"Oh, *no*!" Frank returns, "You don't pray for me, pal, I pray for you!"

Robert chimes in, "OK, Dad," talking to Frank, "take it easy."

"No," states Frank, "this guy wants to go; then let's go!" Then he races to the coffee table and kneels to begin his prayer fight face-off.

Mr. MacDougall takes the challenge and kneels as well. Now both families quickly follow. They all awkwardly grab hands and Debra asks Mr. and Mrs. MacDougall to begin.

"Very well," says Mr. MacDougall. "Dear Lord, we ask you in this time of turmoil that we might act in compassion and kindness, that we might act in accordance with your will."

Frank butts in, "I can beat that!"

Debra stops Frank by saying, "Frank, we're not competing."

Mr. MacDougall then adds, "This is hardly worshipful."

"Oh, yeah," Frank returns in animosity, "Who made you the prayer sheriff?"

"I am not the prayer sheriff," Mr. MacDougall says, "but I will not allow you to use our Lord to continue your own arguments. It is sacrilegious."

"You're right," Frank says, now more defiant, now turning in prayer again. "Dear Lord, please keep this in-law family the hell away from me."

"Fine." says Mr. MacDougall, now heated himself. "Then you stay the heck away from me."

Frank comes back, "You can say 'heck' all you want, but we know you mean 'hell.'"

"Whether I say it or not," says Mr. MacDougall, "it doesn't change that that's where I think you're going."

"How about I take you with me!" asserts Frank.

PRAYER AND COMPETITION

This very funny scene points to an important reality; Frank and Mr. MacDougall pray, they enter into the practice, but the practice itself leads to further animosity and almost violence. The practice of prayer was impotent in this comedy because it had been taken over by competition, and competition breeds in the lukewarm water of individualism. Frank and Mr. MacDougall pray over and against each other not to encounter personhood but to justify themselves. Their prayer does not reveal each other's personhood but hides it in a religious act of competition.

In chapters thirteen and fourteen I've made a case that the way to live into a ministry of sharing in each other's person, as a way of sharing in God's life, is to become communities of personal encounter through prayer. I made such a significant case for prayer because it is the most direct gift given to the church for divine and human indwelling. Therefore, I've advocated prayer by making a case for us to see education as teaching people to pray by teaching them to tell their stories, connecting those stories to Scripture. I've also pushed for us to see preaching as proclamation born from and within the congregations' spoken prayers, and from their stories that give way to prayer, as we together inductively reflect on the text.

Prayer is a transforming action because prayer unveils personhood, but only when negative emotions don't contaminate the practice (e.g., using prayer as a power game or weapon, using it to infuse others with anxiety). It unveils personhood when we are able to indwell each other, which leads to the indwelling of God. The practice itself holds little power and can be used as a religious billy club without the encounter of personhood, without the movement away from competition and to sharing (competition that asks "What will others think of me?" destroys the ability to be honest, like Psalms of Lament, in our own prayers). Prayer and personhood, then, are interconnected. Persons pray, and personhood is uncovered in prayer, not only because we seek relationships with God and petition for the relationships that are us, but even more so because in prayer the person of Jesus Christ participates in and with us, connecting his Spirit with our own, inviting us into the relationship that is Jesus (the trinitarian love of the Father to the Son in the Spirit).

PRAYER AND LEADERSHIP

But this then raises an important issue, what is vividly exposed in the dust-up between Frank and Mr. MacDougall: an issue of leadership. How can the pastor keep the ground of prayer from becoming frozen by competition, anger and conflict?[1] So many pastors I know would love to move their communities in this direction but feel it is such an uphill battle to do anything, sensing that people are either apathetic or directly against change. And when the people say they're ready for such a change, the larger structures they live in (e.g., denomination, economic situation or historical memory of the congregation) still resist us.

This is an issue of leadership. How do we invite people into a new reality, as Max De Pree would say, to engage structures and care for each other's person? This is such a struggle that we often set our sights lower; instead of shaping a view of reality, let's just keep things going. When this happens, participating in the life of God by participating in the spirit of each other is no longer central to ministry; instead, pastoral leadership defaults to running the church: managing the programs, building and staff. When this happens, the pastor is viewed as a manager, as someone responsible for productivity, as someone who manages individuals toward an institution's interest. Such pastoral leadership has little to do with persons. And even the practice of prayer or worship can become the battleground of competing interests in the congregation.

THE MANAGER

The pastor as manager, taking on functions, can easily be mesmerized by data. When leadership is bound in a management mentality, the pastor becomes obsessed with how-tos, clouding her or his ability to imaginatively see the spiritual reality of indwelling, and settling instead for techniques of management.

When primarily a manager, the pastor is ultimately a problem solver, seeking answers to why people don't come, or what will make the institution more successful. Like any manager, it feels like most of the pastor's job is cleaning up messes that are standing in the way of productivity—whatever the productivity might be.

The pastor is more of a cleaner than someone discerning God's action by helping shape a narrative of sharing within and outside the community, someone pushing and praying for the structures themselves to be more conducive to personhood. And this management mentality, the pastor as cleaner, pulls us like a magnet to see relationship as influencing people, because what counts is managing programs, making our institution more productive, getting people committed.

The other problem is that managers, especially those hell-bent on success, tend not to say thank you. They may say "good job," but to say thank you is to be in need; it is to be thankful that another person has shared with you, has made a space for you. So often it is hard for us to get people on board with congregational change because we rarely say thank you. Changing structures starts with saying thank you, by being open enough to understand, listen and recognize. We rarely seek to listen and be with *persons*, understanding them, appreciating them and assuring them that this is a church, even in its (structural) change, that has a place for their person.

Ronald Heifetz and Marty Linsky explain that people resist change not because they are curmudgeonly jerks (not all the time) but because they fear loss, *they fear that the change will be a threat to their person.* Heifetz and Linsky explain that our views are often connected to people. To change positions can be hard for some because they first learned these views inside a personal relationship.[2] Change then can be hard because it messes with our person, with our present or past relationships.

Kara made a huge change in our little church a few years back. Joining me on a lecture tour in London and Oslo, Kara visited a number of small, unique churches. None of these diverse new-paradigm churches met every week. So sitting in the Heathrow airport we wondered why our church needed to meet every Sunday. Wasn't there a way to honor the personhood of our congregation by meeting on Sundays every other week, giving people space to actually rest on the alternate Sunday? They could enjoy sabbath, which is to remember and lean into the relationships that we are (with God and neighbor). After several months of conversations and prayer, the congregation decided to alter their worship schedule to meet the first and third weeks on Sundays as usual, and second and fourth weeks to meet on Saturday evening, with a prayerful service and shared meal, together setting aside the following day as a sabbath, a Sunday day of rest.

You can imagine that it was an uphill task to convince this congregation to make this fairly radical change, a change that would interrupt some people's sixty-year-long routine. But to Kara's surprise, for the most part, the change happened quite smoothly. But it only happened without spilled blood because she and the elders took the time to meet with every congregation member to say thank you, to hear their stories and to share in their person in several different formats (one on one, in small groups, etc.). Not coincidently, those she never met with because of scheduling problems remain resistant to the change.

After spending time with the persons of the congregation, Kara was not only far more wise in knowing how this change needed to happen to honor their persons, but having shared in her they were much more willing to trust her. Kara took on a significant form of leadership as personhood by simply but profoundly saying thank you, by listening intently to people's stories, by being a person to them and inviting them to be the same to her. In this way the change became a reflection of their shared story, their personhood as a whole, as they were able to reimagine their vocation as a congregation and live into their next era in a way that differed from the past. Not surprisingly, sharing in each other's stories became not just a method to reach some kind of change but the very fabric of their ongoing life together—as is reflected in the times of prayer in worship.

BEING A PERSON: GRATITUDE

The pastor, then, leads not as a manager, a functional title bound in the logic of individualism, but as a person, inviting people to pray as a way of sharing, and to share as a way to pray. The heart of leadership for the pastor then is focusing not on *tasks* but *personhood*, on the personhood of God by imaginatively speaking of God's new reality and the personhood of each other by saying thank you. The only response to the new reality of sharing given in the hypostatic union and the sharing of relationships with others, that leads us to say thank you, is to live in gratitude.

This means that pastoral leadership starts in gratitude; it starts in the joy that you, *that you*, the pastor, are blessed with speaking and witnessing to the mystery and beauty of God's action of sharing God's own person. And blessed that you, *that you*, are called to these others to share life with. The very core of pastoral leadership then is to live in gratitude *yourself*. And to live in gratitude is to live as a person with others. This then is the central action of pastoral leadership: stop focusing so intently on how to function and focus instead on your *being*, on your person. We set the environment for personal encounter by being persons ourselves—this is the essential form of leadership in the new energy regime we find ourselves in.

Without you living in gratitude for your relationships with others, for the privilege of speaking of the mystery of the indwelling of the hypostatic union, there is little reason, little point, to doing pastoral ministry. What should get us out of bed in the morning is not the possibility that today we will make our church productive, today we will be the success that makes us the envy of the denomination. This can only lead to frustration, burnout and cynicism (which fairly describes pastors of the last few decades). Rather, the reason to get out of bed is *gratitude* that you have been called to share, to share the gospel by sharing in the humanity of others. But *this gratitude is only possible if you are willing to be a person.* So the first step in pastoral leadership is to focus on your own personhood.

PASTOR AS PERSON

At first glace this seems self-centered; it is anything but. To focus on your own person, to commit to being a person, is to recognize and live the fact that you are your relationships. It recognizes that you are bound to others and others are bound to you in action, language and brokenness.

You are your relationships, but as such, you are *you*, and when you change, so too do the relationships that are you.[3] This means that the most significant way to change a system (a relational group of people) is for one of the persons who shares in the others to change, to claim his or her personhood and to invite others to share in it.

Even business leadership gurus have begun teaching (from empirical examination) that good leaders focus on themselves, tend to their own person by attending to their emotions. Award-winning business books like *Deep Change, A Failure of Nerve* and *The New Leader*[4] explore the need for leaders to focus on their own person, to have enough emotional intelligence to be in touch with their self, so that they might be in touch with others.

These business theories advocate this because even in the business setting we are our relationships; *systems* can only change when persons change. Or systems (companies, churches and families) are radically transformed when someone (Friedman believes *anyone* with some significance in the system) changes.

Recently, a young pastor was being shadowed for a day by a college student. The college student joined the young pastor as she had coffee with a congregation member and dropped off a Sunday school project made for a shut-in and prayed for him. He joined the pastor at a community safety meeting and stood by as the pastor talked for fifteen minutes with a person who came to the church office looking for money. At the end of the day, upon reflection, the shadowing student said to the pastor, "I guess today I learned what a pastor does. Well, I mean, I guess what I really learned is that a pastor is like a professional *person*."[5]

And maybe in some ways this is the best description of pastoral leadership; we are professional *persons*, persons blessed with the gift (the financial, professional gift) of tending to our personhood as a way of tending to others. If we are persons, then focusing on our own personhood, committing to be a person, is at the same time to be with and for others; it is to speak the language of sharing of Godself in the incarnation. We focus on being persons not by seeking some self-help or spiritual workout plan, but by learning to share, by focusing on what it means to share ourselves in a way that is not for us but for others. It is not for us but nevertheless blesses us.

LEADERSHIP AS EMOTIONAL INTELLIGENCE

We focus on being persons by learning to interpret our own feelings, but recognizing that our feelings, in part, are for others (our feelings are the signals that connect our brains); but they remain ours, and to share them we must be in touch with them, honestly wrestling with them. We must choose as a mark of discipleship to be radically honest with ourselves about ourselves, all for the purpose of knowing ourselves, so that we might be known and know others, allowing for the indwelling of our spirit with others". "Self-awareness . . . plays a crucial role in empathy, or sensing how someone else sees a situation: If a person is perpetually oblivious to his own feelings, he will also be tuned out to how others feel."[6] Daniel Goleman continues, "Simply put, self-awareness means having a deep understanding of one's emotions, as well as one's strengths and limitations and one's values and motive."[7]

Inviting people to pray their stories and taking the sensitive move of preaching people's prayers demands that the pastor be a self-aware *person*. The pastor must not shy away from facing his or her own feelings, trusting that feelings communicate personhood. And to embrace feelings is to embrace him- or herself, sure, but more so it sends the pastor like a vortex to share in others, inviting others to feel safe enough to be with others by opening their person through their own feelings.

If the pastor's job is to teach people to pray and to preach people's prayers, if the point of the Christian life is relationships of sharing, then the pastor's primary job will be to feel the emotions of the community (again, emotional intelligence is needed here, and seminary education needs to focus on it!) so that the pastor might intervene or encourage relationships to flow.

The flow of relational sharing is the mark of the church (its very witness to the world), meaning the pastor must do the work of keeping the relational flow going by being in touch with people's emotions, confronting and attending to emotional cutoffs, overfunctioning and triangulation. It is not the pastor's job to solve these problems or completely heal them in individuals, but to confront relational blockages so that the environment might be set for sharing.[8] "The leader acts as the group's emotional guide."[9]

This tending to the emotional currents of our congregation is not unsimilar to prayer. It involves feeling our way into an environment, honestly facing what is keeping people from feeling safe or energized enough to share in each other.[10] To get Frank and Mr. MacDougall to honestly pray means getting them to honestly name their feelings of fear, frustration and exclusion. Prayer can only be a dead religious practice when personhood is absent, and personhood can only be revealed when Frank and Mr. MacDougall find a way to deal with their emotions. It might be that these issues are too complicated to easily solve. The pastor's job is not to solve Frank's and Mr. MacDougall's psychological issues but to make sure that their issues don't lead to a negative emotional contagion that blankets the community and pulls people apart. The apostle Paul's ethical teaching can be interpreted not as moralistic laws but as action, needed at that time and in that place, so that relationships might flow, so that the church might share in each other as a way to share in God.

ANXIETY

What destroys sharing, what makes relationships fray and sometimes die, is so often anxiety. Anxiety is a cancer to sharing, because anxiety keeps us from being open enough to share ourselves. Anxiety keeps us from being ourselves, fearing we need to please everyone. Anxiety pushes us to cut off, to protect ourselves, to overfunction, to be what others want us to be, or to triangulate to pass anxiety on. Anxiety has a kind of zombie effect; it seeks to pass its state on to others, to spread itself. Friedman says, "Chronic anxiety might be compared to the volatile atmosphere of a room filled with gas fumes, where any sparking incident could set off a conflagration. And where people would then blame the person who struck the match rather than trying to disperse the fumes."[11]

Anxiety is so powerful and dangerous to communities because it can so easily be passed from one person to another. Anxiety can so easily hide in our action and language like cancer in cells, but this cancer is contagious because it lives in the emotional connections between us, in the invisible wires that connect our brains.[12] Anxiety is so potent because it grows near our brokenness, making our brokenness no longer the invitation to share in our person, but festered wounds that promise to infect your own person at the vulnerable point of *your* brokenness.[13]

Anxiety, not suffering, is demonic to personal relationships. Suffering, mutual brokenness, leads to indwelling, but anxiety pushes us away from each other. Sensing the anxiety coming into our own being, we enter a state of fight or flight.

People so often move into fight or flight because they are anxious.

Anxiety pushes us to run or swing. The pastor's job as leader is to deal with feelings of anxiety so that people need not respond with a sprint or punch, but can share themselves in story so they can pray and hear the Word preached.

"That is precisely the function of a leader within any institution: to provide that regulation through his or her non-anxious, self-defined presence."[14] But it is impossibly hard for pastors to embrace a non-anxious presence if they slide into a form of individualism that sees the pastor as meeting some interest. The focus on interest will almost always produce anxiety, because it heightens competition by making winners and losers, or big important churches and small insignificant ones.

THE FINAL WORD: BE OPEN AND CLOSED

To lead in gratitude, focusing on your own person in a way that allows relationships to flow and avoids anxiety, is to be open and closed—a pastor that is a person, inviting others to also be persons, living among a congregation in an open and closed manner. Balancing open and closedness allows for sharing and brackets out anxiety.

All relationships of personhood are actually contingent on persons being open with each other. But just as important as openness, persons in relationship need to be closed with each other. We can only have openness, we can only have personhood, when we are also closed to each other, when we are able to differentiate, when we are able to have a healthy sense of ourselves.[15] Bonhoeffer has articulated this open and closedness as the essence of true relationship: "Thus the 'openness' of the person demands 'closed-ness' as a correlative, or one could not speak of openness at all."[16]

Without this open and closedness we have only enmeshment, where we lose our personhood in our overwhelming connection. Here anxiety encircles us. Without differentiation, without closedness, there can be no gratitude, for your neighbor can never be a gift to you, but only a burden to your freedom or an object to possess.[17]

The pastor is a person to his congregation, to his community, by being open to them, sure, but more importantly by being closed to them, by communicating her or his need for vacation, rest, family time and viewing lowbrow movies. Closedness is a boundary that exists as a gift, because when we are closed to each other we can give to each other our person.

When we are always and continually open, our people get the impression that we exist to meet their wants, that the pastor, like a functional manager, is here to make the customer happy. But when we say no (not the no of "that is not our policy" but the no of *I'm tired, I'm disappointed, I'm needing a break, I'm needing study and prayer*), we become persons to the others in our church, persons with others (like children, spouses and friends) that make us *us*. When we are at times closed, our openness becomes the doorway into our personhood.

But this closedness also works another way. Because we are persons who are both open and closed, no one in the congregation has a right to overcome or violate another's personhood. We must all respect each other's boundary of closedness; there can simply be no relationship of sharing without respecting our shared and personal boundaries.[18] In many ways the pastor's leadership is to protect people and help them, both personally and communally, to communicate their boundaries so they might know that their boundaries will not be crossed, making them free to share and be shared in.[19]

This open and closedness, then, is about responsibility, about the pastor responsibly setting the environment for the sharing of persons. This essential open and closedness keeps our focus on empathy from allowing the anxious to set the terms for the community. But this can happen only if the pastor first lives out of the open and closed reality. Then, as a person, the pastor is free and empowered to confront those who violate personhood by either making the time of prayer their personal open mic gripe session or by belittling people like Dave did before his confession.

And this very open and closed reality exists within Godself. God is open to us in the very person of Jesus Christ; Jesus is bone of our bone and flesh of our flesh (Gen 2:23). But this same Jesus Christ, while open to us by sharing our human nature, is closed to us, because his person simultaneously shares in the very nature of God. God promises that we too can share in his nature, but only by us being our broken selves, by joining him in this open and closed reality, and sharing in the person of our neighbor by being with them, by being open to them, but also closed to them, by being our unique selves that are nevertheless bound to them.

IN CONCLUSION AND BENEDICTION

We have taken quite a journey in this project. I have made the assertion that the very conception of the pastor is changing as we enter a new energy regime, a regime in which sharing is central. This sharing, I've argued, will fundamentally be a sharing of personhood, pushing past our present forms of individualism that have led pastoral ministry into so many cul-de-sacs. To escape this we will need to redefine our very selves as persons who are not our interest but our very relationships.

This understanding of personhood is bound within the heart of the Christian commitment. Through the hypostatic union God has acted for us by sending Jesus the Christ, who is one *person*, making personhood essential to Christianity, in two natures. Jesus' personhood is the linking of divine and human, the human participating in the life of the divine. I have argued then that the way we participate in the life of God is by upholding personhood, by sharing in it spirit to spirit through the Spirit. And as we share in it we share in Christ, who is found forever with and for us, binding his person to ours.

Sharing, then, becomes the heart of pastoral ministry. We invite people to pray as a way of sharing and share as a way to pray. Teaching and preaching become molded around prayers of sharing.

So may we go and share in the humanity of each other as the very joyous journey of sharing in the life of God.

Appendix

Portraits of Relational Pastors

The following vistas and practices have been written by pastors of various communities who are seeking to live into the themes of this book. They are collected here to spark ideas for, and recognition of, the many ways communities of faith share in Christ by sharing in each other.

BUS STOP COFFEE

One Sunday during announcements after worship, someone said, "I think we should pick one day a week and give away coffee at the city bus stop on this corner. We need to extend our hospitality outside the doors."

Everyone shrugged and said, "Okay." So that very week, at 7:00 a.m., three people showed up with thermoses of coffee, donuts and fresh bread spread out on a little folding table. For an hour, they greeted people waiting for their morning bus. One of their regulars came to worship last week. And then the next Friday, he came to help serve the coffee.

The next week, they did it again. Week after week. Pretty soon, they learned names. Now they have regulars. Their presence is weird and surprising and usually awkward. But it's also beautiful and brave.

We don't put out signs or pass out information about our congregation. Most people don't know we are from a church. Displaying signs or fliers would undermine the whole reason we are there: because we love our neighbors and want to make the bus stop a place of hospitality and conversation.

LITTLE RASCALS

A few of us were setting up for worship, chatting outside on the sidewalk. A couple of kids wandered by, pulling a cooler on wheels—a brother and sister (I presume), ages five and eight. The eight-year-old poked her head in the door and asked, "Hey, what is this place?!"

"Well, it's a church service."

"Oh. Can I sign up?" she asked.

"Um, you can just come. You don't need to sign up."

"Okay." Then, she turned and yelled down the sidewalk to her little brother, "You wanna go to this thing?"

So they wheeled in the cooler and assisted with setup. They asked a lot of questions. I asked where they were coming from when then wandered by our doorway. They had been hanging out next door at Joe and Stan's (a bar). "We went for a kiddie cocktail. Well, my brother had water; he wanted orange juice, but they said that breakfast time was over." Perfect sense.

One of the congregation's folks took them under his wing—he sat with them and guided them through the service. We heard the eight-year-old sing and knew she was disappointed when she found out that we sing collectively (she was hoping for a solo). We learned that the five-year-old likes to listen to Eminem. I told them I like to eat M&Ms. Then we giggled at how lame I am.

After worship, back outside on the sidewalk, we were munching on leftover communion bread. The eight-year-old pulled out a refillable restaurant-style ketchup bottle from her wheelie cooler and doused the bread with it. (I liked this display of preparedness.) Plans were made to return in two weeks. Goodbyes were exchanged as they continued down the road.

This was the moment that those of us who were left couldn't stop laughing. It was all so normal and strange and joyful and weird. "You know, this church has a certain *Little Rascals* vibe to it," one person said. "Oh my word. That's exactly it," said another.

Then with heads shaking at what it was we got to witness, we headed to our cars.

BACK TO SCHOOL FORMAL, BLESSING AND DANCE

We spent three solid months building relationships with neighborhood families. We played games in the park every Thursday evening. We blessed bikes and danced to rock and roll. We ran away for a weekend together in the woods. We spent another weekend working on five homes in our area that needed repairs and painting. Then we spent a whole week building community and eating dinner together in our public park.

Now all these young students and families were preparing for the beginning of a new school year. Since only a couple of households in this wide neighborhood network are part of our worship life, it just didn't make sense to do a backpack blessing. We did that last year, and it was pretty lame because it meant we missed out on all those people who do not worship with us. And we knew that asking them to come to worship would mean compromising what we just spent a summer building: relationships with no strings attached.

Finally, we hit on an idea that met this community where it lives: a back-to-school formal, blessing and dance. We texted parents: "Want to take part in a back-to-school dinner where we all dress up and serve the kids a meal? Then we will do a blessing for the new school year and end with a dance?" They immediately responded with zeal: "Yes!" "Best idea ever!"

The family with the biggest yard volunteered to host. A menu was planned. Parents quickly lobbied for the coolest jobs—bartender (Shirley Temples), DJ, servers—and then the rest of us cooked, set up and cleaned up. One person printed up invites and walked them around to each house. Another dad volunteered to teach the Moonwalk.

As we were preparing for the event, one adult said, "We have to do this every year. This is the *first annual* back-to-school formal, blessing and dance."

The kids arrived, wearing lipstick, ties and skirts. One young man had a squash blossom tucked into his vest—freshly plucked from his mom's garden. They found a banquet table set with mismatched Goodwill dishes and tablecloths, fresh flowers in jars, name cards and ridiculously excited adults. Everyone milled about with pink fizzy drinks; one mom wandered around with trays of pigs in a blanket. A big pack of our youngest kids wrestled in the corner of the yard.

Finally, we had everyone find their seat, and we sang grace. The meal was served. At the end of the meal, all the adults surrounded the table and divided into small groups. Everyone answered two questions:

- What are you most excited about at the beginning of school?

- What are you most nervous about?

We said prayers of thanks for teachers and our schools and asked Jesus to help us with our nervousness. Then we danced.

That night we were church together—asking Jesus to be with us as we navigated another wildly scary transition with our kids, and giving thanks for the village of adults standing around those Goodwill banquet tables.

CREATING SPACE

During the season of Lent, our congregation has the tradition of inviting members to preach at our Wednesday evening service. Each lay preacher is asked to "tell their story" as it relates to our Lenten theme. For years this tradition has been a sacred fixture in the worship of our people; it is so beloved in part because we get to hear the stories—the triumphant highs and the desperate lows—of each other, fellow members in the body of Christ. Hearing these stories helps us to see each other in new ways and brings us closer together. We would never think about changing this tradition of lay preaching in Lent.

Until, one week last year, we had to change our tradition. On the last Wednesday in Lent, on the verge of Holy Week, we found ourselves without a preacher. Not sure of what to do, our senior pastor opted for an "open mic night." We invited anyone to share their story or to comment on those stories that we had heard from other members earlier in the Lenten season.

This invitation could have been a grand failure (Midwest Lutherans are not known for sharing emotions before others); it was instead the most powerful Lenten service of which I have been a part. Through tears and laughter, person after person commented on how someone's story had resonated with their own lives, how they had experienced

Christ through this sharing in another's story, and how they had been drawn into a new relationship through this experience of the other.

You could feel the connections being made; you could feel the Spirit at work. This unexpected space to share had become the space in which Christ was powerfully present, bringing people together in profound ways.

RELATIONSHIPS CHANGE EVERYTHING

Throughout seminary, I had a secret identity as the lead singer in a punk rock band. We played dozens of gigs across the Twin Cities, often sharing the stage with the same half-dozen other punk bands in the metro area.

Our frequent encounters with these other musicians did not bring us closer together; in fact, the more we played together, the more we began to *dislike* each other—especially each other's music. Not knowing one another, it was easy to pass off each other's music as cliché, simplistic, poser-sounding noise (or any other distanced and judgmental assessments we could think up after a pint). In fairness, our music was overworked, confused, poser-sounding noise to them!

But then one evening, perhaps despite our best efforts, we found ourselves sharing a table—and a few pints—with "The Ugly Fat Kids." As we got to know each other, we found out that we had a lot of the same musical interests, a lot of the same passions, a lot of the same hopes and history and struggles and joys. In short, we found out that both bands were filled with people—real people—and we sort of liked these real people.

The next time "The Ugly Fat Kids" hit the stage, I heard their music for the first time. And I loved it. Without the barriers, without the prejudice, without the competition (and, most importantly, *with* a new relationship), I heard and saw *persons* up on stage, and they were brilliant.

SUNDAY NIGHT CHEF SCHOOL

We gather. We prep. We cook. We eat. We clean up. We go home. In between, we talk. Sometimes we remember to say grace. Our most noticeable youth event each month, "Sunday Night Chef School," isn't so much a program as a space.

Sure, there are outcomes: after a year of banging around a commercial kitchen, teenagers know how to handle knives or navigate a crowded range, or work an industrial dishwasher; but the term *school* in the title isn't intended to suggest a curriculum other than that supplied by space and time and something to do with our hands. Our use of the environment and equipment provided by our congregation's big kitchen includes an education of sorts: we make crepes and sausage, and we can pickles in brine. One month we made tamales from scratch, hand-tying *masa* into corn husk bundles to be steamed while we sat on the countertops and shared about school and friendships.

An activity as basic as making a meal provides a human and humanizing scale to hanging out together. It provides a purpose without supplying an agenda. By sharing work and food and time, we share in each other.

INTERGENERATIONAL, ALL-CONGREGATIONAL TALENT SHOW

Our call as Christians includes the ancient and always-needful practice of almsgiving, and there are myriad ways to do it. We decided to share ourselves with each other.

We gathered, ostensibly, to raise some money to help address disaster and famine half a world away. Our talent show was titled "Two Minutes to Help Haiti." We invited anyone and everyone to do or share something amusing or amazing that would take no longer than two minutes. In and among the acts were opportunities to give toward the cause. Our talent show blended audience and performer into one all-ages stew of laughter and beauty and grace.

Whether it was two-year-old Amy's single-leg-in-the-air "handstand" (which garnered an ovation), or the organist's fitted sheet-folding exhibition, or ninety high-energy seconds of Nerf basketball shooting, we celebrated each other's unique abilities and recognized each other as persons—as gifts of great value, made for sharing.

KEEPING THE FAITH

One day we gathered for a very different kind of get-together—one none of us had ever done before. "Welcome to our 'Keeping the Faith Ceremony,'" I said.

There was a basket to drop notes into at the door and candles spread throughout the space. The communion table was left conspicuously open, the cup and platter in one back corner, a couple of candles in the other. In the center of an open space was a big, soft chair with a homemade quilt over it and a puffy footrest. It was flanked by rocking chairs and pews extending from there, forming an intimate semicircle bracketed on either end by the baptismal font and the communion table.

There were packs of Kleenex in all the pews. People came in with more tissues in their pockets or purses. Some couldn't bring themselves to come at all, but those who came entered timidly, quietly, apprehensively. Then she came in, walker slowly pushed in front of her. She was guided to the special seat, her feet propped up on the plush cushion.

We proceeded to acknowledge that our dear sister was dying, that her life was coming to an end, and that we had been blessed beyond measure to share it with her.

We read Scripture and sang a hymn; we prayed, and then the time came for us to fill the table. And we did. People brought items up that had stories attached to them—memories of her. Trinkets, symbols, laughter and tears. One person brought a film clip from forty years earlier, 8mm footage of a family celebration at the lake, ending with our guest of honor cheekily dancing at the camera. Some brought flowers; a few brought "just myself and my words" and shared with her what she had meant to them, what she had been for our community. Some merely stood and told her how deeply they loved her, and that she could read the rest of what they had to say in the note they had left in the basket.

When the sharing was finished, we gathered around her and laid our hands on her. We prayed for peace and God's presence. We poured out our gratitude for her life and our sadness to be losing her. We anointed her with oil and blessed her, just as she had been anointed at her baptism, claimed by God and marked as Christ's own forever. We hugged her and returned to our seats to listen to sweet sopranos sing a song of blessing: "May the Lord bless you and keep you . . ."

And then it was over. Except nobody wanted to go. We lingered nearly an hour. Someone rustled up some cookies; someone else made coffee. We placed them with a jug of cider and some paper cups on the communion table, and lingered in the sacramental fellowship of love, the sacred space held by the Spirit of God. In the shadow of death, we will fear no evil. For Thou art with us.

Two weeks later she died; her baptism was complete. And we held in sacred gratitude that day we had spent celebrating her life with her.

CIRCLE OF PRAYER

Transitions, losses, change, joy—our lives are filled with them and God is met within them. So it makes no sense that so often we hold them inside as we sit in our pews, sharing it with a few close people here and there in our lives, but not bringing these essential experiences into worship.

As our congregation has practiced praying for one another, naming aloud our joys and pain in prayer, we've gotten more comfortable bringing ourselves, just as we are, into the same space to be held by God and the community. Now, after checking first with the person before worship (and I have never had someone say *no*), we invite the person facing surgery, a move, a new job or a scary transition to come to the center of our space during our prayer time. We gather around them in a circle of prayer. It's not long or wordy, and it is about as charismatic as our largely well-behaved Presbyterians can be. We simply place our hands on the person, or on someone whose hand is on the person, and one person lifts before God in words what all of our hearts lift in that moment: this brother or sister in their need.

When we do, I always feel a sense of deep gratitude at the gift of standing with another, and a sense that the burden has now been gently spread over the whole circle so that we can bear it together. At the *Amen*, we lift our heads and look for a moment at each other, and head back to our seats, and our brother or sister leaves knowing that, come what may, they are not alone.

SPIRITUAL DISCIPLINES AS EMPATHY

My wife and I are copastors at a small church. Every year during the Lent and Easter seasons, our congregation learns a new spiritual discipline. We have explored prayer circles, group spiritual direction, biblical study, meditations on the writings of Dietrich Bonhoeffer, and prayer circles again (some of us apparently forgot how to pray). The main purpose of a spiritual discipline is to connect our hearts to God's heart, to make our minds into the mind of Christ, to invite the guidance of the Holy Spirit.

While we hope these lofty goals have been facilitated by our exercises, the more amazing thing to me is how we have become connected to each other as we have sat in silence, learned to pray, struggled with a hard text and listened to each other's stories. While reaching out to God, we more often than not found the person sitting next to us.

WORSHIP PRAYER RITUALS

Each time someone in our community is in transition, we put them in the center of our "Prayers of the People" during worship. We invite them to sit in the middle of the gathered; often those seated or standing round them will lay hands on them, but sometimes everyone keeps their hands to themselves (we are primarily a church of introverts and reluctant to put anyone into creepy situations). The pastor prays and then leaves space for others to pray. Each prayer ends with "Lord, in your mercy . . ." and the community's response, "Hear our prayer."

Usually the petitions are raw and beautiful and personal. For those who are moving, for those whose lives are crumbling because of divorce, for students and teachers entering or ending a school year, for kids leaving for camp, for those beginning a new job: "Lord, in your mercy . . ."

We are a fluid church—with people coming and going all the time—but it took a few years for us to recognize that this liturgical act is incredibly important for the entire body. Of course, it sends those who are leaving out with a blessing. For those people who are left—who are not moving anytime soon—this tiny moment recognizes that our community will not be the same. We grieve the loss. We are excited about new adventures for our beloved.

In July, we sent five third-graders to sleep-away camp for the first time. When we told them that they would be sent off with prayers and a blessing, one said, "*Yes!* I have been waiting for my turn to be in the middle of the prayers."

Notes

Chapter 1: Reshifting Pastoral Ministry

[1]Martin Buber, *I and Thou* (London: Continuum, 2004), p. 22.

[2]Jeremy Rifkin points to the personal and how attention to the person has started to show itself in a number of fields. See his *The Empathic Civilization* (New York: Jeremy P. Teacher/Penguin, 2009), p. 20.

[3]Dietrich Bonhoeffer says, "It is not merely a means to an end but also an end in itself. It is the present Christ himself; and this is why 'being in Christ' and 'being in the church-community' is the same thing; it is why Christ himself bears the sins of the individuals, which are laid upon the church-community" (*Sanctorum Communio* [Minneapolis: Fortress Press, 1998], p. 190).

[4]Rifkin, *Empathic Civilization,* p. 166.

[5]The call for people to have a personal relationship with Jesus is right and truly theologically evangelical as it calls people to see Jesus as a person. Yet, even in the language of Jesus being a person, the one who is to assimilate Jesus into his or her life is not a person but a free-will individual that is asked to make an epistemological conversion, to become loyal to the brand of Jesus.

[6]I introduce and unpack this concept in *Revisiting Relational Youth Ministry* (Downers Grove, IL: InterVarsity Press, 2007). In this project I continue with the thesis started there. With different tools and perspectives, this project allows me to deepen the theoretical ground and broaden the audience of that earlier project.

Chapter 2: New Energy, New Communications, New Consciousness . . . New Ministry

[1]Andrew Walls call this process "translation." He states, "Each phase of Christian history has seen a transformation of Christianity as it has entered and penetrated another culture. There is no such thing as 'Christian culture' or 'Christian civilization' in the sense that there is an Islamic culture, and an Islamic civilization. There have been several different Christian civilizations already; there may yet be many more. The reason for this lies in the infinite translatability of the Christian faith" (*The Missionary Movement in Christian History* [Maryknoll, NY: Orbis, 2009], p. 22).

[2]Particularly, some Catholic thinkers, such as Thomas Rourke and Christian Smith, have pushed for the personal in political science and sociology respectively, both giving credit to the Christian tradition for moving their thinking in this direction (as well as the direction of their predecessors).

[3]Rifkin's work crosses fields in the social sciences, moving between history, political science and more. But also Rifkin's work crosses the boundary between scholarly guild writing and a broader audience. This is a great strength of Rifkin's work but also opens it to critique. It doesn't take much to see that both in academic journals and newspaper op-eds, some find Rifkin's history too expansive and are quick to point out the many nuances, curves and twists in the historical trail he blazes.

[4]Rifkin's history is broad, as is my contribution to it. Some may argue that Rifkin's attention to energy regimes and communication systems gives too much attention to middle- or upper-class people and therefore ignores the poor. But putting attention for transition here is in line with Max Weber, who observed that "prophetic movements have not been primarily movements of economic protest, motivated mainly by the economic interests of the disadvantaged classes. Middle classes of various types and solid handicraft groups have been very prominent. Generally the poorest classes have not" (Talcott Parsons, introduction to Max Weber, *The Sociology of Religion* [Boston: Beacon Press, 1963], p. xli).

[5]Rifkin, *Empathic Civilization*, p. 34.

[6]Ibid., p. 37.

[7]"The collection of the prophetic religious revelations or, in the other case, of the traditionally transmitted sacred lore, may take place in the form of oral tradition. Throughout many centuries the sacred knowledge of the Brahmins was transmitted orally, and setting it down in writing was actually prohibited, . . . the reason being that this knowledge was meant to be possessed only by qualified persons, namely the twice-born" (Max Weber, *Sociology of Religion* [Boston: Beacon Press, 1991], p. 67).

[8]See ibid., p. 17.

[9]See ibid., p. 18. Weber is not beyond critique. Yet, my focus in this chapter is not to provide an airtight history but to simply play with a few perspectives for the purpose of sparking the creative imagination of the pastor.

[10]See ibid., p. 17.

[11]Rifkin, *Empathic Civilization*, p. 564.

[12]In comparison to hunting and gathering, which could have been the main energy regime for millions of years.

[13]Talcott Parsons, introduction to Weber's *Sociology of Religion*, p. xxxviii.

[14]Rifkin calls this "theological consciousness." However, I think this is a mistake and find it more helpful to restate it as "religious."

[15]"The term 'priest' may be applied to the functionaries of a regularly organized and permanent enterprise concerned with influencing the gods, in contrast with the individual and occasional efforts of magicians. Even this contrast is bridged over by a sliding scale of transitions, but as a pure type the priesthood is unequivocal and can be said to be characterized by the presence of certain fixed, cultic centers associated with some actual cultic apparatus" (Weber, *Sociology of Religion*, p. 28).

[16]Weber takes us deeper here, giving important grounding to my point, "Yet another distinguishing quality of the priest, it is asserted, is his professional equipment of special knowledge, fixed doctrine, and vocational qualifications, which brings him into

contrast with sorcerers, prophets, and other types of religious functionaries who exert their influence by virtue of personal gifts (charisma) made manifest in miracle and revelation. . . . Rather, the distinction between priest and magician must be established qualitatively with reference to the different nature of the learning in the two cases" (ibid., p. 29). Continuing, Weber states, "The development of priestly education from the most ancient charismatic stage to the period of literary education has considerable practical importance in the evolution of a faith into a scriptural religion, either in the complete sense of an attachment to a canon regarded as sacred or in the more moderate sense of the authoritativeness of a scripturally fixed sacred norm, as in the case of the Egyptian Book of the Dead. As literacy becomes more important for the conduct of purely secular affairs, which therefore assume the character of bureaucratic administration and proceed according to regulations and documents, education passes from the hands of secular officials and intellectuals into those of literate priests. The latter, for their part, occupy offices the functions of which involve the use of writing, as in the chancelleries of the Middle Ages" (ibid., p. 70).

[17]Ibid., p. 23.

[18]Weber's point here connects to my argument that evangelism in this period happened through civilization. The priest was supported by the system of civilization, and in some ways we can say that priest served the system as much as God (see ibid., p. 29).

Chapter 3: Transitioning from the Pastor as Self-Help Entertainer

[1]See Ann Swidler, *Talk of Love* (Chicago: University of Chicago Press, 2001).

[2]All the transitional periods are more complicated and nuanced than is possible to discuss here. For instance, our Western conception of the self is a more curved road than there is room for discussing here. For more see my *Children of Divorce* (Grand Rapids: Baker, 2010), chaps. 2-3.

[3]See George Marsden, *Reforming Fundamentalism* (Grand Rapids: Eerdmans, 1995), and D. G. Hart, *That Old-Time Religion in Modern America* (Chicago: Ivan R. Dee, 2002).

[4]In one sense the pastor in this period could be called a prophet, especially as we relate it to the priest as Weber explained. The pastor was not the one devoted to managing divine things but an example, giving vision of how to live in this new regime. Parsons explains, "The exemplary prophet provides a model for a way of life which can be followed by others, embodying in a religious sense what is defined as a higher level of personal virtue" (Parsons, introduction to Max Weber, *Sociology of Religion* [Boston: Beacon Press, 1963], p. xxxv).

[5]I'm following and then adapting Weber here (see ibid., p. 75).

[6]Of course some non-Western nations too found themselves in this new coal and steam energy regime, but it was much more rare to send missionaries to these places. Rather, more often missionaries were sent to places in Africa, the Pacific islands or South America.

[7]Anthony Giddens, *The Transformation of Intimacy* (Stanford, CA: Stanford University Press, 1992).

[8]Rifkin actually calls it psychological consciousness (*The Empathic Civilization* [New York: Jeremy P. Teacher/Penguin, 2009], p. 392).

[9]See Martin Gross, *The Psychological Society* (New York: Touchstone, 1979), and Philip Rieff, *The Triumph of the Therapeutic* (Chicago: University of Chicago, 2006).

[10]"Fifty years ago, the critic Philip Rieff announced that the twentieth century was the era of 'Psychological Man.' This conception of who we are, he suggested, was the latest in a historical series that began with Political Man in Classical times, giving way to Religious Man in the Christian Middle Ages and then to Economic Man in the Enlightenment. Now, rather than understanding ourselves in terms of our place in the social order, our relationship with God, or our rational pursuit of self-interest, we looked to Freud's theory of psychoanalysis and its conception of a complex psyche balancing its instinctual origins with the demands of civilization" (Steven Pinker, *How the Mind Works* [New York: W. W. Norton, 2009], p. vii).

[11]"The dominant metaphors of leadership in our time have been either pastoral (caring for the flock of God, counseling, and spiritual care) or entrepreneurial (the leader who knows where the church needs to go and has the vision, passion, and strategy to take it there)" (Alan Roxburgh and Fred Romanuk, *The Missional Leader* [San Francisco: Jossey-Bass, 2006], p. 6).

[12]While this may sound heavy-handed; it fits with the psychological consciousness Rifkin highlights of this period. It may make us cringe, but only because we either never connected with this form of consciousness or more likely this period too is coming to a close, therefore making room for critique.

[13]See Charles Taylor, *Sources of the Self* (Cambridge, MA: Harvard University Press, 1989).

[14]I think the missional church movement is a right response to this very reality. Their most convincing argument (through the missio Dei) is that evangelism in the church became something to do, something individuals either did as a program or called people to come to, rather than something that God was in Godself doing.

[15]For more on this see Christian Smith, *Evangelicalism* (Chicago: University of Chicago Press, 1998).

[16]And this might have been altruistic in a sense. What I mean is that a parent may decide to go to a certain church because of what it offers their teenager. But even in this altruistic choice, it is individualism that is the driver. Participation in this church is decided on because of what it individually offers the teenager.

[17]For much more see my book *Revisiting Relational Youth Ministry* (Downers Grove, IL: InterVarsity Press, 2007), chaps. 1-2.

[18]See Rifkin, *Empathic Civilization*, p. 520.

[19]See ibid., p. 518.

[20]"The point is that the increasing connectivity of the human race is advancing personal awareness of all the relationships that make up a complex and diverse world. A younger generation is beginning to view the world less as a storehouse of objects to expropriate and possess and more as a labyrinth of relationships to access"(ibid., p. 594).

[21]Ibid., p. 575.

[22]Ibid., p. 589.

[23]See Tony Jones, *New Christians* (San Francisco: Jossey-Bass, 2008).

[24]It is interesting, as I've unfolded this history, to see how male-centric *all* the models of ministry, pastor and evangelism are at their core. Only since the middle twentieth century have female pastors been a possibility. Yet history reveals why they've often felt like they've been swimming upstream. These very conceptions seem to demand that they play the ministry game like boys. What is interesting is that more women are filling the seats of moderate seminaries, in some places becoming the majority. Conservative pastors like Mark Driscoll see this as a sign of an apostate church, a weak church, an unfaithful church. I see it rather as a sign of contextual change that Rifkin points to, and a very positive one at that. A sign that we are moving into a consciousness of personhood where the pastor will need to be a facilitator of empathetic encounter, making female leadership essential. While I'm not intending to essentialize gender, it just may be that the reason our seminary classes are filled with women is because the Spirit is preparing the church for the kind of leadership it needs in a distributive energy regime where the new consciousness is around personhood.

Chapter 4: Sipping the Sweet, Hard Liquor of Individualism

[1]I understand that those connected to certain leadership perspectives are disturbed with my negative conception of influence. I'll address this in chapter fifteen.

[2]I'm following Christian Smith in placing my thought squarely within European personalism. This perspective will take a radical theological turn in chapters eight through ten. Smith sums up this perspective well, and I find myself within his own "I" statement. "Yet I believe the personalism of the early twentieth century—particularly the realist personalism of Europe, more than the more idealist personalism of Boston—bequeaths an intellectual and moral legacy, despite ambiguities and problems, that is worth retrieving, amending, and developing today" (Christian Smith, *What Is a Person?* [Chicago: University of Chicago Press, 2010], p. 102).

[3]Christian Smith explains the contrast that I am seeking to make here for pastoral ministry. "Persons are self-governing centers of social communication.... Personalism thus rejects the human image constructed and promoted by individualistic liberalism, libertarianism, social contractarianism, rational choice theory, and exchange theory. Persons do not exist first as self-contained selves who subsequently engage and exchange with other selves in order to secure some outcome or consume some benefit. Persons, instead, are originally, constitutively, and inescapably social, interactive, and communicative in origin and being. Sociality helps constitute the essential character of personhood" (ibid., pp. 67-68).

[4]See Thomas Rourke and Rosita Rourke, *A Theory of Personalism* (Lanham, MD: Lexington Books, 2005), p. x.

[5]For more see Thomas Frank, *The Conquest of Cool* (Chicago: University of Chicago Press, 1998).

[6]See Karl Barth, *Prayer* (Philadelphia: Westminster Press, 1946).

[7]John Macmurray explains, "If one person treats another person impersonally, he treats him as if he were an object and not a person. He negates the personal character of the other, then, that is to say, his freedom as an agent; and treats him as completely condi-

tioned in his behaviour, as if he were not free but determined" (*Persons in Relation* [London: Faber & Faber, 1961], p. 34).

[8]From this point forward I'll be using the concept of "dwell" or "indwell." I take this perspective as a theological and biblical concept that points to the depth of seeing human beings as embodied spirit. I think the word has psychological, biological, neurological and social connections, but I'm drawing on (and defining) it first and foremost theologically. Or maybe even better, spiritually; I see indwelling as the spiritual anthropological core to human beings.

[9]This is not to denigrate material. As I said earlier, material can be transformed into something significant when it is drawn into the person-to-person encounter. The dress my wife wore on our wedding day is sacred, not because it is spirit and therefore can encounter me. It cannot. But it does represent her sprit to me, and therefore reminds me, witnesses to me, that I have been encountered, that I have stepped into that thin space of person to person relationship.

[10]It is true that Heidegger contends that things, practical things, are essential to our *Dasein*. I've discussed this at length in *The Children of Divorce*, asserting that lost rooms become an ontological shaking reality, because we know ourselves around this material. I'm not backtracking here, but simply stating that even so, even when material objects can wear the residue of *Dasein*, they remain objects and are in the end, like the previous footnote states, only significant for how they mediate *mit-Sein* (being with), how they represent the stuff of person-to-person encounter. But let us not forget, they remain objects.

[11]There are ways by definition that my perspective rests in idealism. I'm contending that there is more than material reality to existence, that there is a spiritual thrust to our lives. But this spiritual thrust, á la Bonhoeffer, is seeking to provide a spiritual existence for the human that is not primarily metaphysical. Rather it is through the personal, in relationship one-to-another in our day-to-day lives, that we encounter the spiritual. It is not bound metaphysically but socially.

[12]John Macmurray, *The Personal World: On Self and Society* (Edinburgh: Floris Books, 1996), p. 184.

Chapter 5: All the Lonely People

[1]Clifford Green explains that for Bonhoeffer "The image of God is understood not as an individualistic attribute but as a particular social relationship between persons, based on the relationship of God to humanity"(*Bonhoeffer* [Grand Rapids: Eerdmans, 1999], p. 190).

[2]Martin Buber, *I and Thou* (London: Continuum, 2004), p. 22.

[3]Christian Smith here discusses emergence theory, a foundational concept that comes from his own mining of personalism. His statement here supports my argument that we are our relationships: "The novel reality takes existence not through the parts but through their relationships and interactions. Reality is thus significantly constituted through relationality, not merely composition" (*What Is a Person?* [Chicago: University of Chicago Press, 2007], p. 30).

⁴Bonhoeffer says it this way, "The I comes into being only in relation to the You; only in response to a demand does responsibility arise. 'You' says nothing about its own being, only about its demand" (*Sanctorum Communio* [Minneapolis: Fortress Press, 1998], p. 54).

⁵John Macmurray, *Persons in Relation* (London: Faber & Faber, 1961), p. 150.

⁶David Brooks picks up on this familial analogy to make a similar point. He also points to neuroscience and its new relational understanding of the brain that we'll attend to in chapter eight. "That is to say, people don't develop first and create relationships. People are born into relationships—with parents, with ancestors—and those relationships create people. Or, to put it a different way, a brain is some thing that is contained within a single skull. A mind only exists within a network. It is the result of the interaction between brains, and it is important not to confuse brains with minds" (*The Social Animal: The Hidden Sources of Love, Character, and Achievement* [New York: Random House, 2011], p. 43).

⁷"Meeting, sharing, engagement, fellowship, and communion are constituting activities of personhood—not functional means or afterthoughts" (Smith, *What Is a Person?* p. 73).

⁸"Through the Thou a man becomes I" (Martin Buber, *I and Thou* [New York: Charles Scribner's, 1958], p. 28).

⁹Smith helps define what I mean by love, placing it in the personal. "By 'loving,' I mean relating to other persons and things beyond the self in a way that involves the purposive action of extending and expending of oneself for the genuine good of others—whether in friendships, families, communities, among strangers, or otherwise. Human persons are such that their very selves are centered in and grow out of relationships of genuine care for each other that are not purely instrumental but require genuine giving of the self in love in various ways for the good of others" (*What Is a Person?* p. 73).

¹⁰Kathryn Tanner, *Christ the Key* (London: Cambridge University Press, 2010), p. 3.

Chapter 6: What Is a Person?

¹It shouldn't be missed that throughout this project when I use the word *person* I mean it in both a singular and plural way. Following Bonhoeffer, who follows Paul, personhood has the depth to encompass both the singular and the collective. Paul contends that the singular Adam represents the collective of all humanity, just as the singular Christ represents the collective of the new humanity. Bonhoeffer, drawing not only from this biblical perspective but also from the social theory of Hegel and Simmel, contends that the I-you can be understood in the singular or collective. In most of the stories and analogies of this project I'll lean on the singular, such stories tend to be more helpful in illustrating points. But it should be understood that this perspective also has a collective logic to it.

²These words, *without confusion* and *differentiation*, are the very language of Chalcedon. It was in this council that the church became clear on how the two natures of Christ indwelt one another.

³I'm hesitant in the text itself to call "sharing by indwelling persons" as a metaphor for

ministry in our time. I'm reluctant because I think it is a reality much deeper than a simple metaphor. But metaphors can possess power in themselves and we do use metaphors to articulate reality. So I think it is fair to say that "sharing as indwelling" becomes an essential metaphor for ministry in the new energy regime that is emerging, with the very power to set terms for human consciousness. *Sharing* is already a word we use with the new communication system. We share files; we share information online. Something being wiki means it is shared content. Yet what has been missing in church literature is seeing wiki church, or sharing church as something more than functional. Here I'm pushing us to see it as an inner reality of God's action. Rifkin explains how these metaphors move across time. "Even the metaphors we use to describe our sense of selves and our sense of reality are borrowed from our organizing relationships. Hydraulic agricultural civilizations envision the world in hydraulic metaphors. The First Industrial Revolution cobbled together ideological consciousness using mechanical metaphors. The Second Industrial Revolution re-envisioned the cosmos in electrical terms" (Jeremy Rifkin, *The Empathic Civilization* [New York: Jeremy P. Teacher/Penguin, 2009], p. 182).

[4]Smith points to the centrality of action for defining personhood. "A central characteristic of personal being is possessing the capacity to cause one's own actions and interaction. Humans everywhere, in every culture, understand that persons are at least in part responsible for their own actions" (Christian Smith, *What Is a Person?* [Chicago: University of Chicago, 2010], p. 69).

[5]Ray Anderson says, "The reality of a person is in his action with the Other, because this action includes his individuality. When the Other agent 'knows' me in my action. He knows the real me. In effect. I transcend myself, my individuality, in my action. My transcendence of the Other is not my withdrawal from him into the inaccessible realm of individuality, but my action with him by which he knows me as a person in relation. In the same way, the transcendence of the Other is his action and inter-action with me by which I can really know him" (*Historical Transcendence and the Reality of God* [Grand Rapids: Eerdmans, 1975], p. 197).

[6]Ibid., p. 17.

[7]See John Macmurray, *The Personal World* (Edinburgh: Floris Books, 1996), p. 89; and Smith, *What Is a Person?* p. 72.

[8]"Personalism takes the emphasis on social communication one step further, however. From a personalist perspective, persons are not simply social creatures. Nearly everyone grants as a truism that humans are naturally social. But wolves, bees, hyenas, and ants are also highly socially interactive. Social communication does not make for personhood. What humans experience in their social interactions that sets them apart as persons is the relating at a deeper level of intersubjective understanding, what some personalists call 'communion.' Personalist theorists define communion as a type of shared human existence and reciprocal action that advances the personal fulfillment of those involved through relationships of mutual confirmation and affirmation. Communion involves the mutual giving of personal selves as gifts of fellowship and love for the good of each person concerned" (Smith, *What Is a Person?* p. 68).

[9]"To our knowledge, we are unique among the animal species in that we are the only ones who tell stories. We live by narrative. The narrative changes with each new stage of consciousness. But what remains constant is the central theme. We communicate with each other and listen to each other's stories because we seek each other's company and are predisposed to intimacy and affection, relationships, and sociability. Conversation, whether it be oral, script, print, or electronic, is our means of exposing ourselves to others and entering their realities, and by so doing, incorporating parts of their reality into our own" (Rifkin, *Empathic Civilization,* p. 184).

[10]Smith defines narratives, showing how they are laced with meaning that often reveals personhood, opening the door for mutual sharing and indwelling. See his *What Is a Person?* p. 50.

[11]Bonhoeffer, among others, pushes hard for this understanding of the person as spirit: "Human spirit in its entirety is woven into sociality and rests on the basic-relation of I and you. 'Only in interaction with one another is the spirit of human beings ever revealed; this is the essence of spirit, to be oneself through being in the other.' In infinite closeness, in mutual penetration, I and You are joined together, inseparable from one another forever, resting in one another, intimately participating in one another, empathizing, sharing experiences, bearing together the general stream of interactions of spirit" (Dietrich Bonhoeffer, *Sanctorum Communio* [Minneapolis: Fortress Press, 1998], p. 73).

[12]James Loder explains how the face of the mother becomes the invitation into the personal. See his *The Transforming Moment* (Colorado Springs: Helmers & Howard, 1989), p. 163. Macmurray affirms this; see his *Persons in Relation,* p. 63.

[13]Object relations psychology in the work of Ronald Fairburn and Donald Winnicott particularly has shown the importance of personal encounter of the mother for our humanity. Here Rifkin discusses Winnicott, "What Winnicott is saying is that a relationship precedes an individual, not the other way around. In other words, individuals don't create society. Rather, society creates individuals. This simple observation challenged the very core of modernity, with its emphasis on the self-contained, autonomous individual exerting its will on the world" (*Empathic Civilization,* p. 62).

[14]See Bonhoeffer's *Sanctorum Communio.*

[15]"By virtue of their personhood, persons are quite able to climb past themselves to attend to and devote themselves to that which is beyond themselves. According to personalist theory, the ultimate form of self-transcendence is love for and communion with other persons" (Smith, *What Is a Person?* p. 65).

[16]Macmurray highlights the significance of the mother-child relationship and then contrasts that with the instincts of nature. See his *Persons in Relation,* p. 62.

[17]Jürgen Moltmann, *The Source of Life* (Minneapolis: Fortress Press, 1997).

[18]See Anderson's take on Barth's significant point here, in Ray S. Anderson, *Theology, Death and Dying* (New York: Basil Blackwell, 1986).

[19]"That is why we put persons on trial for crimes, but not bears. Bears do not commit crimes. Bears do not engage in meaningful actions. Bears merely behave" (Smith, *What Is a Person?* p. 69).

²⁰See Steven Pinker, *How the Mind Works* (New York: W. W. Norton, 2009).

²¹See Gary Thomas, *Sacred Parenting* (Grand Rapids: Zondervan, 2004); and Dawn Alitz, "And a Little Child Shall Lead Them: The Advent and Event of Parenting as Spiritual Journey," *Lifelong Faith* 5, no. 3 (2011): 17-25.

²²Though scientists are starting to tell us that our brains are social organisms and therefore one sick flesh may have an impact on others. But this just shows the depth of the personal indwelling.

²³"The . . . relation to the human 'other' is precisely the form in which people encounter the divine 'Other' " (Clifford Green, *Bonhoeffer* [Grand Rapids: Eerdmans, 1999], p. 35).

²⁴Smith discusses the fundamental level of brokenness in seeking an understanding of personhood (see *What Is a Person?* p. 77).

²⁵Dietrich Bonhoeffer, *Creation and Fall* (Minneapolis: Fortress Press, 1997).

²⁶In John 6 Jesus uses words like *consume* in his passage about being the bread of life. Yet the emphasis in that text is much different than what I'm drawing out here. In John 6 Jesus is not asking his disciples to possess him (to violate his personhood) but rather to do the opposite, to take his personhood (because he is the bread) deep into their own spirits. In many ways it is the reversal of the issue that appears in this Genesis text, where Adam possesses God and therefore excludes God.

²⁷Another important biblical image for this point is the parable of the prodigal son. Many, including Barth, see this passage as the articulation of God's love for humanity, that God responds in extravagant love when seeing our need, even a need and brokenness that we thrust upon ourselves.

Chapter 7: Empathy, It's a Spirit Thing

¹Throughout this chapter and the next I'm defining *empathy* as more than just the ability to place oneself in another's shoes, but more radically to feel the other, to indwell the other. Unlike Martha Nussbaum, who defines *sympathy* as deeper than empathy because it is closer to compassion, I'm reversing this assertion (so I can more fully enter into a neuroscientific dialogue), claiming that empathy is deeper than sympathy—in the end this is simply a distinction in definition. See Martha Nussbaum, *Cultivating Humanity* (Cambridge, MA: Harvard University Press, 1997).

²"Empathy is an attempt to experience the inner life of another while retaining objectivity. In other words, we hold our own perspective in mind while simultaneously imagining what it is like to be the other" (Louis Cozolino, *The Neuroscience of Human Relationships* [New York: W. W. Norton, 2006], p. 203).

³Dietrich Bonhoeffer, *Ethics* (New York: Simon & Schuster, 1995), p. 67.

⁴"Our bodies and minds are made for social life, and we become hopelessly depressed in its absence. This is why next to death, solitary confinement is our worst punishment. Bonding is so good for us that the most reliable way to extend one's life expectancy is to marry and stay married. The flip side is the risk we run after losing a partner. The death of a spouse often leads to despair and a reduced will to live that explains the car accidents, alcohol abuse, heart disease, and cancers that take the lives of those left behind. Mortality remains elevated for about half a year following a spouse's death. It

is worse for younger than older people and worse for men than women" (Frans de Waal, *The Age of Empathy* [New York: Three Rivers Press, 2009], p. 10).

[5]Jeremy Rifkin, *The Empathic Civilization* (New York: Jeremy P. Teacher/Penguin, 2009), p. 153.

[6]See Waal, *Age of Empathy*.

[7]Rifkin makes an interesting point here about truth and the core of relationships. What is informative is the need to attend to emotion—he may too quickly critique faith here, but nevertheless these are interesting thoughts. "All of our truths are just a systemizing of our existing relationships and commonly shared understandings. The truth of our existence is that it is inseparable from our relationships. In this sense, an embodied philosophical approach is a radical departure from faith and reason, both of which discount our experiential existence" (*Empathic Civilization*, p. 156).

[8]"Moreno argued that the human imagination is tapped into by empathic engagement. It is by imagining and experiencing the feelings and thoughts of others as if they were one's own that one unleashes personal creativity. But he didn't regard empathy simply as an instrumental means to advance the individual creative spirit. Rather, he believed that empathy was at the very core of what it means to be a fully aware and responsible human being. That awareness can't help but spark one's 'creative faculties,' which is just another way of saying one's 'self-development.' The more empathic one is, the more self-developed one becomes" (ibid., p. 401).

[9]Issues of gender come up here as well. Throughout this work I've made a tentative assertion that in this new period empathy will be the driving pastoral need and gift, making the comment that just maybe there is a reason that women have become the majority in many seminary classrooms. Standing by that assertion the focus on empathy does not eliminate men. "While it is often assumed that gender plays a prominent role in empathy—women are believed by many to be more attentive to (Hermann, 2007) or better than men at 'reading' other people's thoughts and feelings—the evidence indicates that male and female observers are equally capable of empathy, but only when both groups are sufficiently motivated (Ickes, Gesn, & Graham, 2000; Hodges & Klein, 2001)" (Liesbet Goubert, Kenneth D. Craig and Ann Buysse, "Perceiving Others in Pain: Experimental and Clinical Evidence on the Role of Empathy," in *The Social Neuroscience of Empathy*, ed. Jean Decety and William Ickes [Cambridge, MA: MIT Press, 2011], p. 160).

[10]"An important aspect of emotions is their social function. Emotions, both primary and categorical, serve as the vehicles that allow one person to have a sense of the mental state of another" (Daniel Siegel, *The Developing Mind* [New York: Guildford Press, 1999], p. 148).

[11]Waal, *Age of Empathy*, p. 65.

[12]Nussbaum connects emotions and imagination. "What this means is that the emotions typically have a connection to imagination, and to the concrete picturing of events in imagination, that differentiates them from other, more abstract judgmental states" (*Upheavals of Thought: The Intelligence of Emotions* [New York: Cambridge University Press, 2001], p. 65).

[13]The definitions and comparison-contrast of *empathy* and *sympathy* is tangled in the literature. Some authors see them as synonymous, some as two distinct perspectives, others as enemies of each other. Here I'm simply using *sympathy* in a flat manner to draw out the distinct texture of *empathy* that I hope to present. I admit my definition of *sympathy* is far too narrow, but the realities my narrow definition points to I believe are valid.

[14]Steven Johnson takes us deeper into the phenomenon of laughter. "Understanding the roots of laughter requires a kind of hybrid of the Darwinian and Freudian models. We laugh primarily because laughter is a crucial component of the emotional glue that connects parent and child during the most vulnerable years of development. Children who laugh and roughhouse and tickle with their guardians create powerful bonds of affection with those grown-ups, and the bonds help them survive. But natural selection is notoriously conservative with its designs: when you build a mechanism for bonding into the child's brain, the accompanying impulses don't necessarily disappear in adulthood or when children aren't around. So the difficulties of child-rearing created the capacity for—and the deep pleasure of—laughing, and once that capacity was installed, we came upon other applications for it. So when we laugh at the Chaplin film, we have childhood to thank for it. Not our individual childhood in the Freudian sense, but childhood itself and its unique challenges" (*Mind Wide Open* [New York: Scribner, 2004], pp. 127-28).

[15]Daniel Goleman, *The New Leaders* (London: Sphere, 2002), p. 13.

[16]See ibid., chap. 14.

[17]"Empathetic consciousness would be strangely out of place in either heaven or utopia. Where there is no mortal suffering, there is no empathic bond" (Rifkin, *Empathic Civilization*, p. 168).

[18]This is where Rifkin misses the importance of the cross in the Christian confession. "Mature empathy is a unique phenomenon that only living, mortal beings can experience. That's why it's possible to obey and serve God but impossible to empathize with his spirit because we cast it in perfection. God is immortal and not of the flesh and therefore can't feel the pain and struggle of a unique mortal being. We have no way to empathize with the divine, but one might add that God has no way to empathize with us either" (ibid.).

[19]See Morna Hooker, *From Adam to Christ* (Eugene, OR: Wipf & Stock, 1990).

[20]This is where Rifkin unknowingly connects with a Pauline theology. "Empathy is, after all, the ability to experience another's struggle as one's own and is only possible if one is aware of the fragility of their existence and the mortality of their being" (*Empathic Civilization*, p. 162).

Chapter 8: Can I Read Your Mind?

[1]I'm following Kathryn Tanner's wonderful articulation of noncompetitiveness presented in *The Economy of Grace* (Minneapolis: Fortress Press, 2005), and *Jesus, Humanity, and the Trinity* (Minneapolis: Fortress Press, 2001).

[2]See Søren Kierkegaard, *Works of Love* (New York: Harper Torchbooks, 1962).

³See Matthew Boulton, *God Against Religion* (Grand Rapids: Eerdmans, 2008).

⁴"This study suggests that the experience of love is a combination of at least two processes. The first is that it greatly decreases activation of the fear systems, as demonstrated by the 'standing down' of the amygdala and the environmental processing of the posterior cingulate and other cortical areas. Love is a relief from scanning the outer world for threat and our inner world, for shame. Love turns off the alarm, cancels our insurance, and frees us from worry" (Louis Cozolino, *The Neuroscience of Human Relationships* [New York: W. W. Norton, 2006], p. 316).

⁵Martin Luther defined sin as *homo incurvatus in se*, "to be curved in on yourself," in other words, to dehumanize yourself by giving away your personhood, to choose isolation over relationship because of fear or pride.

⁶See Daniel Goleman, *The New Leaders* (London: Sphere, 2002), p. 7.

⁷Daniel J. Siegel, *Mindsight* (New York: Bantam, 2010), p. 63.

⁸"Scientists have had to expand their thinking to grasp this idea: The individual neuron or a single human brain does not exist in nature. Without mutually stimulating interactions, people and neurons wither and die" (Cozolino, *Neuroscience of Human Relationships*, p. 11).

⁹"Our brains rely on other brains to remain healthy, especially under stress. When faced with illness, catastrophe, or loss, we turn to each other for comfort, regulation, and stability. Resiliency—our ability to cope with life's ups and downs—is closely tied to the extent and quality of our support systems. We appear to be capable of coping with just about anything when we are connected to those for whom we care and who care for us" (ibid., p. 229).

¹⁰See Steven Pinker, *How the Mind Works* (New York: W. W. Norton, 2009).

¹¹Cozolino, *Neuroscience of Human Relationships*, p. 50.

¹²Siegel, *Mindsight*, p. 185.

¹³Siegel deepens these thoughts, "Empathy is the capacity to create mindsight images of other people's minds. These you-maps enable us to sense the internal mental stance of another person, not just to attune to their state of mind. Attunement is important, but the middle prefrontal cortex also moves us from this resonance and feeling-with to the more complex, perceptual capacity to 'see' from another's point of view: We sense the other's intentions and imagine what an event means in his or her mind" (ibid., p. 28).

¹⁴Richard Restak, *The Naked Brain* (New York: Three Rivers Press, 2006), p. 60.

¹⁵"The brain's capacity to echo the perception of the faces and gestures of others and code them immediately in visceromotor terms, supplies the neural substrate for an empathic sharing that, albeit in different ways and at diverse levels substantiates and directs our conduct and our inter individual relationships" (Giacomo Rizzolatti and Corrado Sinigaglia, *Mirrors in the Brain* [Oxford: Oxford University Press, 2006], p. 192).

¹⁶Ibid., p. 104.

¹⁷Restak explores further, "In a paper entitled 'Unconscious Facial Reactions to Emotional Facial Expressions,' the authors found that when we look at another person's facial expression we tend to unconsciously adapt the same expression on our own face, even though we aren't consciously aware that we're doing so. This is called emotional

contagion" (*Naked Brain,* p. 103).

[18]Marco Iacoboni, *Mirroring People* (New York: Picador, 2009), p. 119.

[19]Cozolino, *Neuroscience of Human Relationships,* p. 198.

[20]"The field of 'embodied' cognition is still very much in its infancy but has profound implications for how we look at human relations. We involuntarily enter the bodies of those around us so that their movements and emotions echo within us as if they're our own. This is what allows us, or other primates, to re-create what we have seen others do" (Waal, *Age of Empathy,* p. 60).

[21]"Healthy relationships, life challenges, loss, and personal growth seem capable of re-shaping the circuits of the social brain in both positive and negative ways" (Cozolino, *Neuroscience of Human Relationships,* p. 325).

Chapter 9: New Visions of Incarnational Ministry

[1]James Loder, *The Transforming Moment* (Colorado Springs: Helmers & Howard, 1989).

[2]"God comes to a person not as an idea, a philosophy, a religion, but as a human being" (Clifford Green, *Bonhoeffer* [Grand Rapids: Eerdmans, 1999], p. 158).

[3]See Craig Slane, *Bonhoeffer as Martyr* (Grand Rapids: Brazos, 2004), pp. 166ff.

[4]I'm following Torrance here in my commitment to the speaking of the Word as person. For example Robert T. Walker says of Torrance, "It is also supremely important for Torrance that the Word is a person and that therefore all knowledge of the Word is personal knowledge, knowledge of the Word in his person as the second person of the Trinity, the eternal Son" (Robert T. Walker, introduction to Thomas F. Torrance, *Atonement* [Downers Grove, IL: InterVarsity Press, 2009], p. lxx).

[5]See my *Revisiting Relational Youth Ministry,* chap. 3, for examples of this use of language.

[6]Douglas John Hall, *Confessing the Faith* (Minneapolis: Augsburg Fortress, 1998), p. 185.

[7]Thomas Torrance, *Incarnation* (Downers Grove, IL: InterVarsity Press, 2008), p. 108.

[8]Here I am in agreement with Todd Billings' argument in chapter five of *Union with Christ* (Grand Rapids: Baker, 2011). Though unlike Billings, I'm not willing to completely throw out the practice.

[9]This is both the problem and potential of practices in the church (better to call it the recovery of liturgical and traditional practices). They have the potential to provide space for the encounter of persons. They can become routines that allow us to encounter each other and God. But they also run the danger of being routine actions that lack the indwelling power of persons. I can ignore the broken humanity of my neighbor to get to the Communion table.

[10]Kathryn Tanner, *Jesus, Humanity, and the Trinity* (Minneapolis: Fortress, 2009), p. 68.

[11]Jeremy Rifkin argues that we need to expand empathy to all human beings, and if we are unable to do this we find ourselves in ecological and economical trouble. Rifkin believes we've already pushed past religious/theological consciousness, where we extend empathy to only those that share our religious perspective. However, what I think Rifkin misses, at least from a Christian perspective (and he may miss this because the church has failed to substantially live it out), is that the incarnation itself propels us

to have empathic connection with all humanity—the very thing Rifkin hopes for. Incarnation makes all human beings brothers and sisters. Barth says as much: "Thus the so-called 'outsiders' are really only 'insiders' who have not yet understood and apprehended themselves as such. On the other hand, even the most persuaded Christian, in the final analysis, must and will recognize himself ever and again as an 'outsider.' So there must then be no particular language for insiders and outsiders" (Karl Barth, *The Humanity of God* [Louisville, KY: John Knox Press, 1960], p. 59).

[12]T. F. Torrance explains that this understanding of sharing, of union, doesn't eliminate the reality of sin but rather radicalizes it. "The astonishing thing here is that the more God gave himself to this people, the more he forced it to be what it was in its sin and self-will, to be in truth what it actually was, a rebel. The very self-giving of God in holy love not only revealed Israel's sin, but intensified it: it intensified the enmity between Israel and Yahweh and intensified the contradiction between Yahweh and Israel— hence the suffering servant" (*Incarnation*, p. 48).

[13]Tanner, *Jesus, Humanity, and the Trinity*, p. 69.

[14]"What happens in the incarnation is the union of God and man" (Torrance, *Incarnation*, p. 105). The incarnation is the gift of revealing God's very person; it is the invitation to share in God's life. And the incarnation reveals that this union is the union of persons. God has no agenda in the incarnation outside of giving God's very self to our person.

[15]See Dietrich Bonhoeffer, *Christ the Center* (San Francisco: HarperCollins, 1960), p. 104.

[16]See Bonhoeffer's *Discipleship* (Minneapolis: Augsburg Fortress, 2001), p. 59.

[17]Clifford Green, *Bonhoeffer* (Grand Rapids: Eerdmans, 1999), p. 235.

[18]"God does not even need creatures to be with him in this way. It is not just that God does not need us to do something for 'him'; God does not need us at all. God does not need us for company; the trinitarian Persons have all they need in and among themselves" (Tanner, *Jesus, Humanity, and the Trinity*, p. 69).

[19]This is Moltmann's very point in *The Crucified God* (Minneapolis: Fortress Press, 1974).

[20]I mean this very much as a *theologica crucis*. For more on how the Trinity is united around death and invites us to share in God's life through death see my *The Promise of Despair* (Nashville: Abingdon, 2010).

[21]Tanner explains this ministry of the Spirit, "The Holy Spirit in the Trinity, pushing beyond the dyadic self-enclosure of Father and Son, opens that Trinity outward to what is other than God. Reinforcing the unity of being between Father and Son by a unity of love and joyful affirmation, the Holy Spirit is the exuberant, ecstatic carrier of the love of Father and Son to us. Borne by the Holy Spirit, the love of the Father for the Son is returned to the Father by the Son within the Trinity; so the triune God's manifestation in the world is completed in Christ through the work of the Spirit who enables us to return the love of God shown in Christ through a life lived in gratitude and service to God's cause" (Tanner, *Jesus, Humanity, and the Trinity*, p. 14).

Chapter 10: Relational Ministry as Gift

[1]Philip Rolnick discusses the possibility of the gift in his book *Person, Grace, and God*

(Grand Rapids: Eerdmans, 2007), dealing directly with Derrida.

[2]Ibid., p. 176.

[3]Kathryn Tanner, *Jesus, Humanity, and the Trinity* (Minneapolis: Fortress Press, 2001), p. 9.

[4]"In him we have the divine mercy or compassion translated into flesh and blood in our midst. The term the epistle to the Hebrews used here is *sympathesai*, sym-pathy, compassion, feeling-with. It is another term, but essentially the same idea is conveyed, for Jesus is spoken of as gathering up our weakness and sins upon himself and bearing them before God in compassion and sympathy and solidarity with us sinners" (T. F. Torrance, *Incarnation* [Downers Grove, IL: InterVarsity Press, 2008], p. 133). Torrance never uses the word *empathy* here, but he easily could have, drawing from its very entomology of "feeling with" or "feeling into," which is the very theological point I'm making.

[5]Torrance explains that "making perfect" is not to be understood in moralistic frameworks, which is necessary if we are to see God's act as mobilized by God's rage for human purity. Torrance shows that "making perfect" refers to the perfect sharing of our lives, the perfect gift of bearing our reality. "'The making perfect' refers to his ordeal of consecration when before the cross he entered more and more into compassionate and sympathetic solidarity with lost and guilty sinners, bringing his relation of solidarity with them to its purposed end or completion on the cross. 'Making perfect' does not mean some process of moral perfecting in Jesus, but the completing or perfecting of a process into which he solemnly entered at his baptismal consecration and which continued in his relations with those he came to save" (ibid., p. 138).

[6]Tanner explains how God's gift giving becomes the paradigm for true person-to-person gift giving. See her *Jesus, Humanity, and the Trinity*, p. 81.

Chapter 11: Sharing Is More Than What You Learned in Kindergarten

[1]Bonhoeffer states, "I do not know who the man Jesus Christ is unless I can at the same time say, 'Jesus Christ is God'; I do not know who the God Jesus Christ is, unless I can at the same time say, 'Jesus Christ is man.' The two factors cannot be isolated, because they are not separable. God in timeless eternity is not God; Jesus limited by time is not Jesus. Rather we may say that in the man Jesus, God is God. In this Jesus Christ, God is present. This one God-Man is the starting point for Christology" (Dietrich Bonhoeffer, *Christ the Center* [San Francisco: HarperCollins, 1960], p. 45).

[2]"Dunn agrees with von Loewenich, 'Paul's teaching is not that Christ dies "in the place of" others so that they escape death (as the logic of "substitution" implies). It is rather that Christ's sharing their death makes it possible for them to share his death. . . . [There is] a sense of a continuing identification with Christ in, through, and beyond his death which . . . is fundamental to Paul's soteriology'" (Rosalene Bradbury, *Cross Theology* [Eugene, OR: Pickwick, 2011], p. 98).

[3]The concept of the "hypostatic union" was worked out at Chalcedon; the term came later. Bradbury discusses Luther's perspective: "The two natures of Christ in the one hypostasis interpenetrate each other and cannot be abstracted from each other, so that what happens to Jesus Christ affects both his natures. In this, as the crucicentric theo-

logians before him, Luther stands in marked opposition to the classical Greek insistence on divine impassibility. But he also departs from other major Reformers, and notably John Calvin (1509-1564), who are sympathetic to the Greek view" (ibid., p. 96).

⁴Torrance gives some helpful background. "Both Lutheran and Reformed theologians rightly accepted the centrality of the doctrine of the hypostatic union, but they sought to give that doctrine a more dynamic interpretation by drawing out the implications of the unio or union in terms of communio and communication. That is to say, they sought to understand the hypostatic union not simply in terms of a state of union, but in terms of a divine movement of grace, which was translated into the history of the man Jesus Christ" (T. F. Torrance, *Incarnation* [Downers Grove, IL: InterVarsity Press, 2008], p. 215).

⁵"The place of the mystery of Christ in our understanding can only be stated and guarded in negative terms. The mystery is that in Jesus Christ true God and true man are united in one person—that is the doctrine of the hypostatic union. But we must mark out, on either side of that mystery, what it is by saying what it is not. In this way we allow the mystery to declare itself to us, and to keep on declaring itself to us without hindering the depth and breadth of its self-disclosure by positive man-made definitions of what it actually is. This is the Chalcedonian doctrine of Christ. In this statement we say that God and man are united in Jesus Christ, divine and human nature in one person, in such a way that (a) there is no impairing or diminishing of either deity or humanity in the union; and (b) there is neither separation of the natures nor confusion between them" (ibid., p. 83).

⁶Ibid., p. 191.

⁷Torrance continues, "but personal union here means union in the one person. That is a personal union unlike any personal union we know even at its most intimate in marriage, which is union in one flesh, but union of two persons in one flesh. But this is such a union of natures and acts that they are united in one and only one person" (ibid., p. 191).

⁸See ibid., p. 222.

⁹One shouldn't miss the connection to Luther's *Freedom of the Christian* here.

¹⁰See Karl Barth's *Church Dogmatics* I/1 (Edinburgh: T & T Clark, 1936).

¹¹"Just as the Spirit makes us Christ's own so that we may be sons like him, the Spirit makes Jesus' own humanity that of the Son of God. In much the same fashion, in fact, the Spirit makes the bread and wine of the Eucharist into the body and blood of Christ that we eat and drink. There is an effective power here of the Spirit to join—the humanity of Jesus to the Word, us to Christ, and the bread and wine to the body and blood of Christ respectively—sufficient to give all of the former a new identity, the very identity of the latter" (Kathryn Tanner, *Christ the Key* [London: Cambridge University Press, 2010], p. 164).

¹²Ibid., p. 166.

¹³"The incarnation is the coming of God 'down' to humanity, to assume human flesh and to be one with man in the person of Christ. The ascension is Jesus' taking of our humanity in his person into the presence of God into the union . . . of the love of the Trinity" (Robert T. Walker, introduction to Thomas Torrance, *Atonement* [Downers

Grove, IL: InterVarsity Press, 2009], p. iii).

[14]Tanner, *Jesus, Humanity, and the Trinity,* p. 62.

[15]Tanner, with dense biblical citations, articulates this union through the Spirit. See her *Christ the Key,* p. 160.

[16]Tanner, *Jesus, Humanity, and the Trinity,* p. 54.

[17]See Jouette Bassler, *Navigating Paul* (Louisville, KY: Westminster John Knox Press, 2007), p. 39.

[18]Tanner, *Jesus, Humanity, and the Trinity,* p. 79.

[19]Torrance, *Atonement,* p. 72.

[20]"More subtly perhaps, the incarnational model of the atonement undercuts the sense of vicariousness in the satisfaction and penal models. In the claim that Jesus dies for us, the primary meaning of 'for us' is benefit rather than legal substitution; Jesus dies to benefit us so that we will no longer have to live as we do in a sin-afflicted, death-ridden world. Jesus, as the Word incarnate, does act on our behalf: he steps into our place to act as our advocate and thereby does for us what we cannot do for ourselves" (Tanner, *Christ the Key,* p. 258).

[21]Torrance, *Incarnation,* p. 196.

[22]Tanner helpfully reminds us that our ministry is not to save people. This is God's own work. Rather, our calling is to participate in union with our neighbor, to share in the neighbor's life as a way of witness, as a way of participating in God's life; trusting that this participation has the ramification of salvation. See her *Jesus, Humanity, and the Trinity,* p. 55.

Chapter 12: The Place Between

[1]This is Emanuel Levinas's critique of Heidegger. See his *Totality and Infinity* (Pittsburgh: Duquesne University Press, 1961).

[2]For this distinction of the concreteness of transcendence that leads to the face, I'm leaning on Levinas. See *Totality and Infinity.*

[3]See Steven Johnson, *Mind Wide Open* (New York: Scribner, 2004), p. 23; and William Ickes, "Empathic Accuracy: Its Links to Clinical, Cognitive, Developmental, Social, and Physiological Psychology," in *The Social Neuroscience of Empathy,* ed. Jean Decety and William Ickes (Cambridge, MA: MIT Press, 2011), p. 60.

[4]Steven Johnson, *Mind Wide Open,* p. 25.

[5]Giacomo Rizzolatti and Corrado Sinigaglia, *Mirrors in the Brain* (Oxford: Oxford University Press, 2006), p. 115.

[6]Of course this point I am drawing has huge ramifications for online communities and culture. Another book would be necessary to unpack these issues. But I do think they are issues. However, I tend to believe that the Internet, particularly, is not a disembodied tool as much as a way to broadcast our bodies across time and space. Therefore, the Internet doesn't necessarily need to be seen as faceless. Though it clearly runs that danger.

[7]See chapter eight.

[8]The one exception to this is the eyes. The eyes are powerful ways of mediating empathy

and sometimes people can recognize each other by just seeing the eyes.

[9]"But for the most part, facial recognition is the commonest way for one person to recognize another. And since perceiving and identifying another person's face is so basic to social interaction, we are at a great disadvantage when we aren't certain who we are dealing with: We don't know how we should relate to the person, interpret his or her responses, or plan responses of our own" (Richard Restak, *The Naked Brain* [New York: Three Rivers Press, 2006], p. 98).

[10]Thomas F. Torrance, *Space, Time and Incarnation* (London: T & T Clark, 2005), p. 24.

[11]Most Old Testament scholars would argue that the God of Israel has always sought relationship over containers. Hence, one of the reasons graven images are anathema. The God of Israel cannot be placed in a container.

[12]This is part of the emphasis of Chalcedon. Jesus' divine and human natures cannot be divided, placed in two containers, because they are bound in the one person through relationship.

[13]"Christ is the mediator as the one who exists pro me. That is his nature and his mode of existence" (Dietrich Bonhoeffer, *Christ the Center* [San Francisco: HarperCollins, 1960], p. 60).

[14]Torrance articulates beautifully Jesus' action of place sharing. See his *Atonement* (Downers Grove, IL: InterVarsity Press, 2009), p. 152.

[15]I'm attempting to hold to the commitments of Chalcedon, particularly through the work of Torrance. But through Bonhoeffer I'm also trying to move in a more positive Christological direction that imagines the presence of Christ in our lives. This positive Christological move is essential for ministry. For some context, Clifford Green says of Bonhoeffer and his view of Chalcedon: "Bonhoeffer wants to go beyond Chalcedon with good historical reason he treats the conciliar Christological formulations as 'critical or negative Christology;' their intent was chiefly to exclude heretical theological content and unsuitable forms of thought and expression. It is the responsibility of individual theologians, however, to produce a positive Christology, but always with reference to the limits established by the conciliar decisions" (*Bonhoeffer* [Grand Rapids: Eerdmans, 1999], p. 208).

[16]See ibid., p. 212; and James Loder, *The Transforming Moment* (Colorado Springs: Helmers & Howard, 1989), p. 120.

[17]"For his own positive Christology Bonhoeffer proposes a way forward in his conceptuality of sociality. 'The relation of God and human beings cannot be conceived as a relationship of things but only in the relationship of persons.' It is persons who ask of other persons the question: 'who?'" (Green, *Bonhoeffer*, p. 209).

[18]This is a huge Christological debate that I am deciding to circumvent. Mainly because I don't think it adds to the pastoral heart of this project. But it should be said that I am trying to walk the thin line between the Lutheran and Reformed debate (a line that runs straight through my person) about whether the finite can encompass the infinite. The Lutherans say yes and the Reformed no. I have argued that Jesus is present in the space between persons. This has the potential (though more work is needed) of saying that the finite human person does not encompass the infinite but nevertheless fully

shares in the infinite through the neighbor. The neighbor doesn't become Jesus to us (as Luther liked to say—or better, as Lutherans like to quote him as saying); the neighbor remains the neighbor. But in the encounter of our spirits, in the sharing of our spirits, the infinite becomes present, not as substance in us but as a relationship that binds us. We remain finite humans, but in our place sharing we experience the infinite.

[19]Martin Luther, quoted in Kathryn Tanner, *Jesus, Humanity, and the Trinity* (Minneapolis: Fortress Press, 2001), p. 63.

[20]"United with Christ, we are thereby emboldened as ministers of God's beneficence to the world, aligning ourselves with, entering into communion with, those in need as God in Christ was for us in our need and as Christ was a man for others, especially those in need" (ibid., p. 9).

Chapter 12¾: A Quick Pauline Excursion

[1]See Morna Hooker, *From Adam to Christ* (Eugene, OR: Wipf & Stock, 1990), p. 25.

[2]Bassler gives examples of all this *in* language in Paul. "In Gal 2:19-20 Paul says, 'I have been crucified with Christ; and it is no longer I who live, but it is Christ who lives in me.' In 2 Cor 5:17 he proclaims, 'So if anyone is in Christ, there is a new creation!' In Rom 6:3 he asks, 'Do you not know that all of us who have been baptized into Christ Jesus were baptized into his death?' In Rom 8:10 he asserts, 'But if Christ is in you, though the body is dead because of sin, the Spirit is life because of righteousness.' And in Gal 3:27 he instructs, 'As many of you as were baptized into Christ have clothed yourselves with Christ' " (Jouette Bassler, *Navigating Paul* [Louisville, KY: Westminster John Knox Press, 2007], p. 35).

[3]Hooker, *From Adam to Christ,* p. 19.

Chapter 13: Will You Pray for Me?

[1]"What counts is the leader's presence and being, not technique and know-how" (Edwin Friedman, *A Failure of Nerve* [New York: Seabury, 2007], p. 17).

[2]Ibid., p. 96.

[3]Dietrich Bonhoeffer, *Prayerbook of the Bible* (Minneapolis: Fortress, 1987).

[4]Bonhoeffer states, "One cannot ask whether it is the Christian who prays, or the Church. There is no alternative, for when the Christians pray, it is the Church; and when the Church prays, it is the Christian. Between these two there can be no opposition" (ibid., p. 11).

[5]Bonhoeffer explains Calvin's phrase: "Calvin even says that we pray through the mouth of Jesus Christ, who speaks for us because of what he has been, because of what he has suffered in obedience and faithfulness to his Father. And we ourselves pray as though with his mouth, inasmuch as he gives us access and audience, and intercedes for us. Thus, fundamentally, our prayer is already made even before we formulate it. When we pray, we can only return to that prayer which was uttered in the person of Jesus Christ and which is constantly repeated because God is not without man" (ibid., p. 22).

[6]See ibid., p. 156.

7"As the work of Jesus Christ, prayer is truly divine work; and as the work of Jesus Christ, it is truly human work as well. It is the work of humanity-with-God, the perfect reversal and reconciliation of leitourgia. In Jesus Christ, at once Son of God and Son of humanity, all attempts at separation between creature and Creator are overcome, that is, overcome exactly insofar as Christ undertakes these very attempts and refashions them" (Matthew Boulton, *God Against Religion* [Grand Rapids: Eerdmans, 2008], p. 167).

8"God is the Father of Jesus Christ, and that very man, Jesus Christ, has prayed, and he is praying still. Such is the foundation of our prayer in Jesus Christ. It is as if God himself has pledged to answer our request because all our prayers are summed up in Jesus Christ; God cannot fail to answer, since it is Jesus Christ who prays" (Karl Barth, *Prayer* [Philadelphia: Westminster Press, 1946], p. 22).

9"God gives all things; genuine human beings live as beings-in-gratitude. They do not offer God gifts in comic and tragic parodies of divine generosity. They are grateful. In short, they are human" (Boulton, *God Against Religion*, p. 110).

10Robert A. Fryling quotes De Pree, saying, "Max's profound and succinct definition of leaderships [is] 'defining reality and saying thank you'" (*The Leadership Ellipse* [Downers Grove, IL: InterVarsity Press, 2010], p. 188).

11"What we focus on becomes our reality. When an organization gives its attention to some aspects of the corporate life, those aspects tend to define the whole. The 'reality' of an organization is defined by whatever participants think about, talk about, work on, dream about, or plan" (Mark Lau Branson, *Memories, Hopes, and Conversations* [Nashville: Alban Institute, 2004], p. 25).

12Eugene Peterson, *The Contemplative Pastor* (Grand Rapids: Eerdmans, 1989), p. 93.

Chapter 14: What This Looks Like

1The end of this line is stolen from Justin Vernon's (Bon Iver) song "Holocene," an artistic and beautiful statement that we are our relationships, that we are persons.

2"'Formal generalization is overvalued as a source of scientific development.' Sometimes the most interesting phenomena are 'found in the most minute and most concrete of details. In-depth case study and narrative (without theoretical comment) are often more useful than either factual "findings" or the high-level generalizations of theory'" (Bent Flyvbjerg, cited in Bonnie Miller-McLemore, presidential address to the Academy of Practical Theology, Amsterdam 2011, pp. 49-50).

3Eugene Peterson, *The Contemplative Pastor* (Grand Rapids: Eerdmans, 1989), p. 89.

4See Alan Roxburgh and Fred Romanuk, *The Missional Leader* (San Francisco: Jossey-Bass, 2006), p. 69.

5"When we share stories, we strengthen our links to other people. Within a group—any group, from family to office to cult—stories establish norms and articulate a defining myth" (Frank Rose, *The Art of Immersion* [New York: W. W. Norton, 2011], p. 205).

6Frank Rogers explains how central narrative is to our very personhood in *Finding God in the Graffiti* (Cleveland: Pilgrim Press, 2011), p. 57.

7"In a command-and-control world, we know who's telling the story; it's the author. But digital media have created an authorship crisis. Once the audience is free to step out into the fiction and start directing events, the entire edifice of twentieth-century mass media begins to crumble" (Rose, *Art of Immersion*, p. 83).

[8]"Online, the simple act of linking would help foment a culture of participation that manifests itself in blogs, YouTube, Wikipedia, and the whole host of user-generated media known as Web 2.0. 'The hyperlink is one of the greatest inventions of mankind,' Kelly reiterated when I saw him at his home in the Oceanside village of Pacifica, just south of San Francisco" (ibid., p. 124).

[9]There is significant reason for the church to do catechesis in this perspective of ministry as the sharing of persons in empathetic encounter. The reason for catechesis, however, is bound in prayer as story. Because Scripture itself is a story—the story of who God is and what God is up to—we need this very story to connect us to the life of God and the person of Jesus Christ. But the point of reading the Bible and knowing the Christian tradition is not to possess more information but to make connections, to link our own story with God's.

[10]Richard Bauckham and Trevor Hart discuss how science fiction leads to eschatological imagination. See their *Hope Against Hope* (Grand Rapids: Eerdmans, 1999).

[11]"It turns out that the memories contained in our stories are also evolving. Memories are not a file of notes; they are stories that are told, reorganized, and recreated with each telling. Each time a memory is accessed, it can be modified (both in its narrative and neurology) by new experiences that increase its relevance to current conditions" (Louis Cozolino, *The Neuroscience of Human Relationships* [New York: W. W. Norton, 2006], p. 334).

[12]"There are two camps when it comes to explaining memory. One holds that memory is like a videotape you play back whenever you need to. On the other side is the reconstructive camp, which holds that memories are assembled by the brain on the fly as we try to summon them up. Hassabis thought the latter explanation made a lot more sense. If memory were like a videotape, it would almost certainly be a lot more reliable than it is" (Rose, *Art of Immersion*, p. 285).

[13]See ibid., p. 304.

[14]Daniel Siegel, *The Developing Mind* (New York: Guildford Press, 1999), p. 6.

[15]See Doug Pagitt, *Preaching Re-Imagined* (Grand Rapids: Zondervan, 2005).

[16]Barth had his own contextual reasons to be enamored with the Baptizer's strong stance. His was a time, in the shadow of world wars, to stand and proclaim, proclaim and proclaim!

[17]There may be some similarities here with Fred Craddock's inductive method of preaching; though, through prayer, I've pushed it even further. Craddock says, "In the inductive method it is essential that the minister really be a member of the congregation he serves" (*As One Without Authority* [Enid, OK: Phillips University Press, 1974], p. 83). Craddock continues, "We are considering the minister's capacity for impression as the necessary prerequisite for expression. An empathetic imagination means, first, having the wisdom and grace to receive the images of life about us and then, secondly, the freedom and confidence to reflect these with appropriate expressions. Such honest receptivity and reflection is fundamental to the nature and movement of inductive preaching, concerned

as it is with the concrete realities within human experience (ibid., p. 90).

[18]Craddock explains the importance of the congregation's participation. I'm trying to push this even further: "What is here suggested, however, is that the participation of the hearer is essential, not just in the post-benediction implementation, but in the completion of the thought, movement and decision-making within the sermon itself. The process calls for an incompleteness, a lack of exhaustiveness in the sermon. It requires of the preacher that he resist the temptation to tyranny of ideas rather than democratic sharing. He restrains himself, refusing to do both the speaking and listening, to give both stimulus and response, or in a more homely analogy, he does not throw the ball and catch it himself" (ibid., p. 64).

Chapter 15: I've Got to Run the Church Don't I?

[1]For resources on moving churches from conflict to communion see the work of Theresa Latini at Luther Seminary: www.luthersem.edu/faculty/fac_home.aspx?contact_id= tlatini001.

[2]"People hold on to ideas as a way of holding on to the person who taught them the ideas" (Ronald Heifetz and Marty Linsky, *Leadership on the Line* [Boston: Harvard Business School Press, 2002], p. 28).

[3]This is Friedman's point in his groundbreaking book *A Failure of Nerve* (New York: Seabury, 2007).

[4]Robert Quinn, *Deep Change* (San Francisco: Jossey-Bass, 1996). See also Daniel Goleman, *The New Leaders* (London: Sphere, 2002), and Edwin Friedman *A Failure of Nerve*.

[5]Thanks to pastor Jodi Houge for this anecdote.

[6]See Goleman, *New Leaders,* p. 38.

[7]Ibid., p. 49.

[8]"Our congregations are living systems. We are emotionally wired together with our brothers and sisters in the family of God (Romans 12). Our behavior and choices affect each other in ways of which we are often unaware" (Jim Herrington, Robert Creech and Trisha Taylor, *The Leader's Journey* [San Francisco: Jossey-Bass, 2003], p. 33).

[9]Goleman, *New Leaders,* p. 5.

[10]"When leaders are able to grasp other people's feelings and perspectives, they access a potent emotional guidance system that keeps what they say and do on track. As such, empathy is the sine qua non of all social effectiveness in working life" (ibid., p. 63).

[11]Friedman, *Failure of Nerve*, p. 58.

[12]See Louis Cozolino, *The Neuroscience of Human Relationships* (New York: W. W. Norton, 2006), p. 202.

[13]"The same effect holds in the office, boardroom, or shop floor; people in groups at work invariably 'catch' feelings from one another, sharing everything from jealousy and envy to angst or euphoria. The more cohesive the group, the stronger the sharing of moods, emotional history, and even hot buttons" (Goleman, *New Leaders,* p. 9).

[14]Friedman, *Failure of Nerve*, p. 151. "By leader I do not mean someone who tells others what to do, but someone who can maintain the kind of non-anxious, well-principled

presence" (ibid., p. 89).

[15]"Relationality—not only in the case of this, but in all relationship—presupposes both identity and difference, and the two poles must be understood in dynamic, dialectical tension one with the other" (Douglas John Hall, *Confessing the Faith* [Minneapolis: Augsburg Fortress, 1998], p. 56).

[16]Dietrich Bonhoeffer, *Sanctorum Communio* (Minneapolis: Fortress Press, 1998), p. 74.

[17]Friedman is quite hard on empathy in *A Failure of Nerve*, and I think for good reason in how he defines it. He sees it as a way of abdicating to unhealthy people, allowing them to keep a system from running in a healthy way. This kind of empathy is openness without closedness and I would therefore agree with him. See his *The Failure of Nerve*, pp. 133ff.

[18]"Research has taught me that if we really want to practice compassion, we have to start by setting boundaries and holding people accountable for their behavior" (Brené Brown, *The Gift of Imperfection* [Center City, MN: Hazelden, 2010], p. 17).

[19]Friedman powerfully articulates the need for this open and closedness and the impact it can have. See his *Failure of Nerve*, p. 14.

Index

IVP PRAXIS
EQUIPPING LEADERS FOR MINISTRY

"...TO EQUIP HIS PEOPLE FOR WORKS OF SERVICE,
SO THAT THE BODY OF CHRIST MAY BE BUILT UP."

EPHESIANS 4:12

God has called us to ministry. But it's not enough to have a vision for ministry if you don't have the practical skills for it. Nor is it enough to do the work of ministry if what you do is headed in the wrong direction. We need both vision *and* expertise for effective ministry. We need *praxis*.

Praxis puts theory into practice. It brings cutting-edge ministry expertise from visionary practitioners. You'll find sound biblical and theological foundations for ministry in the real world, with concrete examples for effective action and pastoral ministry. Praxis books are more than the "how to" – they're also the "why to." And because *being* is every bit as important as *doing*, Praxis attends to the inner life of the leader as well as the outer work of ministry. Feed your soul, and feed your ministry.

If you are called to ministry, you know you can't do it on your own. Let Praxis provide the companions you need to equip God's people for life in the kingdom.

www.ivpress.com/praxis